THE COMPLETE ILLUSTRATED GUIDE TO
JAPANESE COOKING

SACHIYO HARADA

THE COMPLETE ILLUSTRATED GUIDE TO
JAPANESE COOKING

TECHNIQUES, INGREDIENTS & RECIPES

Hardie Grant

NORTH AMERICA

CONTENTS

HOW TO USE THIS BOOK

ESSENTIALS

Discover the recipes and basic ingredients of Japanese cooking.
An infographic is included with each essential concept, accompanied
by a detailed explanation of the preparation method.

RECIPES

Use the essential concepts to make Japanese recipes. For each recipe,
you can refer back to the essentials, use the infographic to understand the
composition of the recipe, and follow the step-by-step photographs.

ILLUSTRATED GLOSSARY

Deepen your understanding of tools and ingredients and explore essential
techniques through pictures.

CHAPTER 1
ESSENTIALS

Understand
JAPANESE RICE

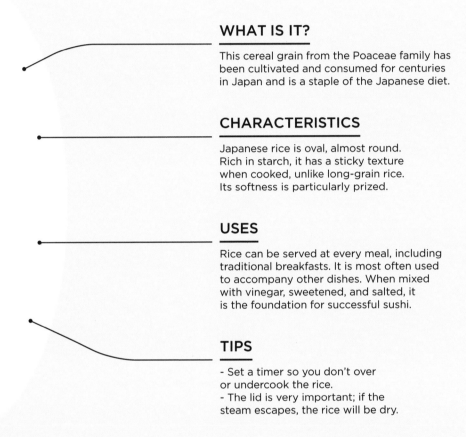

WHAT IS IT?

This cereal grain from the Poaceae family has been cultivated and consumed for centuries in Japan and is a staple of the Japanese diet.

CHARACTERISTICS

Japanese rice is oval, almost round. Rich in starch, it has a sticky texture when cooked, unlike long-grain rice. Its softness is particularly prized.

USES

Rice can be served at every meal, including traditional breakfasts. It is most often used to accompany other dishes. When mixed with vinegar, sweetened, and salted, it is the foundation for successful sushi.

TIPS

- Set a timer so you don't over or undercook the rice.
- The lid is very important; if the steam escapes, the rice will be dry.

CULTIVATION

Rice is planted in spring and the harvest (inekari) takes place in autumn. Each spring, the planting of the first rice plants is celebrated and accompanied by ceremonies to ensure a bountiful harvest. Rice is sacred to the Japanese. Since ancient times, it has served as an offering to the gods (shinto).

WHITE & BROWN RICE

White rice (Uruchimai): the most widely consumed. It is obtained by polishing brown rice. After it is washed, it can be cooked in a rice cooker, clay pot, or cast-iron pot. It is white and sticky.
Brown rice (Genmai): whole grain, less polished, only its outer hull is removed; the bran is retained. Its high fiber content makes it more nutritious. It takes longer to cook and is a little chewier.

Both types are available pre-cooked in a sealed microwavable package.

OTHER VARIETIES

There are over a hundred varieties of Japanese rice. Some of the most popular:
Koshihikari Rice: one of the most well-known and well-liked varieties, it has an exceptional flavor;
Akitakomachi Rice: premium rice, due to the quality of the Akita prefecture's soil and water;
Sasanishiki Rice: noteworthy for its ability to retain its flavor even when cold;
Yumepirika Rice: known for its rich sweetness and strong flavor.

HOW TO STORE

Raw: rice is most flavorful when just harvested. It is therefore preferable to consume it quickly, though it can be stored for several months once the package has been opened. Keep it perfectly dry in an airtight container away from humidity and light.
Cooked: when the rice is still hot, separate it into equal portions and wrap in plastic wrap. Cool to room temperature, then freeze. Defrost in the microwave for 4 to 5 minutes at 600 W.

Learn

TOTAL TIME
Prep time: 10 minutes
Cook time: 15 minutes
Soak time: 30 minutes in summer; 1 hour in winter
Rest time: 15 minutes

EQUIPMENT

Cast-iron pot with lid
Wooden spatula

FOR 5 CUPS / 960 G OF COOKED RICE

2¼ cups / 450 g Japanese rice
2½ cups / 600 ml cooking water

1   To wash the rice, place in a bowl and add plenty of cold water. Stir quickly with your hand, then discard the water immediately. Pour in more water, stir again with your hand for 1 minute, then discard the water. Repeat several times until the water runs clear.

2   Cover the rice with water (1¼ inches / 3 cm above the height of the rice). Set aside to allow the rice to absorb the water (30 minutes in the summer, 1 hour in winter). The rice should turn white and no longer be translucent.

3   Drain the rice and place in the pot. Add the cooking water and cover the pot.

4   Bring to a boil over high heat, and cook for about 3 minutes. Then reduce heat to low and simmer for 10 minutes. Remove from heat and let rest for 15 minutes, keeping the lid on the entire time, so that the rice can finish cooking in its own steam.

5   Remove the lid, and stir with a damp wooden spatula.

SUSHI RICE

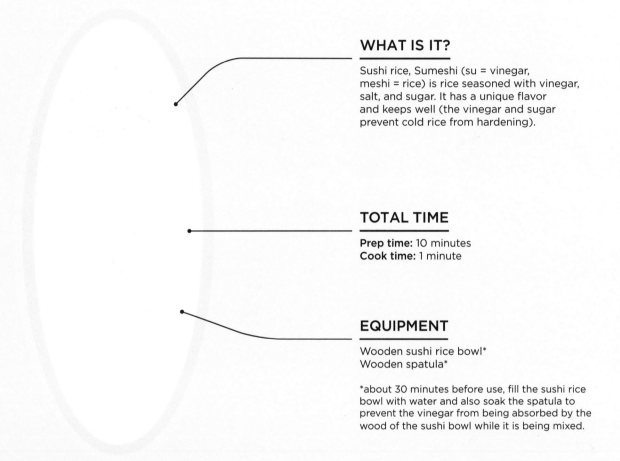

WHAT IS IT?

Sushi rice, Sumeshi (su = vinegar, meshi = rice) is rice seasoned with vinegar, salt, and sugar. It has a unique flavor and keeps well (the vinegar and sugar prevent cold rice from hardening).

TOTAL TIME

Prep time: 10 minutes
Cook time: 1 minute

EQUIPMENT

Wooden sushi rice bowl*
Wooden spatula*

*about 30 minutes before use, fill the sushi rice bowl with water and also soak the spatula to prevent the vinegar from being absorbed by the wood of the sushi bowl while it is being mixed.

TIPS

- Choose non-glutinous short-grain rice (white round rice). Once cooked, it retains its firm shape while becoming soft and sticky.
- While the rice is still hot, pour in the vinegar and mix quickly. Once the sushi vinegar has been absorbed by the rice, leave to cool.
- In Japan, an Uchiwa (a round paper fan with a handle) is traditionally used to cool the rice. This technique evaporates excess moisture and prevents the vinegar's flavor from disappearing under the effect of heat.

Learn

FOR ABOUT 5 CUPS / 960 G OF COOKED RICE

2¼ cups / 450 g Japanese
    short-grain rice
⅓ cup plus 4 teaspoons / 100 ml rice
    vinegar or Japanese grain vinegar
7 teaspoons / 30 g sugar
1¾ teaspoons / 10 g salt

1 Cook the rice (page 10). In a small saucepan, melt the salt and sugar in the vinegar over low heat (without boiling, otherwise the acidity and flavor will disappear). Turn off the heat when the sugar and salt have dissolved. Leave to cool. Place cooked rice in a damp sushi bowl and drizzle with sushi vinegar.

2 Fold in the vinegar without smashing the rice. Start by turning over the rice with the spatula to incorporate the vinegar that has sunk to the bottom.

3 Slice into the rice to incorporate the vinegar into the chunks that have formed. Do not stir the rice - stirring can crush the grains, leading to mushy rice.

4 Cover with a damp kitchen towel and allow to cool before using.

UDON NOODLES

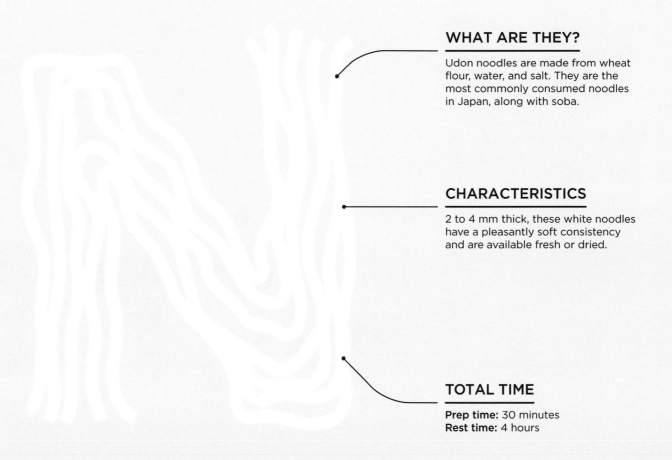

WHAT ARE THEY?

Udon noodles are made from wheat flour, water, and salt. They are the most commonly consumed noodles in Japan, along with soba.

CHARACTERISTICS

2 to 4 mm thick, these white noodles have a pleasantly soft consistency and are available fresh or dried.

TOTAL TIME

Prep time: 30 minutes
Rest time: 4 hours

EQUIPMENT

Rolling pin
Knife: udon kiri or nakiri

STORAGE

Dry udon noodles, like other noodles, can be kept for months in their packaging (if opened, use within the year) away from heat, light, and humidity. Fresh udon can be kept for 3 days in the refrigerator.

THE DELICATE PART

To cut the noodles, fold the dough over itself in thirds, like you're folding a letter.

USES

Served hot, in a dashi broth (nabeyaki udon, page 220), with tempura (tempura udon), or fried tofu (kitsune udon). Served cold (cold chicken udon, page 216) with mentsuyu dipping sauce.

TYPES

The shape and thickness of udon vary from region to region in Japan: in Gunma Himokawa prefecture, udon noodles are very thin and wide, like lasagna noodles. In Tochigi, udon are short and are ear-shaped. In Hokkaido, the wheat flour is replaced by potato starch (gosetsu udon).

Learn

SERVES 4

¾ cup plus 2 teaspoons / 190 ml water
2½ teaspoons / 15 g fine salt
3⅓ cups / 400 g pastry flour
¾ cup / 100 g cornstarch for dusting

1   Pour the water into a bowl, add the salt, and stir until dissolved. Place the flour in a large bowl and incorporate the salted water a little at a time. Mix the dough until it becomes homogeneous.

2   Knead for 5 minutes and form into a ball. Cover with plastic wrap and leave to rest for 1 hour.

3   Dust the work surface. Place the dough on the surface and spread it out, kneading for 5 minutes with your fingertips (as with bread). Shape into a disk.

4   Roll the dough over onto itself by hand and smash it down. Wrap it with plastic wrap and leave to rest at room temperature for 1 hour.

5   Knead again for 5 minutes then form a ball and leave to rest again for 1 hour.

6   Dust the rolling pin and roll out the dough into a large square, rolling vertically and horizontally, while rotating the dough.

7   Roll out the dough to a thickness of 3 mm.

8   Dust the dough and fold it into thirds without applying pressure. Cut into slices ¹⁄₁₆-inch / 2 mm thick with a sharp knife then unfold the udon.

9   Place the noodles in a dusted tray.

SOBA NOODLES

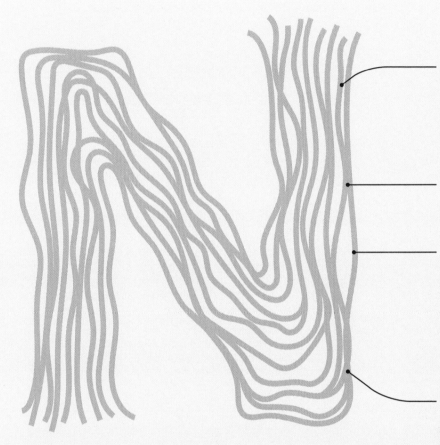

WHAT ARE THEY?

Soba noodles are made from buckwheat flour (mainly produced in Hokkaido) mixed with a small amount of ordinary wheat flour. They are among the most popular in Japan.

ORIGIN

They are uniquely Japanese.

CHARACTERISTICS

They are usually thin (about 2 mm in diameter) and light brown. They are available dried or fresh. Each year, with the first buckwheat harvest, new soba are offered for sale in shops or restaurants under the name shin (new) soba; they are particularly sought after.

NUTRITION

Soba noodles are considered healthy because they are low in calories, nutritious (rich in fiber and protein), and have antioxidant effects.

USES

Hot: in a dashi broth, on their own or with tempura (tempura soba), or fried tofu (kitsune soba). Cold: with mentsuyu dipping sauce.

STORAGE

Dry soba will keep for months in their packaging (if opened, use within the year), away from heat, light, and humidity. Fresh soba can be kept for 3 days in the refrigerator.

HOW TO COOK

Bring a large pot of water to a boil. Once boiling, add the soba noodles in a fan shape. Stir occasionally with chopsticks and cook for about 5 minutes, according to package directions. Drain the noodles and rinse well with cold water.

IMPORTANT

If the noodles are not cooled immediately, they will continue to cook, absorbing additional water, leading them to swell and turn gummy.

SOMEN NOODLES

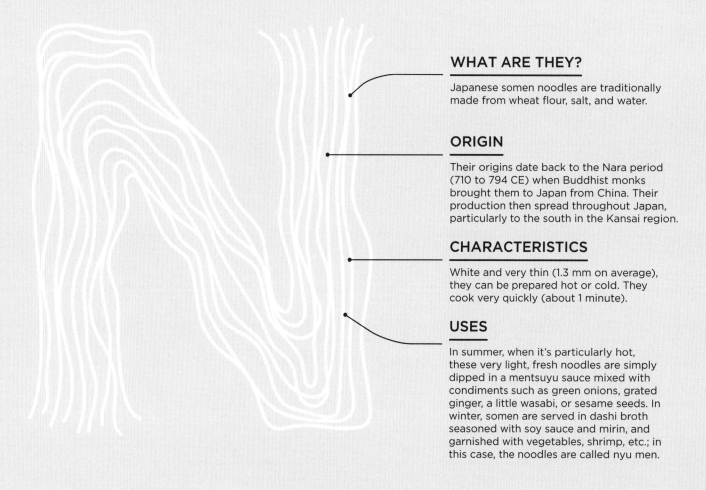

WHAT ARE THEY?

Japanese somen noodles are traditionally made from wheat flour, salt, and water.

ORIGIN

Their origins date back to the Nara period (710 to 794 CE) when Buddhist monks brought them to Japan from China. Their production then spread throughout Japan, particularly to the south in the Kansai region.

CHARACTERISTICS

White and very thin (1.3 mm on average), they can be prepared hot or cold. They cook very quickly (about 1 minute).

USES

In summer, when it's particularly hot, these very light, fresh noodles are simply dipped in a mentsuyu sauce mixed with condiments such as green onions, grated ginger, a little wasabi, or sesame seeds. In winter, somen are served in dashi broth seasoned with soy sauce and mirin, and garnished with vegetables, shrimp, etc.; in this case, the noodles are called nyu men.

STORAGE

Dry somen noodles can be stored for months in their packaging (if opened, use within the year) away from heat, light, and humidity.

HOW TO COOK

Bring a large pot of water to a boil. Once boiling, add the noodles in a fan shape. Stir occasionally with chopsticks and cook for 1 to 2 minutes, according to package directions. Drain the noodles and rinse well with cold water.

IMPORTANT

After cooking, always rinse the somen in cold water, otherwise, the starch remaining on the surface of the noodles will make them sticky and will also dissolve in the soup, making it cloudy.

Understand

UMAMI

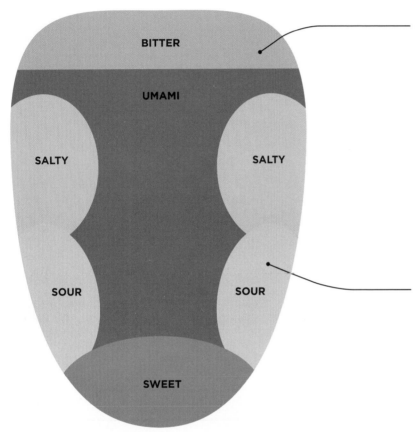

BITTER

UMAMI

SALTY

SALTY

SOUR

SOUR

SWEET

WHAT IS IT?

Umami means "savory taste" in Japanese; it's a fifth taste in addition to sweet, salty, bitter, and sour. This deep flavor is round in the mouth and envelops the palate while enhancing taste.

ORIGIN

Umami was identified in Japan in 1908 by the Japanese researcher Ikeda Kikunae after consuming a seaweed broth. The taste comes from an amino acid, glutamate, present in certain foods. In its natural state, glutamate is highly beneficial to health, as it is a neurotransmitter that enables cells to exchange information. However, manufactured glutamate as an additive is not recommended.

WHERE TO FIND IT?
Japanese sauces and condiments: soy sauce, ponzu sauce, mirin, fermented foods like miso paste, dashi broths, and beef or chicken broth.
Fish: sea bream and mackerel.
Meat: beef contains plenty of umami if it is not overcooked.
Vegetables: mushrooms (like shiitakes), onions, and cooked tomatoes.
Preparation methods: fermentation, maturation, and slow cooking.

HOW TO DEVELOP UMAMI
Specific cooking methods can be used to preserve or develop umami:

Okaage (page 284): a method that consists of cooking ingredients (mainly vegetables) in water, or cooking them slowly on low heat, then letting the ingredients rest in a colander without soaking in water. The juice or cooking water is drained off while the ingredients cool. Because the water is drained and the vegetables' umami is not lost, the vegetables develop delicious flavors.

Kobujime (page 285): a method of sandwiching whole fish fillets or sliced sashimi between pieces of kombu to give the fish a rich umami flavor.

Understand

SHOYU
SOY SAUCE

WHAT IS IT?

Soy sauce, or "shoyu" in Japanese, is a fermented condiment essential to Japanese cuisine. It is made from a mixture of soybeans, wheat, grains, and sea salt.

CHARACTERISTICS

Rich in "umami" amino acids, it is dark brown and has a pronounced salty taste.

HOW TO CHOOSE

Look for the words "naturally brewed" or "fermented" on the bottle to ensure quality. Also check that the sauce contains no ingredients other than soy, wheat, water, and salt.

STORAGE

Once opened, naturally brewed soy sauce can be refrigerated for 6 months.

TYPES

1. Koikuchi shoyu
Used in many recipes, this is the most common soy sauce and is widely available.
2. Shiro shoyu (white soy sauce)
This is the lightest in color of the varieties. It has a subtle taste but a unique aroma and is used in clear soups and chawanmushi (page 148).
3. Usukuchi shoyu (light soy sauce)
Less dark and fragrant than Koikuchi sauce, but a little saltier. Use for recipes without color, like dashimaki (omelet, page 84) and agebitashi (page 140).

4. Saishikomi shoyu (double fermented soy sauce)
After the first brewing cycle, this soy sauce is fermented a second time. After a total maturing period of 24 to 36 months, it develops complex aromas and a velvety texture. It's an exceptional soy sauce to use with sashimi, sushi, tofu, etc., in order to appreciate its natural flavor.
5. Tamari shoyu (Tamari soy sauce)
This uses the soy sauce on the surface of the fermentation tank after a long, natural maturing process (18 months). It is then diluted with water to give it greater fluidity (but remains thicker and more viscous than Koikuchi sauce). The salt content is lower. It is mainly used for sushi and sashimi, due to its intense flavor.

1   2   3   4   5

TOFU

WHAT IS IT?

Tofu is a paste made from soybeans cooked in water, pureed, strained, and filtered. The resulting soy milk is then coagulated with nigari (traditional sea salt), placed in a mold, and pressed.

NUTRITION

Highly nutritious (rich in protein and calcium), it offers numerous health benefits (prevention of heart disease, osteoporosis, and cancer) and supports healthy aging.

TIP

Kinugoshi silken tofu is delicate and fragile, rendering it difficult to cook; it should be used as is.

STORAGE

Tofu is sold in sealed plastic packaging: it can be stored in the refrigerator until the expiration date. Once opened, tofu should be covered with water and refrigerated in a sealed container. It can be kept for 2 to 3 days or consumed as soon as possible.

TYPES

1. Kinugoshi
Silken tofu: very soft, smooth, delicate
Uses: miso soup (page 58), surinagashi (page 68), hiyayakko (page 160).
2. Momen
Firm tofu: compact but still soft, this is the most common variety
Uses: nabe (page 238), agedashi tofu (page 142), steamed red mullet (page 152), salads.
3.Hard
Extra-firm tofu: contains less water
Uses: sautéed, fried, etc.

1   **2**   **3**

Understand

MISO

WHAT IS IT?

Miso is a matured, fermented paste made from boiled or steamed soybeans, rice, or other grains, and a fermentation starter called koji (unique to Japan).

ORIGIN

Miso paste is an ancestral condiment in Japanese cuisine. First imported from China, as "hishio," it has transformed over the centuries into miso.

NUTRITION

Its enzymes and probiotics aid digestion, enrich intestinal flora, and boost immunity.

USES

It is a condiment that can replace salt or soy sauce. Miso adds color, consistency, and flavor, especially to soups and broths (miso ramen), and is an alternative to processed bouillon cubes. It's also the star ingredient in miso soup. Miso is also used in fish and chicken marinades, and even in cakes and cookies.

TIP

To preserve its enzymes, miso paste is added at the last minute to hot dishes and soups, after dissolving it in a little hot water. Add in gradually and taste well between each addition.

STORAGE

Miso paste keeps for 6 months to 2 years in the refrigerator.

TYPES

Miso pastes differ according to the grain used to make them, their more or less salty flavor, their color, and the region in which they are produced:
1. **Shiro miso:** white miso, from rice
2. **Aka miso:** red miso, from rice, salty
3. **Hacho miso:** from soy, 11% salinity, strong taste. It can be used alone or mixed with other types of miso (dengaku page 98)
4. **Inaka miso:** wheat miso, light in color, mild
5. **Sendai miso:** rice, red, salty
6. **Shinshu miso:** white rice miso, sometimes wheat

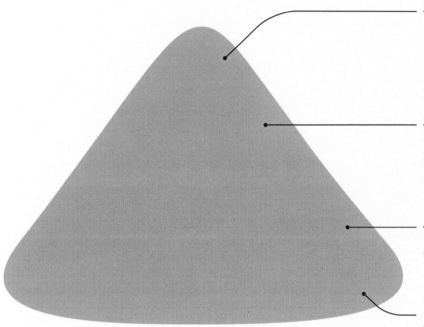

MIRIN

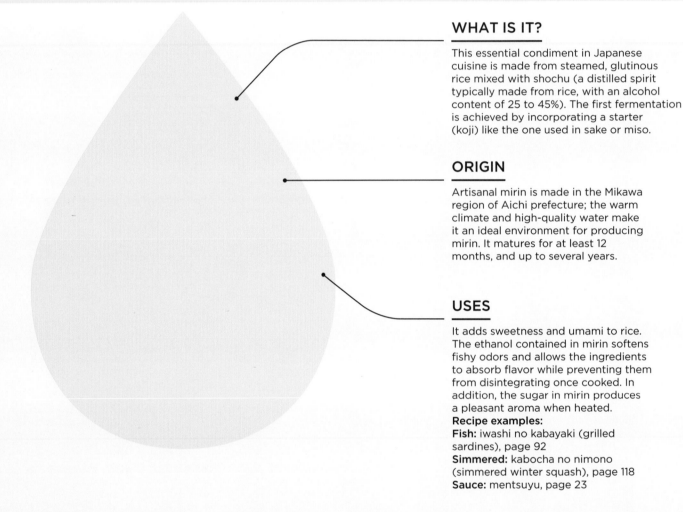

WHAT IS IT?

This essential condiment in Japanese cuisine is made from steamed, glutinous rice mixed with shochu (a distilled spirit typically made from rice, with an alcohol content of 25 to 45%). The first fermentation is achieved by incorporating a starter (koji) like the one used in sake or miso.

ORIGIN

Artisanal mirin is made in the Mikawa region of Aichi prefecture; the warm climate and high-quality water make it an ideal environment for producing mirin. It matures for at least 12 months, and up to several years.

USES

It adds sweetness and umami to rice. The ethanol contained in mirin softens fishy odors and allows the ingredients to absorb flavor while preventing them from disintegrating once cooked. In addition, the sugar in mirin produces a pleasant aroma when heated.
Recipe examples:
Fish: iwashi no kabayaki (grilled sardines), page 92
Simmered: kabocha no nimono (simmered winter squash), page 118
Sauce: mentsuyu, page 23

TIP

Mirin contains alcohol, so if you are going to use it as a seasoning without cooking, evaporate the alcohol first by heating it in a saucepan or in the microwave.

STORAGE

Unopened: 360 to 540 days when kept at room temperature.
After opening: 90 days in the refrigerator.

TYPES

There are several types of mirin:
Hon mirin: considered the best and the most authentic. It is generally the most expensive. It has the longest maturation time and contains 14% alcohol.
Shin mirin: processed and generally less expensive. It is made much more quickly and contains a small degree of alcohol, artificial alcohol, and cornstarch. It has a maturation time of anywhere from one day to several weeks.

Understand

MENTSUYU

WHAT IS IT?

A sauce made from dashi, soy sauce, mirin (or sake), and sugar. You can buy pre-made mentsuyu in Asian grocery stores.

TOTAL TIME

Prep time: 5 minutes
Cook time: 10 minutes
Rest time: overnight

EQUIPMENT

Stainless steel fine mesh strainer
1 pint / 500 ml bottle with lid

USES

In noodle dishes such as soba, udon, and somen. This very versatile sauce can also be used for simmered, stir-fried, tempura, pilaf, and salad dishes.

STORAGE

The sauce can be kept for 3 months in the refrigerator.

VARIATION

Cold version: add 1 tablespoon vinegar and 1 tablespoon toasted sesame oil for ⅓ cup plus 4 teaspoons / 100 ml sauce and serve with a salad or cold noodles.

FOR ABOUT 2 CUPS / 500 ML

1¼ cups / 300 ml soy sauce
1¼ cups / 300 ml mirin
5-inch square piece / 15 g kombu
1⅔ cup / 20 g katsuobushi
        (dried bonito flakes)

1   Pour the soy sauce and mirin into a saucepan and add the kombu. Cover and leave at room temperature overnight.

2   Heat over low heat to bring to a gentle boil. Add the katsuobushi, cook for about 3 minutes, then remove from heat. Leave to cool.

3   Strain the sauce and pour the liquid into a bottle.

Understand
VINEGAR

WHAT IS IT?

Vinegar is an essential ingredient in Japanese cuisine: it is used as a seasoning and in marinades. It also firms the flesh of fish and meat, has a sterilizing effect, and allows products to be preserved for a long time.

TYPES

In Japanese cuisine, 3 different types of vinegar can be used depending on the dish. They each have different compositions and flavors:

1. Japanese grain vinegar
This vinegar, made from a mixture of wheat, sake lees, rice, and corn, is very popular for everyday cooking. It is less expensive than rice vinegar. It has a fairly mild taste.

2. Rice vinegar
Rice vinegar is one of the main condiments of Japanese cuisine. Higher in quality and more expensive, pure rice vinegar only contains rice and water. It is amber in color and has a mellow flavor that will enhance any dish. This vinegar is particularly suitable for fish marinades (such as the one made for mackerel sushi, page 208), sushi rice, and salads. It can also be used to make tsukemono (pickled vegetables, page 170) and gari (page 54).

3. Sushi vinegar
Sushi rice vinegar is already seasoned (salt and sugar) and ready to use. It is used to flavor rice and can also be used on salads and raw vegetables to add a touch of freshness.

1   **2**   **3**

Understand

COOKING
SAKE

WHAT IS IT?

Sake is made from steamed rice to which koji yeast is added for fermentation. The matured mix is pressed and filtered, then the filtered product is heated and distilled. To obtain cooking sake, 3% salt is added to the sake at the end of the process. It has the advantage of being less expensive than drinking sake. It can only be used for cooking.

USES

Cooking sake is indispensable for many Japanese recipes, just as wine or strong spirits are in French cuisine. It adds taste, flavor, and umami:
- it is used, along with other ingredients, in fish and meat marinades (karaage, page 132);
- it is also used to enhance hot pots (page 234 and following);
- in food preparation, such as fish, to reduce odor (prepare fish, page 33; red mullet, tofu, and shiitake mushrooms steamed in sake, page 156);
- in desserts to enhance flavor (dorayaki, page 262).

STORAGE

Unopened cooking sake can be stored for about 9 months to 1 year. After opening, it will keep for about 2 months.

Understand

SEAWEED

WHAT IS IT?

An edible product of the sea, seaweed is essential to Japanese cuisine. It represents the link between nature and the sea that characterizes Japan.

NUTRITION

It provides numerous nutrients, trace elements, and vitamins (iodine, iron, magnesium, calcium, vitamin C).

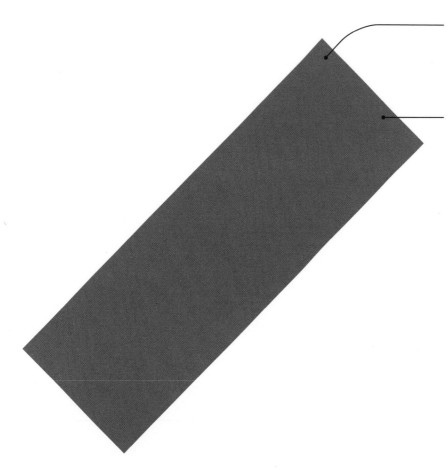

1. AOSA NORI
Small, dried seaweed flakes.
Uses: enhances and accompanies a wide range of dishes such as okonomiyaki (page 88) and stir-fried rice (chahan).

2. WAKAME
Green in color and 1 or 2 meters long, this seaweed grows on submerged rocks before being cut and dried. Rich in vitamins and containing no fat, it is a particularly healthy seaweed. A blend of wakame and other seaweeds is also available.
Uses: dried wakame becomes supple again when soaked for 15 minutes in lukewarm water. Once rehydrated, it can garnish soups and salads.

Storage: dried wakame can be stored in an airtight bag in a cool place.

3. NORI
The most well-known; this dried seaweed in the form of a flat sheet is made from orange-brown algae washed with fresh water and sun-dried. Rich in plant-based protein, vitamins, and minerals, it is widely available in packs of 5 or 10 sheets.
Uses: in sheets for rolling maki, preparing sushi, and wrapping onigiri. Flakes can be used as a decorative garnish, with soba noodles, for example.

1

2

3

Learn

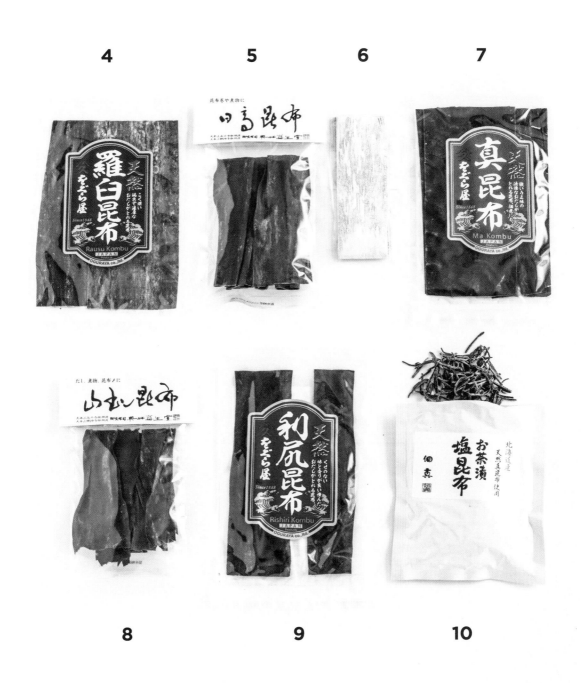

4 **5** **6** **7**

8 **9** **10**

KOMBU

Giant kelp with a briny taste, which grows off the coast of the island of Hokkaido in northern Japan

4. Rausu kombu: wider in shape, it is found on the Pacific coast of the island of Hokkaido near the town of Rausu. It is the main ingredient in dashi, producing a slightly cloudy broth with an intense flavor; ideal for miso or noodle soups.

5. Hidaka kombu: with its pronounced aroma, it is best in simmered dishes. It is also recommended rolled in maki, julienned and cooked with seasonal vegetables, and added to oden.

6. Shiraita kombu: a type of kombu whose surface texture has been shaved off with the blade of a knife. Harvested on the island of Hokkaido, it macerates in distilled vinegar for a full day.

7. and 8. Makombu (or yamadashi): comes from the southern part of Hokkaido near the town of Hakodate. Not as hard as rishiri kombu, it can be used in kobujime and makes a high-quality clear dashi. It is also prepared simmered (nikonbu), particularly in the Osaka region.

9. Rishiri kombu: harvested in northern Hokkaido in the Soya Misaki region near the town of Wakkanai and on the nearby islands of Rebun and Rishiri.

This premium kombu yields a very clear dashi that is used, for example, in traditional Kyoto cuisine.

10. Shio Kombu: finely dried kombu cut into strips that are then cooked in soy sauce with salt and sugar. It is used in onigiri, tsukemono (page 170), ochazuke, and in salads.

Dried kombu: wipe with a damp cloth before soaking in water to soften and clean without removing the white film. This film is similar to a powder called "mannit" and is the umami component of kelp. It is therefore important not to remove it.

DASHI
BROTH

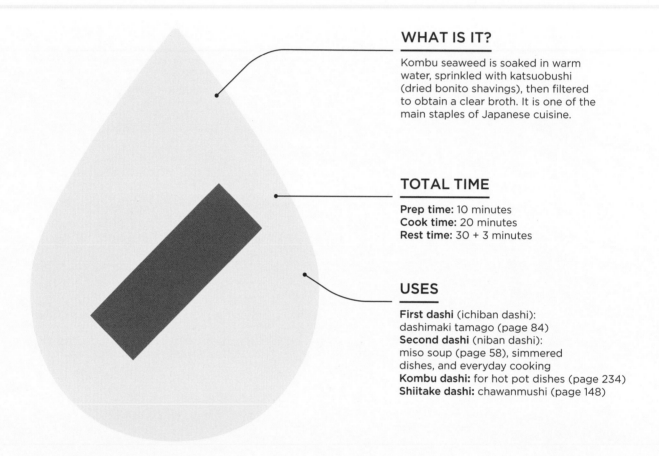

WHAT IS IT?

Kombu seaweed is soaked in warm water, sprinkled with katsuobushi (dried bonito shavings), then filtered to obtain a clear broth. It is one of the main staples of Japanese cuisine.

TOTAL TIME

Prep time: 10 minutes
Cook time: 20 minutes
Rest time: 30 + 3 minutes

USES

First dashi (ichiban dashi): dashimaki tamago (page 84)
Second dashi (niban dashi): miso soup (page 58), simmered dishes, and everyday cooking
Kombu dashi: for hot pot dishes (page 234)
Shiitake dashi: chawanmushi (page 148)

TIPS

To preserve umami, the kombu and katsuobushi used for the first dashi are not thrown away; they are reused in a second dashi. The longer the kombu soaks, the better the dashi. Some chefs therefore recommend soaking the seaweed for up to 24 hours.

DIFFERENT DASHIS

Kombu dashi: with kombu only.
Katsuobushi dashi : with katsuobushi (dried bonito) only.
Awase dashi : a combination of kombu and katsuobushi. This is the most common dashi.

OTHER TYPES

Today, there are also numerous instant dashi variations in powder, liquid, or packet form, allowing for quick and affordable preparation. They are very popular in Japan:
- dehydrated dashi powder (freeze-dried extract of dashi broth made from kombu and katsuobushi);
- liquid dashi (such as Shiro dashi, made with kombu extract, katsuobushi, light soy sauce, mirin, and sugar);
- dashi packets (like tea bags, with a mixture of kombu powder, katsuobushi, and sometimes dried shiitake).

STORAGE

Fresh dashi: 3 days in the refrigerator.
Liquid dashi: 2 weeks to 1 month in the refrigerator, once opened.
Dashi powder or packets: about 2 weeks, once opened.

Learn

FOR 3¾ CUPS / 900 ML OF FIRST DASHI AND 3⅓ CUPS / 800 ML OF SECOND DASHI

FIRST DASHI

4¼ cups / 1 L water
20 g kombu
2½ cups / 30 g katsuobushi
(dried bonito flakes)

SECOND DASHI

4¼ cups / 1 L water
The kombu from the first dashi
1¼ cups / 15 g katsuobushi
(dried bonito flakes)

FIRST DASHI

1 Gently wipe the kombu with a slightly damp cloth.

2 Pour the water into a bowl, add the kombu, and leave to soak: 30 minutes in summer; at least 2 to 3 hours in winter.

3 Pour into a saucepan. Cook for at least 10 minutes over low heat.

4 Remove the kombu with a skimmer or slotted spoon and set aside for the second dashi. Bring to a boil and add the 2½ cups / 30 g katsuobushi. Remove from heat. Leave to stand for 5 minutes, until the katsuobushi settles to the bottom of the pan.

5 Filter the broth through a strainer, reserving the katsuobushi for the second broth.

SECOND DASHI

1 Pour the water into a saucepan and add the kombu and katsuobushi from the first dashi. Bring to a boil, then simmer over low heat for 15 minutes; the broth should reduce by about a third. Add the 1¼ cups / 15 g katsuobushi and remove from the heat.

2 Leave to stand for 3 minutes, until the katsuobushi settles to the bottom of the pan. Strain the broth.

SHIITAKE
& OTHER MUSHROOMS

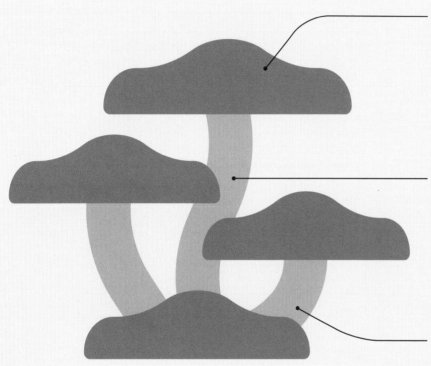

WHAT IS IT?

Shiitake is a widely used mushroom in Japanese cooking.

NUTRITION

Mushrooms are rich in B vitamins and have antioxidant and cholesterol-lowering properties.

GROWING & HARVESTING

Shiitake mushrooms grow twice a year, in spring and autumn, under trees. Japan's mountainous geography and warm, humid climate are ideal for mushroom growth. Shiitake mushrooms are available fresh or dried.

TIP

Allowing fresh mushrooms to dry before use enhances their flavor and umami. Place them, whole or in slices, in a flat-bottomed bamboo basket or sieve; make sure they are evenly spaced to let the air circulate. Leave them to air-dry for 2 or 3 days.

1. SHIMEJI

Characteristics: these mushrooms grow in autumn in bunches with an interconnected base. They are brown or white, with a nutty flavor
Preparation: cut the roots to about 1¼ inches / 3 cm and wash in cold water.
Uses: they should be eaten cooked. Most often sautéed, they can also be used as an ingredient in rice, noodle, tempura, and hot pot dishes.

2. ENOKITAKE

Characteristics: they come in clusters and have a small white cap with a slender stem. With a mild, fruity flavor, they go well with seaweed and bean sprouts.
Preparation: trim off the root section (about 1¼ inches / 3 cm) and wash with cold water.
Uses: they should be eaten cooked. Add into hot pot dishes or Japanese stews. They can also be sautéed in a little oil for 1 to 2 minutes with a drizzle of soy sauce.

3 & 5. SHIITAKE

Characteristics: there are many local varieties. The most well-known are: shii mushrooms (named after the so-called Japanese tree species) (5), the best of which have a dark, velvety brown cap. They are appreciated for their woody flavor and soft texture. The donko shiitakes (winter mushrooms) (3), have a small cracked hat, and are fleshy, swollen, with a woody scent.

Learn

1 2 3

4 5 6

They are the most popular shiitakes.
Uses: shiitake mushrooms accompany meats, mainly beef. They can be grilled or fried into fritters. Dried shiitakes are best cooked in sauce, added to other simmered vegetables, for example in chawanmushi (page 148), or prepared with rice.
Preparation: using an absorbent kitchen towel, remove all traces of soil and trim the toughest part of the stems. For dried shiitakes, soak in lukewarm water for 2 to 3 hours, or for 30 minutes in hot water.
Warning: shiitake mushrooms are potentially toxic if eaten uncooked.

4. KIKURAGE
Characteristics: black mushroom shaped like an ear. They are most commonly available dried.
Preparation: soak in water for 15 to 30 minutes, rinse and drain.
Uses: chewy and firm, they have no pronounced taste, though they easily absorb the flavors of other foods and add texture and consistency to a dish. They are eaten cooked, go perfectly with soups, nages, or fried noodles, and can be used as a base for sauces.

6. ERINGI
Characteristics: a member of the oyster mushroom family, native to southern Europe and cultivated in Japan since the 1990s, eringi mushrooms are eaten in autumn and winter. Choose mushrooms with white stems and smooth caps.
Preparation: wash quickly and slice or mince according to the recipe.
Uses: although not overly fragrant, they are favored for their fleshy texture and can be sautéed or grilled, or used as an addition to soups, pasta, rice, tempura, and hot pot dishes (pages 234 to 246).

FISH PREPARATION

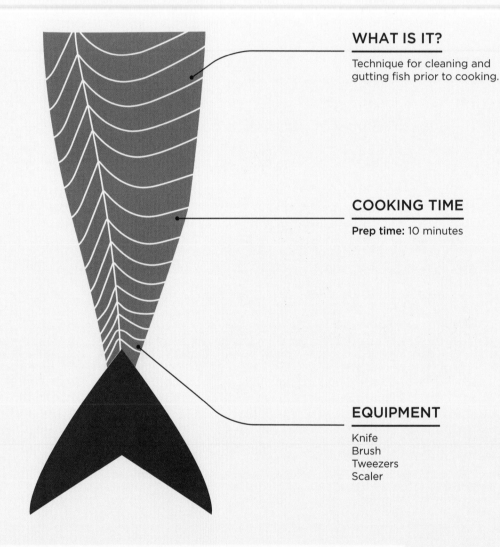

WHAT IS IT?
Technique for cleaning and gutting fish prior to cooking.

COOKING TIME
Prep time: 10 minutes

EQUIPMENT
Knife
Brush
Tweezers
Scaler

USES
This method of cutting fish is called Daimyou oroshi. It is used for fish such as horse mackerel, sardines, and other small fish.

Preparing mackerel / horse mackerel

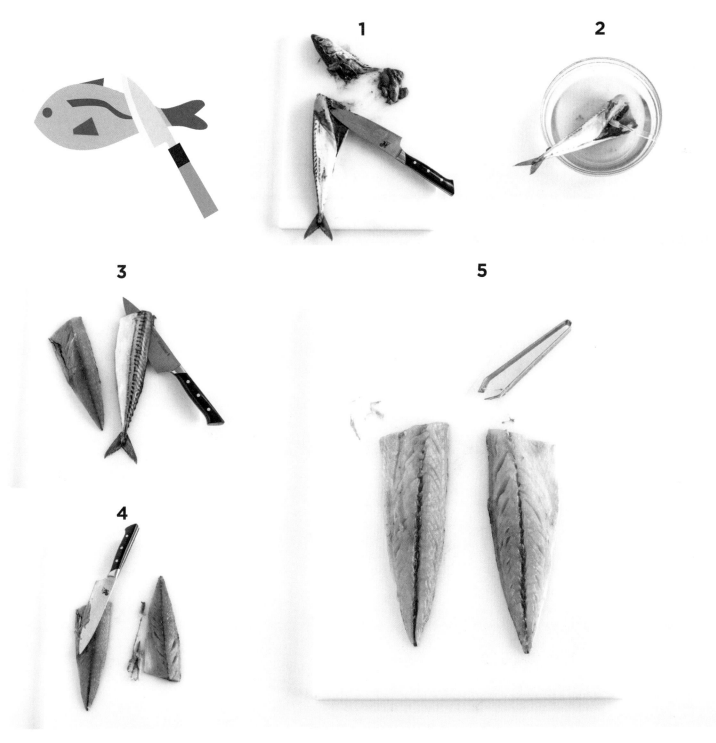

REMOVING THE ZEIGO FROM HORSE MACKEREL

Using a knife, remove the hard scales (zeigo) specific to this fish: slide the tip of the knife over the back, from tail to head, moving the knife in an up-and-down motion, while applying gentle pressure. The zeigo is more prominent towards the head of the fish.

PREPARE MACKEREL / HORSE MACKEREL

1 Between the fish's pectoral fin and ventral fin, holding the knife blade perpendicular to the cutting board, cut right through to the backbone. Turn the fish over and place the knife in the same position as before: make an incision and then cut off the head.

2 Cut along the belly and remove the internal organs. Slice the spinal cord membrane (it contains a lot of blood) all along the backbone. Clean the inside carefully with a brush and wash with water. Wipe dry with paper towels.

FILLET

3 Starting from the head end, insert a knife and slide it over the backbone. While holding the fish with your left hand, cut in one stroke and separate at the tail.

4 Turn the fish over and cut the other side in the same way.

DEBONE

5 Using the tip of a knife, separate the flesh from the abdominal bones in a sliding motion. Use tweezers to remove small bones, checking with your fingers that none remain.

Preparing sea bream for sashimi

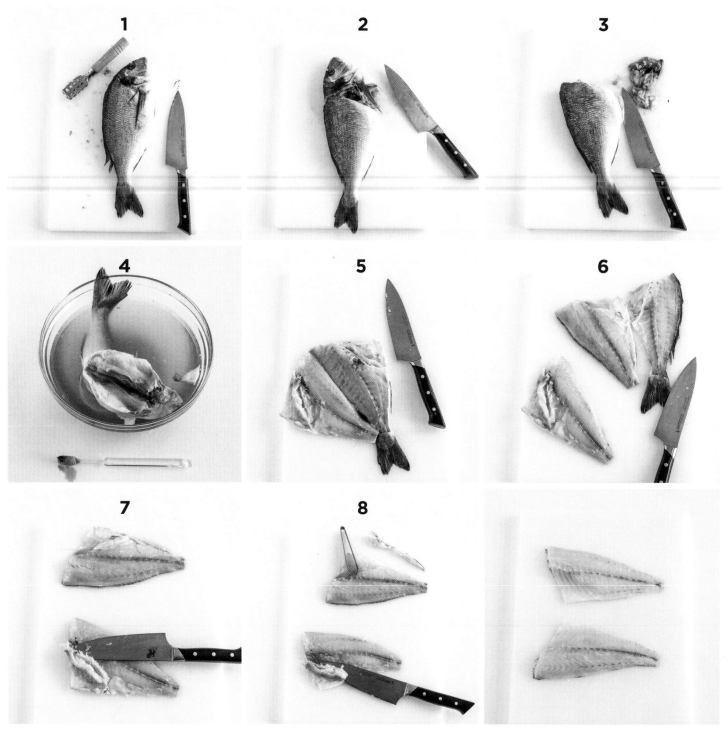

1 Remove the scales using a fish scaler. For the small scales that remain on the sides of the fins, scrape with the tip of a knife. Wash the fish and pat dry with paper towels.

2 Make an incision at the gills. Start behind the pectoral fin and move towards the fish's ventral fin (at the abdomen). Hold the knife blade perpendicular to the cutting board and cut until you reach the backbone.

3 Turn the fish over and place the knife in the same position as before, make the incision, and cut off the head. Continue the incision and cut open the belly. Remove the gills and internal organs. Slice through the spinal cord membrane (which contains a lot of blood) all along the backbone.

4 Clean the inside carefully with a brush and wash with water. Wipe with paper towels.

5 Slice all the way down the abdomen to the tail. Make another incision perpendicular to the base of the tail.

6 While lifting the flesh, insert the knife until you reach the backbone and slide it along the entire length to cut and remove the filleted flesh.

7 Turn the fish over and cut along the dorsal fin until you reach the backbone. Make an incision at the base of the tail. Then slide the knife along the bones to cut and remove the flesh for the second fillet.

8 Using the tip of the knife, separate the flesh from the abdominal bones in a sliding motion. Use tweezers to remove small dorsal bones, checking with your fingers to see if any remain.

Preparing sardines

1   Remove the scales by gently running the blade of the knife along the length of the fish without cutting into it. Scrape off any remaining scales with the tip of the knife. Place the knife at the back of the head and cut it off.

2   Slit the underside of the belly lengthwise and scoop out the internal organs with the tip of a knife or your index finger, sliding it along the backbone. Wash the fish with water and pat dry inside and out with paper towels.

3   Insert your left thumb into the belly of the sardine and slide it, pressing gently along the backbone, working your way towards the tail to open the sardine in two without tearing it. Repeat, this time moving towards the head.

4   With your fingers, pinch the backbone at the base of the tail.

5   Loosen the backbone and pull gently to separate it from the flesh.

6   Along the sides of the sardine, slide the knife in an outward motion to remove the abdominal bones.

Preparing shrimp for tempura

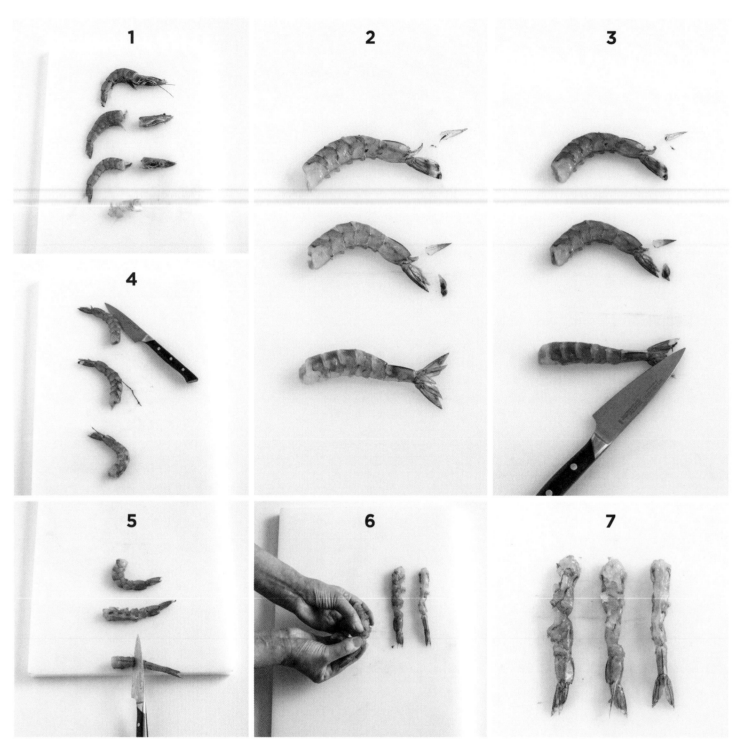

1 Remove the heads. Peel off the entire shell, except the tail.

2 Place the shrimp on a cutting board, remove the top part of the tail, and cut the end of the bottom of the tail at an angle.

3 Place the shrimp on its belly and slide the tip of the knife over the flattened tail to eliminate the water.

4 Make a slit in the back to remove the black vein.

5 Lay the shrimp lengthwise on its back, parallel to the edge of the cutting board. Make a few slits (4 or 5) on the belly. To avoid cutting all the way through, place the knife blade on the edge of the board when cutting.

6 Using your fingers, cut the nerve cord and gently stretch the body lengthwise to prevent it from curling up during cooking. Do the same for the other shrimp.

7 Set on paper towels and refrigerate.

TIPS

The choice of shrimp is important for the success of the tempura: ideally, the shrimp should be between 5 to 6 inches / 13 to 15 cm long. Select wild, fresh, unfrozen shrimp if possible; the peak season is between June and September.

Preparing shrimp for sushi

1   Remove the heads from the shrimp and insert a bamboo skewer lengthwise between the shrimp's shell and the flesh, starting at the top of the body and ending with the tail. Prepare ice water in a salad bowl and set aside.

2   Pour about 2 cups / 500 ml of water into a saucepan and bring to a boil. Add 1 teaspoon salt and 1 teaspoon rice or grain vinegar. Add the shrimp. Cook for about 3 minutes.

3   Drain, plunge into ice-cold water, and leave to cool for 3 to 5 minutes. Once the prawns have cooled, drain.

4   Remove the skewers, then shell the prawns, except for the tails.

5   Place a shrimp on a cutting board. Trim the end of the tail at an angle.

6   Turn the shrimp on its side on the cutting board with the belly to the right. Slice lengthwise.

7   Use the knife to turn the shrimp over onto its back, and strike one time from top to bottom on the board, in an almost rocking motion, taking care not to cut the prawn in half.

8   Pour cold water into a bowl, wash the shrimp, and remove the black vein from the back. Drain.

9   Set the shrimp on a plate lined with paper towels and place in the refrigerator.

Preparing octopus

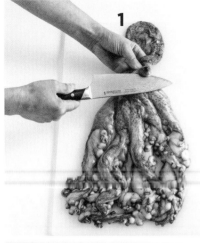

FOR 1 OCTOPUS

1 octopus (about 2.6 pounds / 1.2 kg)
7 teaspoons / 40 g kosher salt
    for cleaning
3½ teaspoons / 20 g kosher salt
    for cooking
1 green tea bag

1 If the octopus's body, which contains internal organs, has not been emptied, turn the round part inside out and remove the organs with a knife or by hand. Rinse thoroughly under running water. Use a knife to remove the eyeballs.

2 Remove the beak with your fingers.

3 Place the octopus and the 7 teaspoons of kosher salt in a bowl. Rub and massage with hands for 5 to 10 minutes to remove impurities and slime.

4 Wash the octopus with water to remove any remaining impurities. Wash the inside of the suckers on the tentacles.

5 In a saucepan, heat 8 cups / 2 L water with 3½ teaspoons of kosher salt and the tea bag. When the water boils, take the octopus by the head and plunge the tips of the tentacles into the boiling water, then take them out again. Repeat this process several times to prevent the tentacles from getting tangled.

Then plunge the whole octopus into the water and wait for it to boil again. Cook over low heat for 5 to 10 minutes, depending on its size. Turn the octopus upside down for the last 1 to 2 minutes.

6 Drain, plunge the octopus into cold water, then drain again. Leave to cool in a colander.

TIPS
The cooking time depends on the weight of the octopus: 5 minutes for 2½ to 3 pounds / 1.2 to 1.3 kilos and 8 minutes for 4½ pounds / 2 kilos. A component called tannin in tea softens the octopus. Tannins also eliminate the odor of the octopus and give it a reddish color.

Preparing squid

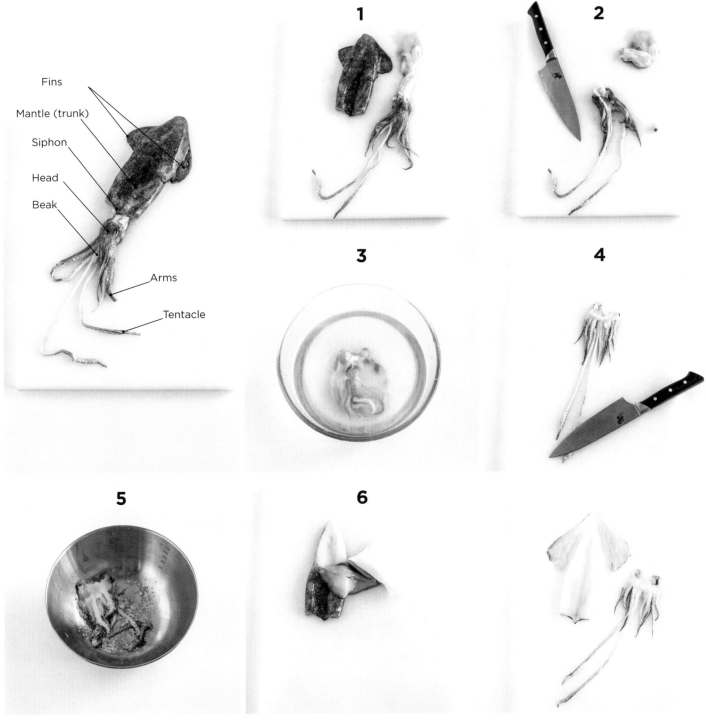

Fins
Mantle (trunk)
Siphon
Head
Beak
Arms
Tentacle

1

2

3

4

5

6

TOTAL TIME

Prep time: 5 minutes

FOR 1 SQUID

1 squid
1 tablespoon kosher salt

1 Insert your thumb into the mantle at the head, lift, and gradually remove the entrails while pulling on the squid's arms.

2 Cut above the head behind the eyes. Make a vertical incision between the eyes and remove the beak.

3 Remove the eyeballs and place them in a bowl of water to prevent the squid ink from spraying out.

4 Scrape off the large suckers from the tentacles with a knife.

5 Place the arms and tentacles in a bowl and sprinkle with 1 tablespoon of salt. Squeeze each squid arm with your fingers to remove the last small suckers. Rinse.

6 Pull the fins towards the body to detach the skin from the entire squid. Finish removing the skin with paper towels. Do the same to strip the skin from the fins. Remove the remaining internal organs from the squid's body and wash thoroughly with water.

Preparing scallops

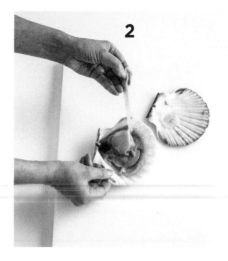

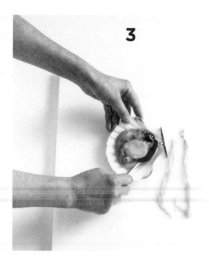

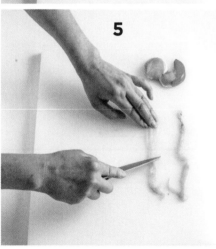

TOTAL TIME

Prep time: 5 minutes

FOR 1 SCALLOP

1 Hold the shell with the flat side up and the domed, concave side in the palm of your hand. Insert a knife into the side of the shell and move it along the top until it comes into contact with the adductor muscle: detach the muscle from the top by sliding the knife blade upwards to open the shell.

2 Remove the top of the shell and examine each part. Remove the frill, all viscera, and any sand. Also remove the black digestive gland (uro) and the gills by pulling with your fingers, then discard.

3 Loosen the white muscle and the coral with a spoon.

4 Remove any blackish residue from the coral with a knife.

5 On a cutting board, hold the frill open with your fingers and gently apply the tip of the knife to scrape off any slime.

6 Place the frill in a bowl, sprinkle with 1 teaspoon of salt, and mix by hand. Once the slime is completely washed off, rinse, change the water several times, and drain. Drain all components: the muscle, coral, and frill, and place on a paper towel.

TIP

A scallop is fresh when it is alive: its shell should be tightly closed, or, when opened, it should close immediately when touched. Avoid scallops with no reaction, those covered with parasites, or those with chipped shells.

Understand

KATSUOBUSHI

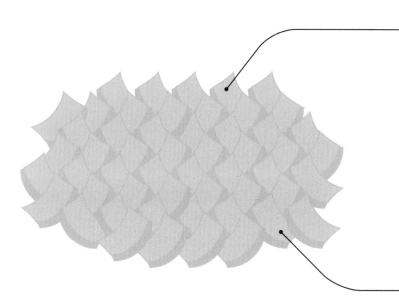

WHAT IS IT?

Japanese condiment made from bonito, also known as skipjack tuna, which has been cooked, dried, fermented, and smoked. It is then finely cut into flakes called hanakatsuo. It is one of the main ingredients in dashi. The umami flavor of bonito flakes is very pronounced and comes from the high content of inosinic acid, which combines with the glutamate in kombu to enhance the umami.

ORIGIN

Katsuobushi is the Japanese name; katsuo = bonito, bushi = boiled and dried fish that have been chopped up (can be called bushi or fushi). Bonito has been eaten by the Japanese since ancient times. Dried bonito is thought to have been used as early as the 5th century. During the Edo period, the torrefaction method became popular, and bonito flakes similar to those we eat today began to be produced.

VARIATIONS

- Different varieties of fish can be used in place of bonito, using the same production process: mackerel, tuna, horse mackerel, anchovies, sardines, etc.
- There are many products made with powdered katsuobushi, such as kombu mixtures, dehydrated dashi, concentrated liquid dashi, and dashi in packets. These are quick and affordable options.
- You can also buy dried bonito fillets and grate the flakes yourself using a special wooden mini-planer available in shops. The flakes will taste even better.

USES

Dashi: katsuobushi is one of the key ingredients, along with kombu. It is also used in miso soup (page 58), Nabeyaki udon (page 220), and mentsuyu sauce (page 23).
As a condiment: sprinkle the flakes directly onto fresh tofu, salad, or okonomiyaki (page 88). Katsuobushi can also be used as an ingredient in onigiri (page 170).

TIP

The fragrance of katsuobushi is its essential element, so it's advisable to use rapidly once the package is opened.

STORAGE

A packet will keep for 1 year. Once opened, close the bag, release as much air as possible, secure with a rubber band, and store in the refrigerator for up to 6 months, ideally no longer than 1 month.

DEBONE
A CHICKEN THIGH

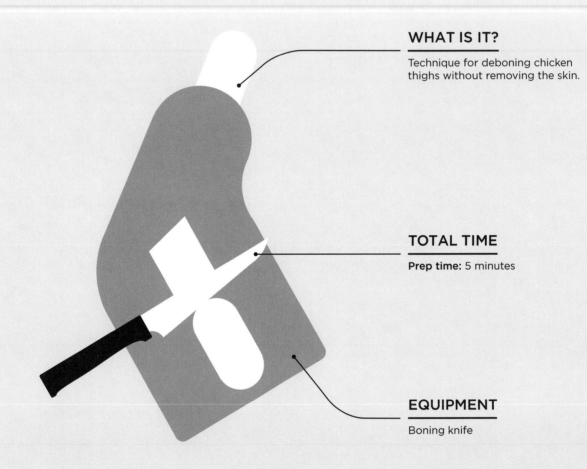

WHAT IS IT?

Technique for deboning chicken thighs without removing the skin.

TOTAL TIME

Prep time: 5 minutes

EQUIPMENT

Boning knife

TECHNIQUE TO MASTER

This fairly simple technique requires a little practice and careful removal of the bones.

TIP

Once removed from the meat, the bones can be used to make chicken stock.

USES

For karaage (fried chicken), yakitori (grilled chicken skewers).

Learn

FOR 1 THIGH

1 chicken leg quarter

1 Remove excess skin and yellow fat from the side of the thigh using the boning knife.

2 The leg is made up of two bones: the tibia and the femur (in the wider part of the leg), with a joint between the two. First, cut lengthwise down the middle of the wider segment and expose the femur by scoring the flesh along its length. Once the bone appears, cut away the flesh on either side to release the bone.

3 Run the knife under the bone and separate it from the flesh. Clear the area around the joint, cut away the remaining flesh, and remove the first bone.

4 For the second bone: cut the flesh down the middle along the bone, from the foot to the joint.

5 Cut into each side as for the first bone. Remove the flesh on each side and run the knife under the bone.

6 Clear away the bone up to the joint.

ANKO
AZUKI PASTE

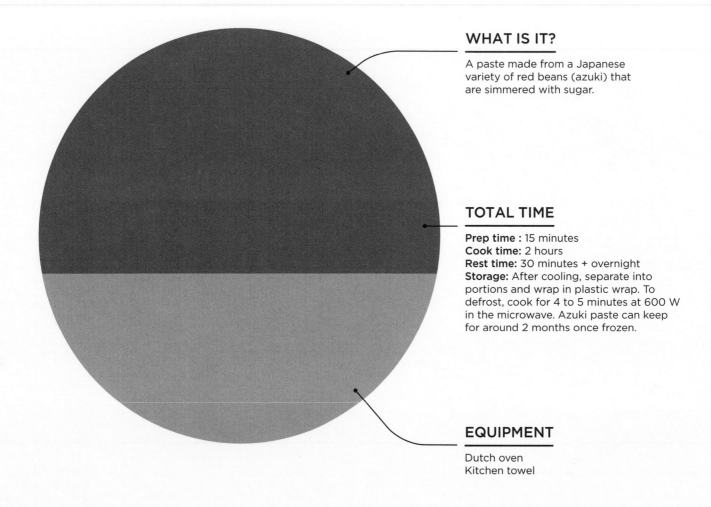

WHAT IS IT?

A paste made from a Japanese variety of red beans (azuki) that are simmered with sugar.

TOTAL TIME

Prep time : 15 minutes
Cook time: 2 hours
Rest time: 30 minutes + overnight
Storage: After cooling, separate into portions and wrap in plastic wrap. To defrost, cook for 4 to 5 minutes at 600 W in the microwave. Azuki paste can keep for around 2 months once frozen.

EQUIPMENT

Dutch oven
Kitchen towel

USES

Japanese desserts

TIPS

- To save time, you can cook pre-blanched azuki beans in a pressure cooker for 20 minutes from the time they are pressurized. Then all that's left to do is mash them, add the sugar and mix.
- The consistency of Azuki paste varies according to how finely the beans have been mashed. It is recommended to strain the beans through a sieve to obtain a very smooth paste.
- Select recently harvested azuki beans by checking the date on the packaging. They will be softer and cook more quickly. If they are too firm, add 1 teaspoon of baking soda.

Learn

FOR 2½ CUPS / 800 G OF PASTE

1½ cups / 300 g azuki beans
1 cup / 200 g raw cane sugar

1   Soak the azukis overnight in a large volume of water.

2   Drain the azukis, place them in a large pot with plenty of water, bring to a boil over high heat, then drain the beans and discard the initial cooking liquid. Refill the pan with water and put the beans back in. Repeat the process twice, replacing the water each time.

3   Place the azukis in the pot and pour in as much water as possible. Bring to a boil over high heat, then reduce to a simmer. Cover and leave to cook for 1 hour. Add water from time to time if necessary - the azukis should remain covered with water.

Check that the beans are cooked; you should be able to crush them with your fingers.

4   When the azukis are done, drain them in a colander lined with a kitchen towel to prevent them from passing through the holes.

5   Return the beans to the pot. Add the sugar and cook uncovered for about 10 minutes over low heat, stirring regularly and mashing the beans with a spatula.

6   When the water has evaporated and the mixture has thickened to the consistency of a paste, remove from heat. Leave to cool at room temperature before storing in the refrigerator.

Understand

TEMPURA BATTER

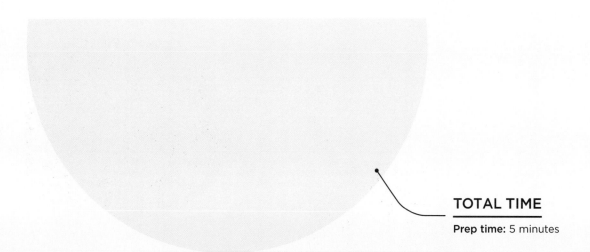

WHAT IS IT?

A batter made from flour, egg, and water which, when fried, forms a thin, crispy crust around the ingredients.

TOTAL TIME

Prep time: 5 minutes

TIP

For perfectly crisp results, use very cold water and refrigerate all the ingredients and containers until you are ready to make the batter. Prepare the batter just before use.

Learn

FOR 4 PEOPLE

100 g pastry flour
1 egg
½ cup plus 2 tablespoons / 150 ml
    cold water
1 pinch of salt

1 Sift the flour and a pinch of salt into
a large bowl.

2   In a separate bowl, pour ½ cup plus
2 tablespoons cold water, add the egg
(well-beaten), and stir with chopsticks
until bubbles appear. The mixture should
be very fluid.

3   Add the water and egg mixture to
the flour bowl. Mix quickly with the
chopsticks, without overworking the
batter - it should still contain a few lumps.

Understand
KIMISU
SAUCE

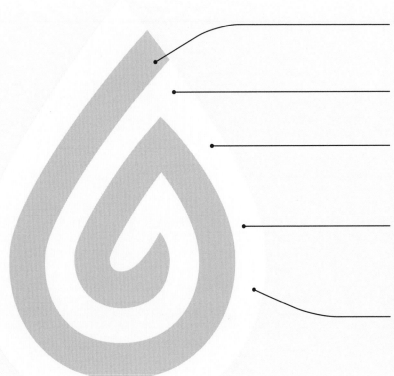

WHAT IS IT?

A cooked then cooled emulsion made with eggs, dashi, rice vinegar, and soy sauce.

ORIGINS

Kimi su kimi = egg yolk, *su* = vinegar.

TOTAL TIME

Prep time: 10 minutes
Cook time: 5 minutes
Storage: 3 days, refrigerated

USES

This sauce can be used like mayonnaise to enhance salads, shellfish, and other seafood. Its yellow color complements asparagus and green spring vegetables.

VARIATIONS

Su miso: add 1 teaspoon of white miso.
Goma su miso: add 1 tablespoon of white sesame paste or tahini.
Karashi su miso: add 1 teaspoon of karashi (Japanese mustard).

FOR ¾ CUP / 180 ML

3 very fresh egg yolks
¼ cup / 60 ml rehydrated dashi
4 teaspoons / 20 ml rice vinegar
   or Japanese grain vinegar
1 tablespoon mirin
1 tablespoon light soy sauce
1 tablespoon sugar
1 pinch of salt
1 teaspoon yuzu or lemon juice

1   Using a fine-mesh sieve and a small spatula, strain the egg yolks into a saucepan. Add all the other ingredients except the yuzu juice and mix with a whisk (without whipping).

2   Prepare a bowl of ice water. Cook the sauce in a bain-marie over medium-low heat, stirring constantly with a spatula for about 3 minutes. When the sauce becomes smooth, remove from heat.

3   Add the yuzu juice and mix. Pour into a bowl and leave to cool, then place the bowl of vinaigrette in the bowl of iced water to chill the sauce. Refrigerate.

SANBAIZU
SAUCE

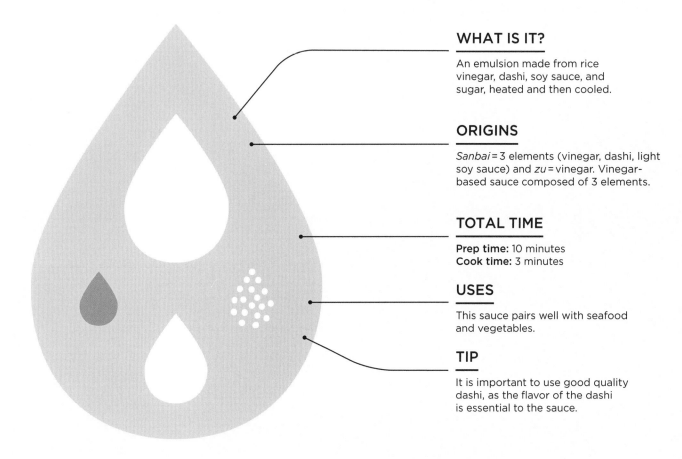

WHAT IS IT?

An emulsion made from rice vinegar, dashi, soy sauce, and sugar, heated and then cooled.

ORIGINS

Sanbai = 3 elements (vinegar, dashi, light soy sauce) and *zu* = vinegar. Vinegar-based sauce composed of 3 elements.

TOTAL TIME

Prep time: 10 minutes
Cook time: 3 minutes

USES

This sauce pairs well with seafood and vegetables.

TIP

It is important to use good quality dashi, as the flavor of the dashi is essential to the sauce.

VARIATIONS

Add ginger juice to the sauce for a different flavor. Yuzu juice and sesame seeds can also be added.

FOR 4 PEOPLE

⅓ cup plus 4 teaspoons / 100 ml
    good-quality dashi
2 tablespoons / 30 ml light soy sauce
1 teaspoon sugar
3 tablespoons / 50 ml rice vinegar

1 Pour the dashi, soy sauce, and sugar into a small saucepan. Bring to a boil, add the vinegar, and remove from heat.

2 Place the pan in a bowl filled with ice water and leave to cool. Pour into a jar. Keep refrigerated.

GOMA DARE
SESAME SAUCE

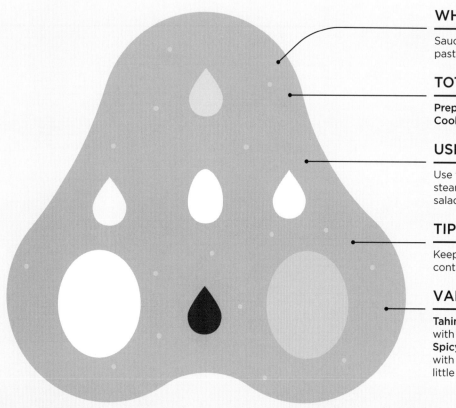

WHAT IS IT?

Sauce made from white sesame paste, heated, then cooled.

TOTAL TIME

Prep time: 10 minutes
Cook time: 2 minutes

USES

Use for shabu shabu sauce (page 234), with steamed or poached chicken, or to season salads or cold noodles in summer, etc.

TIP

Keep for 1 week in an airtight container in a refrigerator.

VARIATIONS

Tahini: replace the white sesame paste with the same amount of tahini.
Spicy: replace the garlic and ginger with 1 teaspoon wasabi or add a little chili paste or chili powder.

FOR OVER 1 CUP / 250 ML

¼ cup / 56 g white sesame paste
2 tablespoons white miso
½ cup / 120 ml dashi (page 28)
2 tablespoons soy sauce
2 tablespoons rice vinegar
2 tablespoons mirin
1 garlic clove
1 (¾-inch / 10 g) piece fresh ginger
2 teaspoons toasted sesame oil

1 Peel and grate the garlic and ginger.

2 In a small saucepan, add the white sesame paste and white miso. Pour in the dashi a little at a time, stirring with a whisk to thin out the sauce.

3 Add in the soy sauce, rice vinegar, and mirin, and bring to a boil.

4 Remove from heat and let cool at room temperature. Add the sesame oil and mix.

5 Pour into an airtight container. Keep refrigerated.

Understand

PONZU SAUCE

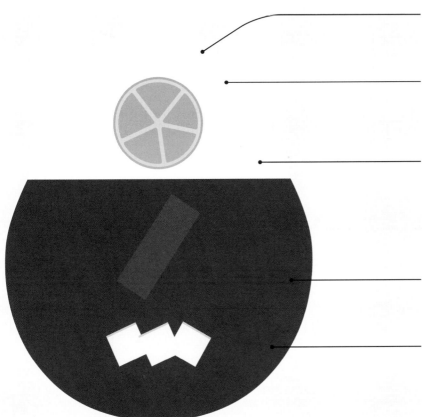

WHAT IS IT?

A vinaigrette sauce made with citrus juice, combined with kombu and bonito for umami.

TOTAL TIME

Prep time: 10 minutes
Cook time: 1 minute
Rest time: 6 hours to overnight

USES

It has a tangy, refreshing flavor and aroma, and helps even high-fat ingredients taste lighter. It can be used for shabu shabu sauce, salads, cold noodles, grilled fish, meat, and vegetables; it's a versatile sauce.

TIP

It will keep for about 1 month in the refrigerator.

VARIATIONS

You can add 1 tablespoon of sesame oil and 1 teaspoon of ginger juice. The oranges can be replaced by other citrus fruits: fresh or bottled yuzu juice, lemon juice, etc.

FOR 2½ CUPS / 600 ML

2 organic oranges
⅔ cup / 150 ml rice vinegar or
    Japanese grain vinegar
3 tablespoons / 50 ml mirin
1 cup / 230 ml soy sauce
4-inch square piece / 10 g kombu
¾ cup / 10 g katsuobushi
    (dried bonito flakes)

1 Bring the mirin to the boil in a small saucepan, remove from heat, and leave to cool to room temperature.

2 Squeeze 2 oranges, filter, and collect ¾ cup plus 4 teaspoons / 200 ml of juice.

3 Place all the ingredients in a container, mix, and leave for at least 6 hours in the fridge (ideally overnight). Pour into a jar. Keep refrigerated.

MITSUWA ZUKE
PICKLED RADISHES

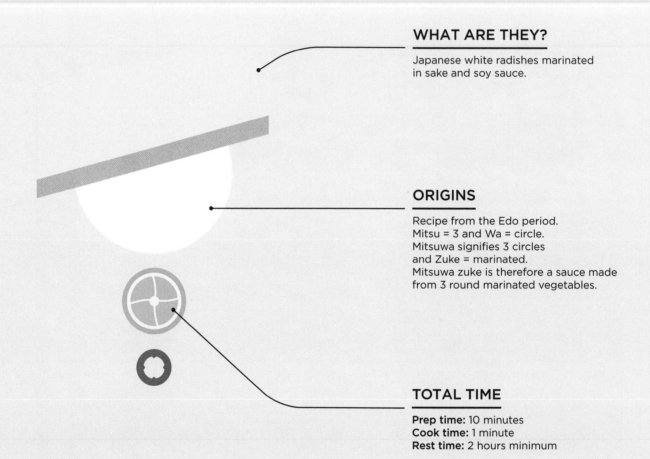

WHAT ARE THEY?
Japanese white radishes marinated in sake and soy sauce.

ORIGINS
Recipe from the Edo period.
Mitsu = 3 and Wa = circle.
Mitsuwa signifies 3 circles
and Zuke = marinated.
Mitsuwa zuke is therefore a sauce made from 3 round marinated vegetables.

TOTAL TIME
Prep time: 10 minutes
Cook time: 1 minute
Rest time: 2 hours minimum

EQUIPMENT
Mandoline

CHARACTERISTICS
Japanese pickles, known as Tsukemono, are a staple in Japan. They come in many varieties and can be fermented in many different ways.

TIP
Make this recipe in autumn/winter when Japanese white radishes are in season.

VARIATIONS
Use carrots and cucumbers instead of radishes, as long as they are cut into slices.

SUBSTITUTIONS
Yuzu is traditionally used in Japan. If you can't find yuzu, you can substitute with kumquats or lemon.

Learn

FOR 4 PEOPLE

10½ ounces / 300 g daikon
    (Japanese radish)
1 red chili pepper
2 kumquats

NIKIRI SAKE

3 tablespoons / 50 ml cooking sake
5 teaspoons / 25 ml soy sauce
¼ teaspoon yuzu or lemon juice

1 To make the sauce, pour the sake into a microwavable container. Put it in the microwave without plastic wrap and heat at 600 W for 50 to 60 seconds to evaporate the alcohol.

2 Mix with the soy sauce and yuzu juice. Set aside.

3 Peel and slice the radish into round slices 1 mm thick using a mandoline. Slice the chili into thin rounds with scissors. Slice the kumquats into rounds 2 mm thick.

4 Spread the radishes out in a shallow dish and pour the sauce over them. Add the chili and kumquat slices.

5 Cover with plastic wrap and refrigerate for at least 2 hours, ideally overnight.

GARI
PICKLED GINGER

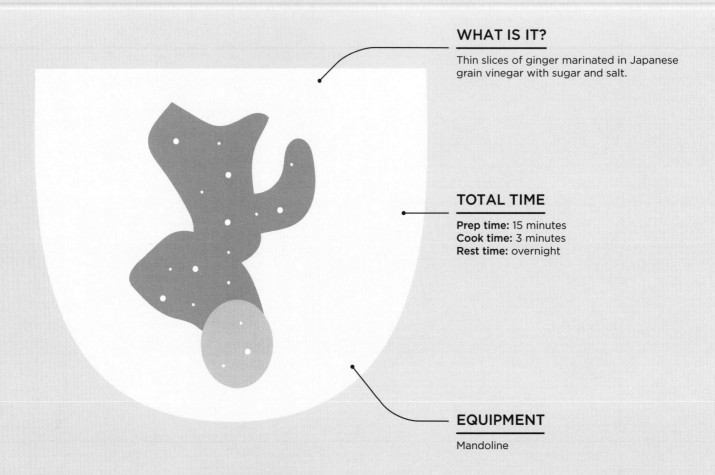

WHAT IS IT?
Thin slices of ginger marinated in Japanese grain vinegar with sugar and salt.

TOTAL TIME
Prep time: 15 minutes
Cook time: 3 minutes
Rest time: overnight

EQUIPMENT
Mandoline

USES
To serve with sushi, etc.

TECHNIQUE TO MASTER
Okaage (page 284) - Japanese resting technique

STORAGE
Store in a well-sealed jar for about 1 month.

VARIATIONS
With young ginger: make the same recipe with blanched young ginger, without salting the slices of ginger; the pickles will be softer.

Learn

FOR 4 PEOPLE

10½ ounces / 300 g fresh ginger

MARINADE

1 cup plus 2 teaspoons / 250 ml rice
    vinegar or Japanese grain vinegar
3 tablespoons / 50 ml water
5 tablespoons / 60 g superfine sugar
2 teaspoons / 10 g fine salt

1 Using a mandoline, cut the ginger into slices 1 mm thick. Place the slices in a large bowl and rinse several times, changing the water each time.

2 Sprinkle with 1 tablespoon of fine salt and massage. Leave to rest for 2 hours, then rinse with water.

3 Squeeze the water out of the ginger by hand, then cook in boiling water for 2 to 3 minutes. Drain and leave to cool in a colander, using the okaage technique (page 284).

4 Place all the marinade ingredients in a small saucepan and cook over low heat until the sugar and salt have dissolved. Remove from heat.

5 Add the ginger to the hot marinade. Leave to cool at room temperature, then pour into a jar. Place in the fridge overnight before using.

CHAPTER 2
RECIPES

MISO SOUP
WITH CLAMS & WAKAME

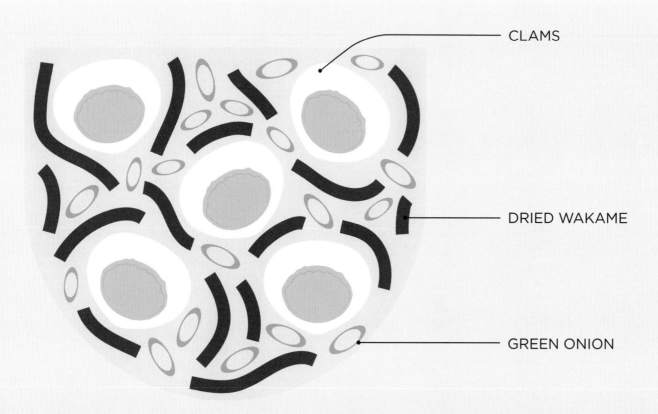

CLAMS

DRIED WAKAME

GREEN ONION

WHAT IS IT?

Dashi with miso, clams, and wakame.

ORIGIN

This dish dates back to the days of the Samurai, for whom it was a breakfast staple. It later gained wider popularity and more versatility. Variations depend on the region, the season, and the type of miso chosen.

TOTAL TIME

Prep Time: 10 minutes
Cook Time: 10 minutes

TECHNIQUES TO MASTER

Preparing dashi (page 28)
Rehydrating wakame (page 283).

WHERE TO ENJOY

Miso soup is served with most home-cooked meals. Restaurants generally offer it with seasonal vegetables.

TIPS

- Miso's saltiness and flavor vary according to the type and the brand, so it's best to taste and adjust as needed.
- To preserve the full flavor of the miso, add the paste at the last minute and do not allow it to boil.

VARIATIONS

Spring: asparagus + spring onion
Summer: cherry tomatoes + zucchini
Fall: eggplant + mushrooms
Winter: kabocha squash + leek

Learn

FOR 4 PEOPLE

10½ ounces / 300 g clams
2 tablespoons dried wakame
2 green onions or ¼ bunch of chives
2 tablespoons white miso
2 tablespoons cooking sake (optional)
3⅓ cups / 800 ml dashi

1 Rub the clams with your hands while washing thoroughly in water. Rinse and drain. Prepare the dashi (page 28). Rehydrate the wakame (page 283).

2 Place the clams in a saucepan and pour in the dashi and sake. Bring to a boil over low heat. When the clams open, skim the broth and turn off the heat.

3 In a ladle, dissolve the miso with a little of the hot stock using a small whisk. Pour the contents of the ladle into the pan and add the wakame. Cook over low heat for 1 or 2 minutes, without boiling (do not cook for too long, otherwise the clams will harden).

4 Serve in individual bowls, sprinkled with green onions.

TOFU NAGE

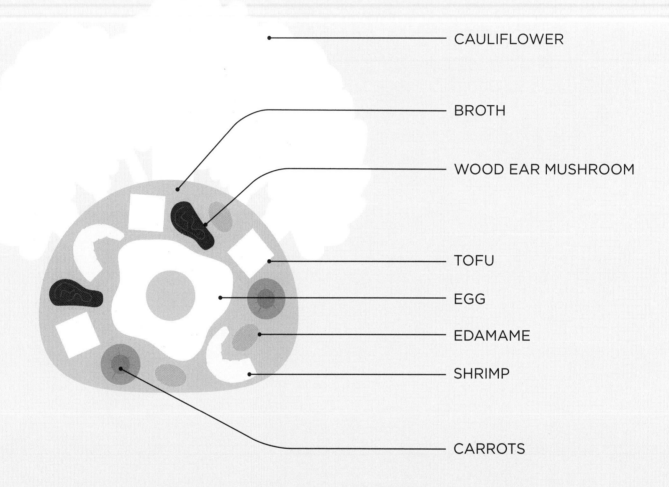

CAULIFLOWER

BROTH

WOOD EAR MUSHROOM

TOFU

EGG

EDAMAME

SHRIMP

CARROTS

WHAT IS IT?

Tofu and shrimp croquettes in broth, with cauliflower and sansho pepper.

ORIGIN

Fried tofu (ganmodoki) was introduced during the Edo period (16th century) when vegetarian Buddhist monks adopted it as a substitute for meat.

TOTAL TIME

Prep time: 30 minutes
Cook time: 20 minutes
Rest time: 1 hour

EQUIPMENT

Mandoline
Deep frying pan
Potato masher or food processor

TECHNIQUES TO MASTER

Cutting vegetables (page 280)
   Hari-shouga (ginger matchsticks, page 281)
Preparing oil for frying (page 284)

TIP

Drizzle boiling water onto the cooled tofu-shrimp croquettes, then drain. Any excess oil from the frying will be eliminated and the broth will be lighter.

VARIATIONS

Udon, soba, or somen noodles can also be added.

Learn

SANSHO PEPPERCORNS
Berries with a lemongrass-like flavor and minty, woody notes.

KIKURAGE
Dried black wood ear mushrooms that absorb the flavors of foods they are cooked with.

EDAMAME
Immature soybeans.

FOR 4 PEOPLE

CROQUETTES
17½ ounces / 500 g extra-firm tofu
6 raw shrimp
1 tablespoon cooking sake
⅔ cup / 100 g shelled edamame
1 small carrot
6 pieces (¼ ounce / 5 g) kikurage
Canola oil
1 teaspoon soy sauce
½ teaspoon fine salt
2 tablespoons cornstarch
1 egg
Canola oil for frying

BROTH
2½ cups / 600 ml first dashi
1 tablespoon soy sauce
1 tablespoon mirin
1 pinch of salt
7 ounces / 200 g cauliflower

FOR SERVING
1 (2¼-inch / 30 g) piece fresh ginger
¼ tablespoon green sansho berries,
        whole or ground

Make

1 Place the kikurage in plenty of warm water. Leave to rest for 20 minutes, then drain. Put the tofu in a colander and top with a plate. Weigh down the plate (with a can of food, for example), and set aside in the fridge for 1 hour to press out excess water from the tofu.

2 Peel and grate the carrot. Drain the kikurage mushrooms, remove the hard parts with a knife, and chop finely. Cut the ginger into slender matchsticks (page 281), soak in cold water, then drain. Set aside.

3 Remove the head and shell from the shrimp. With a knife, slice along the back to remove the vein. Cut into small pieces, place in a bowl, and mix with 1 tablespoon of sake. Cover and set aside.

4 Cut the tofu into pieces, place in a bowl, and mash with a potato masher (or blitz in a food processor, then return to the bowl). Add the egg, cornstarch, 1 teaspoon soy sauce, and ½ teaspoon fine salt and mix. Then add the shrimp, sake, grated carrot, edamame, and chopped kikurage, and mix again. On a cutting board, divide the tofu mixture into 18 small mounds (around 2 tablespoons per ball). Coat your hands with canola oil, then shape the croquettes, arranging them in a tray or dish as you work.

5 Pour the cooking oil into a frying pan (2 inches / 5 cm high) and heat to 320°F / 160°C. In batches of 6 croquettes at a time, fry for 5 minutes. Drain and set aside on paper towels.

6 Wash the cauliflower, then make thin slices 1/16-inch / 2 mm thick with a mandoline.

7 Bring the first dashi to a boil in the saucepan, add the cauliflower, and cook for 3 minutes. Add the tofu croquettes, 1 tablespoon soy sauce, 1 tablespoon mirin, and a little salt. Cook for 2 to 3 minutes over low heat. Divide the croquettes and broth between 4 bowls. Sprinkle with chopped ginger and sansho (whole berries or powder).

TONJIRU

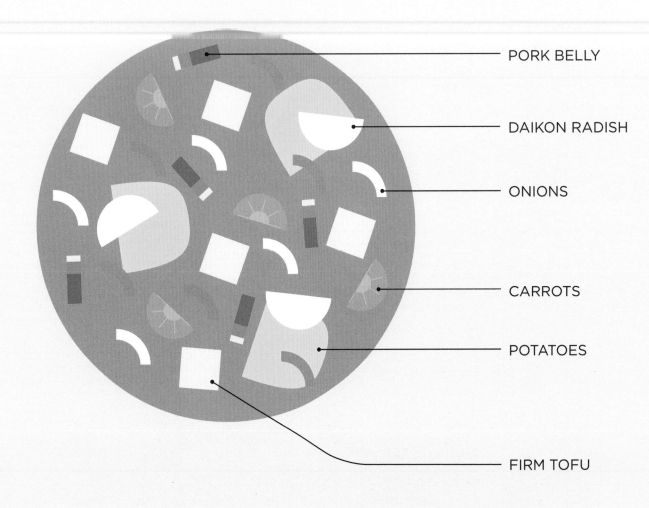

PORK BELLY

DAIKON RADISH

ONIONS

CARROTS

POTATOES

FIRM TOFU

WHAT IS IT?

Miso soup with vegetables and pork.

ORIGIN

Ton = pork; jiru = soup. This restorative soup, made with plenty of root vegetables, is popular during the cold season in Japan.

TOTAL TIME

Prep time: 20 minutes
Cook time: 20 minutes

WHEN TO ENJOY

This everyday winter staple is also appreciated at festive seasonal events (snow festivals, sports competitions, etc.).

TECHNIQUES TO MASTER

Cutting vegetables (page 280)

TIPS

Miso's saltiness and flavor can vary according to the type and brand, so it's best to taste and adjust as needed. To preserve the full flavor of the miso, add the paste at the last minute, and do not allow it to boil.

VARIATION

Kenchin jiru: vegetarian version (without the pork) eaten in zen temples.

ADDITIONS

- Add 1⅔ cups / 400 ml of dashi and ¾ cup plus 4 teaspoons / 200 ml of soy sauce.
- Add seasonal vegetables, like ¼ cup / 40 g of shiitake mushrooms, along with the rest of the vegetables.

Learn

DAIKON

Mild, juicy white radish.

SHICHIMI TOGARASHI

Also known as Japanese seven spice, it contains red chili pepper, sesame and poppy seeds, nori, sansho, ginger, shiso, hemp seeds, and chenpi (mandarin peel).

WHITE MISO

Soybean paste with a short fermentation (between 2 and 8 weeks). Mild and only slightly salty.

KONNYAKU

Jelly-like paste made from konjac (a type of yam). Available in Asian markets.

FOR 4 PEOPLE

SOUP INGREDIENTS

7 ounces / 200 g pork belly
1 onion
● 5¼ ounces / 150 g daikon (Japanese radish)
2 potatoes
1 carrot
● 1 package konnyaku (block of konjac)
½ leek
9 ounces / 250 g firm tofu
1 (¾-inch / 10 g) piece fresh ginger

BROTH

2½ cups / 600 ml dashi (page 28)
● 2 tablespoons white miso
1 tablespoon sesame oil

FOR SERVING

1 green onion, thinly sliced
● Shichimi togarashi

1   Cut the konnyaku into small cubes and blanch in a pan of boiling water for around 2 minutes. Drain.

2   Peel and halve the potatoes, then cut into slices ⅜-inch / 1 cm thick. Set aside in a bowl of cold water until ready to use. Halve and finely chop the onion. Peel the daikon and cut in half lengthwise and then crosswise into medium-sized slices. Cut the carrot in half lengthwise, then into thin slices.

3   Cut the tofu into small cubes. Peel and mince the ginger. Thinly slice the leek and set aside. Cut the pork belly into thin strips.

4   Preheat a large pot over medium heat. Add the sesame oil. Brown the pork belly for about 2 minutes, then add the onions and sauté. Add the carrots, daikon, leeks, konnyaku, and potatoes. Stir. Pour in the dashi until all the ingredients are covered. Stir again, bring to a boil, and reduce heat. Skim. Cover and simmer until the vegetables are cooked, about 15 minutes.

5   Add the tofu cubes, sliced leeks, and minced ginger.

6   Dissolve the miso paste in a ladleful of broth. Pour into the soup. Serve in bowls and sprinkle with thinly sliced green onions and shichimi togarashi.

FAVA BEAN
SURINAGASHI

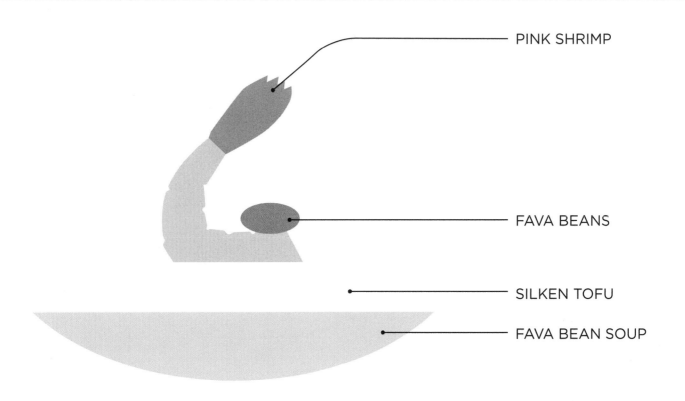

PINK SHRIMP

FAVA BEANS

SILKEN TOFU

FAVA BEAN SOUP

WHAT IS IT?

A cold soup made from fava beans mashed in a mortar and mixed with dashi.

TOTAL TIME

Prep time: 20 minutes
Cook time: 8 minutes
Rest time: 2 hours

WHEN AND HOW TO ENJOY

Surinagashi is a summer soup served either in a lacquer bowl called a wanmono or in a glass bowl. It is served as part of the traditional Japanese multi-course meal known as kaiseki ryori.

TIP

Mainly consumed in summer, this soup is best when prepared in advance and refrigerated before serving.

VARIATIONS

With white asparagus: season with white miso and soy milk.
With edamame: season with white soy sauce. Use pureed edamame.

FOR 4 PEOPLE

2 cups / 250 g shelled fava beans

BROTH

¾ cup plus 4 teaspoons / 200 ml rehydrated dashi
¾ cup plus 4 teaspoons / 200 ml soy milk
1 tablespoon cooking sake
1 tablespoon white miso
1 pinch of fine salt
1 tablespoon kuzu starch
1 tablespoon water

Learn

SOUP TOPPING

5¼ ounces / 150 g silken tofu
4 cooked pink shrimp
4 chives
1 lemon, for zesting

1   Remove the thin skin from the fava beans. Bring 4¼ cups / 1 L water to a boil with 1 teaspoon of salt, then immerse the fava beans in the water for 2 to 3 minutes. Drain and submerge in cold water so that they retain their color. Drain again. Set aside 4 beans for serving.

2   Blend the fava beans with the soy milk. Strain (optional). Keep chilled.

3   Prepare a bowl of ice water. Pour the dashi and sake into a saucepan and cook over medium heat. In a small bowl, mix the kuzu starch and 1 tablespoon of water, then pour the mixture into the saucepan and stir. Leave to cook, stirring, for 2 to 3 minutes. When the dashi becomes transparent, remove from heat. Dilute the miso with a little dashi in a ladle using a small whisk, then pour back into the saucepan. Leave to cool. Place the pan in the bowl of ice water.

4   Add the blended fava beans. Taste and add miso or salt if needed. Leave to cool in the fridge for about 2 hours.

5   Prepare the shrimp. Peel the shell, leaving the tail intact. Cut along the back

and remove the black vein. Cut the tofu into 4 equal parts. Wash, drain, and mince the chives. Set aside. Divide the soup into 4 bowls. Place a tofu part in each bowl, and top with a prawn and a fava bean. Sprinkle with chives and lemon zest.

Understand

TAI NO KOBUJIME

KOMBU SEAWEED

GILTHEAD SEA BREAM

WHAT IS IT?

Marinated gilthead sea bream
(kobujime technique).

ORIGIN

Initially a method for preserving fish,
kobujime later became a special
dish for entertaining, thanks to the
kombu's rich flavor and nutrients.

TOTAL TIME

Prep time: 15 minutes
Rest time: 1 to 4 hours

EQUIPMENT

Sashimi knife
Deep tray
Mandoline

TECHNIQUES TO MASTER

Slicing sashimi (page 282)
Kobujime (page 285) – resting technique

TIPS

It takes 3 to 4 hours for the flavor of the
kombu to fully infuse the sashimi. After
resting for 1 to 2 hours, the fish is lightly
perfumed. After 3 to 4 hours (ideally), the
flesh is firm, translucent, and well-flavored.

VARIATIONS

- Replace the sea bream with another
white fish, such as turbot or bass.
- Use sanbaizu (page 49), soy
sauce, or nikiri sake (page 53)
instead of yuzu kosho.

Learn

KOMBU SEAWEED

Giant seaweed with a briny taste from the genus Laminaria.

YUZU KOSHO

Fermented paste made from green chili peppers and yuzu peel and used as a condiment.

FOR 4 PEOPLE

2 fillets gilthead sea bream (10½ ounces / 300 g)
- 4 large sheets of kombu (4 by 8 inches / 10 by 20 cm)
1 pinch of salt

TOPPING

8 French breakfast radishes
2 spring onions
A few chives

FOR SERVING

- 1 tablespoon yuzu kosho (yuzu pepper)

Make

TAI NO KOBUJIME

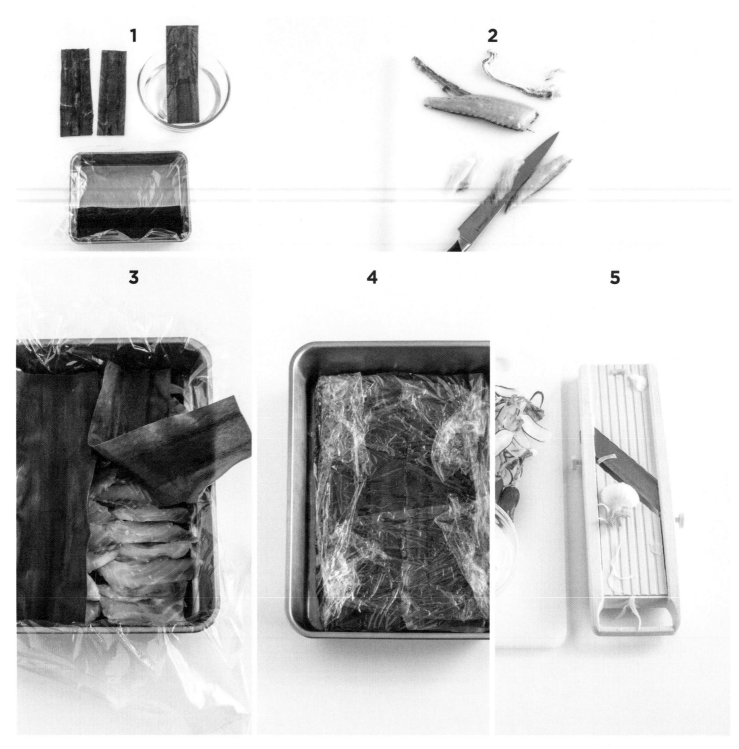

1 Line a tray or dish (8 by 8-inch / 20 by 20 cm) with a square of plastic wrap that is slightly bigger than the dish. Cut 2 kombu sheets so that they fit inside the dish. Rinse the kombu quickly in cold water to moisten, then place the sheets on the plastic wrap.

2 Slice the sea bream sashimi (page 282).

3 Arrange the sea bream sashimi on top of the kombu and sprinkle lightly with salt. Cover with the remaining kombu and wrap tightly in plastic wrap (kobujime technique, page 285).

4 Place the bundle in the dish or tray and set another dish or tray on top so that the fish marinates evenly. Place in the refrigerator for 1 to 4 hours, depending on the desired result.

5 Thinly slice the onion using a mandoline. Soak the slices in cold water for 10 minutes, then drain. Thinly slice the 8 radishes lengthways using the mandoline. Chill, along with the onion. Place the sea bream kobujime on a plate and add the radishes and sliced onions. Serve with the yuzu kosho.

MAGURO NO
TATAKI

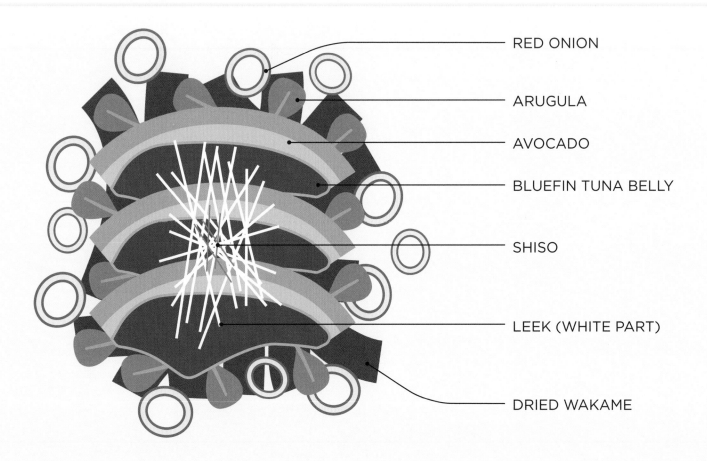

RED ONION

ARUGULA

AVOCADO

BLUEFIN TUNA BELLY

SHISO

LEEK (WHITE PART)

DRIED WAKAME

WHAT IS IT?

Seared tuna served with avocado slices and chopped vegetables.

ORIGIN

The tataki technique is thought to have been invented in the 17th century by a samurai from Tosa, following his encounter with European travelers who were cooking food on a grill at very high temperatures. The method was further developed by Sakamoto Ryōma, a nineteenth-century samurai.

TOTAL TIME

Prep time: 30 minutes
Cook time: 5 minutes
Rest time: 10 minutes

EQUIPMENT

Nonstick skillet
Sashimi knife
Mandoline

TECHNIQUES TO MASTER

Shiraga Negi (page 280)
Rehydrating the wakame (page 283)
Cutting the sashimi (page 282)

TIP

Squeeze lemon juice on the avocado to slow down oxidation.

FOR 4 PEOPLE

10½ ounces / 300 g bluefin tuna belly
1 ripe avocado
1 lemon

TOPPINGS

2 tablespoons dried wakame
1 leek (white part only)
½ red onion
2 cups / 40 g arugula
2 garlic cloves
2 tablespoons olive oil
4 shiso leaves and some shiso microgreens, for decoration

Learn

FOR SERVING

1 tablespoon Yukari
Ponzu sauce
Wasabi

1   Soak the wakame in warm water for 10 minutes, then drain. Wash the arugula. Chop the white part of the leek using the shiraga negi technique (page 280). Thinly slice the onion using a mandoline. Soak in cold water for 10 minutes, then drain. Peel the garlic and cut into thin slices. Cook the garlic in 2 tablespoons of olive oil in a small skillet over low heat until slightly golden and crispy. Set aside.

2   Peel the avocado and cut lengthways into slices ¼-inch / 6 mm thick. Add a squeeze of lemon and seal with plastic wrap.

3   Fill a bowl with water and ice cubes. Lightly oil a frying pan and heat over high heat. Sear the tuna for a few seconds on each side. When the surface of the tuna turns white, plunge it into the ice water. Leave to cool for 3 minutes, then drain and place on paper towels.

4   Cut the tuna into slices ¼-inch / 6 mm thick: place the knife on the right-hand side of the fillet and slide the blade gently up and down towards you. The aim is to cut by pulling rather than pushing the knife.

5   Cut the shiso leaves into thin strips. Combine the wakame, red onion, arugula, and chopped shiso leaves.

6   Divide the toppings into each plate, then alternate with slices of avocado and slices of tuna. Arrange the leeks and shiso in the center and sprinkle with the garlic chips and yukari. Serve with wasabi and ponzu.

Understand

SCALLOP
SASHIMI

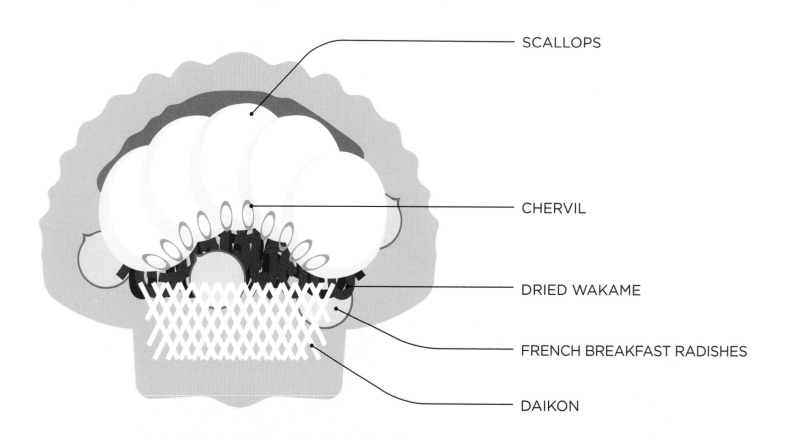

SCALLOPS

CHERVIL

DRIED WAKAME

FRENCH BREAKFAST RADISHES

DAIKON

WHAT IS IT?

Scallop sashimi with vegetables and seaweed.

ORIGIN

Sashi = pierced; mi = body (referencing the action of cutting). This term dates back to the Muromachi period and is thought to be synonymous with slicing.

TOTAL TIME

Prep time: 20 minutes
Cook time: 3 seconds
Rest time: 10 minutes

EQUIPMENT
Mandoline
Grater

TECHNIQUES TO MASTER
Rehydrating the wakame (page 283)
Ken (page 281) – cutting technique
Preparing scallops (page 40)

VARIATIONS
Scallop shimofuri: quickly blanch the scallops and frills in boiling water and then cool in ice water. This method, from scallop-fishing region Hokkaido, gives the dish a completely different texture and more flavor.

Learn

FOR 4 PEOPLE

4 scallops (keep the frills and shells)
2 tablespoons dried wakame
½ bunch of French breakfast radishes
4 inches / 10 cm daikon (Japanese radish)
2 sprigs of chervil
Ume su sauce

1 Rehydrate the wakame in warm water (page 283) for about 10 minutes, then drain. Peel and cut the daikon using the ken technique (page 281). Repeat the process several times, then place the chopped daikon in a bowl of very cold water and drain.

2 Slice 4 radishes into rounds using a mandoline. Grate the rest.

3 Prepare a bowl of ice water. Bring a pan of water to a boil, plunge the scallops and frills into the water for 2 to 3 seconds using a skimmer, then remove immediately. Cool in the ice-cold water. Drain and place on a paper towel.

4 Cut the scallops into slices ¼-inch / 6 mm thick. Cut the frills into 1-inch / 2.5 cm pieces (page 40).

5 Place a little of the sliced daikon in each shell (or on a plate). Add the wakame, radish slices, frills, and chervil. Arrange the scallop slices on top, then top with the grated radishes. Add a little wasabi on the side. Serve with a small bowl of ume su sauce for dipping the sashimi.

NAMEROU

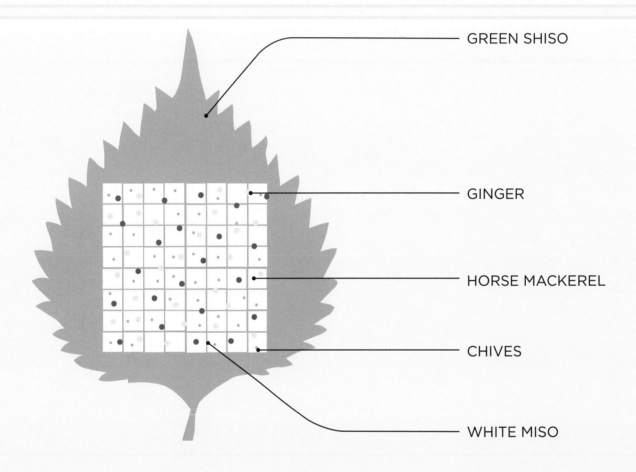

GREEN SHISO

GINGER

HORSE MACKEREL

CHIVES

WHITE MISO

WHAT IS IT?

Horse mackerel tartare with vegetables and miso.

ORIGIN

A local specialty from the coastal areas of the Boso peninsula in Chiba prefecture. This quick 'fisherman's meal' can be eaten while still on the boat. Namerou comes from nameru (to lick), and this tartare is delicious enough to make you want to lick the bottom of the plate.

TOTAL TIME

Prep time: 10 minutes

EQUIPMENT

Sharp knife

WHERE TO ENJOY

Namerou is made at home throughout Japan and is also served in izakaya restaurants.

TECHNIQUE TO MASTER

Preparing horse mackerel (page 33)

TIPS

- Miso is used to season the dish and harmonize the flavors.
- The horse mackerel can be replaced with bonito, sardines, or mackerel.

VARIATIONS

Donburi: place a portion of namerou on a bowl of rice (page 180).
Mago cha: pour some tea or dashi on the donburi.
Sanga yaki: make namerou balls and grill in a skillet.
Sanga age: make namerou balls and fry.

Learn

FOR 4 PEOPLE

14 ounces / 400 g horse mackerel fillets
1 (3-inch / 40 g) piece fresh ginger
1 bunch of chives or 4 spring onions
8 shiso leaves
2 tablespoons white miso

1   Prepare the horse mackerel (page 33). Cut into strips, then into small cubes.

2   Mince half of the ginger for the tartare and cut the other half into matchsticks for the garnish. Mince the chives and the 4 shiso leaves. Set aside.

3   Mix the chopped fish with the ginger, chives, chopped shiso, and the miso.

4   With a knife, mince all the ingredients, turning several times, until the mixture is homogeneous and sticky. Taste and add a little miso if necessary.

5   To serve the namerou, place the remaining shiso leaves on each plate, add the mixture, and top with the chopped ginger.

Understand

BEEF TATAKI
MARINATED IN PONZU SAUCE

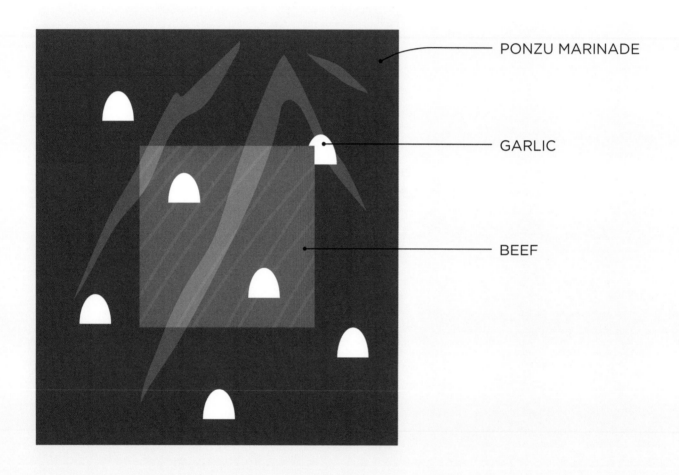

PONZU MARINADE

GARLIC

BEEF

WHAT IS IT?

Seared beef (tataki) served with arugula, cilantro, chives, spring onions, matchstick-cut ginger, and homemade ponzu sauce.

TOTAL TIME

Prep time: 20 minutes
Cook time: 6 minutes
Rest time: 3 hours

EQUIPMENT

Mandoline
Sujikiri or Gyuto knife for cutting meat
Sealable freezer bag

TECHNIQUES TO MASTER

Hari-shouga (ginger matchsticks, page 281)
Tataki (page 284) – cooking technique

TIP

Choose tender cuts such as tenderloin or sirloin.

VARIATIONS

You can make the same recipe with Kobe or Wagyu beef, which are particularly good for tataki because they are extra-tender meats.

Learn

SANSHO OIL
Rice oil infused with green sansho.

PONZU SAUCE
Citrus-based vinaigrette sauce with kombu and bonito for umami.

FOR 4 PEOPLE

BEEF
1 pound 5 ounces / 600 g beef tenderloin
1 teaspoon vegetable oil
Salt
Pepper

MARINADE
• ¾ cup plus 4 teaspoons / 200 ml ponzu sauce, store-bought or homemade (page 51)
1 tablespoon grated ginger
1 clove of garlic, grated
• 1 teaspoon sansho oil

TOPPING
1 (3-inch / 40 g) piece fresh ginger
1 bunch of chives
¼ bunch of cilantro
4 spring onions
1 teaspoon sesame seeds

Make

1   Remove the beef from the fridge and leave at room temperature for 1 hour before cooking. Cut the tenderloin in half. Sprinkle the beef with salt and black pepper and rub it over the whole surface.

2   Heat a non-stick skillet over high heat with vegetable oil and sear the meat for 1 minute on each side.

3   Place the beef in a freezer bag along with the ponzu sauce, grated ginger, grated garlic, and sansho oil. Seal the bag and massage to coat the meat well. Leave to cool at room temperature, then place in the fridge. Marinate for 2 to 3 hours.

4   For the topping, finely slice the ginger using a mandoline, then slice very thinly lengthways to obtain hari-shouga strips (page 281). Soak in cold water for 3 minutes, then drain.

5   Thinly slice the onions using a mandoline. Soak in cold water for around 10 minutes, then drain. Wash the chives and chop into 2-inch / 5 cm pieces. Coarsely chop the cilantro. Set aside.

6   Drain the beef and reserve the marinade. Cut the meat into slices ¼-inch / 6 mm thick. Arrange the meat and vegetables in a dish, drizzle with a little of the remaining marinade, and sprinkle with sesame seeds.

DASHIMAKI
TAMAGO & GRATED RADISH

DAIKON

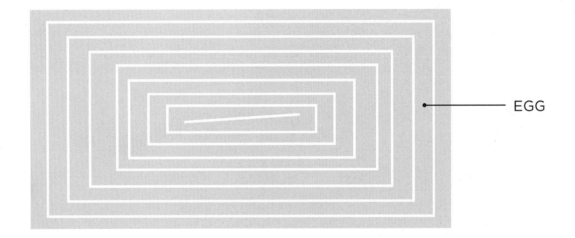
EGG

WHAT IS IT?

Egg and dashi stock are cooked together and rolled into an omelet.

ORIGIN

Dashi = broth; maki = roll.

TOTAL TIME

Prep time: 10 minutes
Cook time: 5 minutes

COOK TIME

Rectangular non-stick skillet
Grater
Makisu (bamboo mat)

HOW TO ENJOY

The omelet tastes better if you roll it when it is still runny. In Japan, this recipe would be for 2 or 3 people because it is served with other dishes.

TECHNIQUES TO MASTER

Making dashi (page 28)

TIPS

- Have paper towels on hand to oil the skillet during cooking (put the oil and some folded paper towels in a small bowl).
- The starch is used to bind the dashi broth inside the omelet during cooking, resulting in a fluffy texture. It will sink to the bottom of the batter, so stir well before pouring the mixture into the skillet each time.

VARIATIONS

- Add chopped spinach, leek, or garlic to the batter.
- Add black sesame seeds or aonori (green seaweed).

Learn

DAÏKON
Mild, juicy
white radish

MIRIN
A Japanese rice wine
used as a condiment;
it is sweeter than sake.

LIGHT
SOY SAUCE
A fermented condiment
that is darker, less
fragrant, and saltier than
traditional soy sauce.

DASHI
Kombu seaweed
broth infused
with katsuobushi
then strained.

FOR 1 PERSON

3 medium eggs
- 6 tablespoons / 90 ml cold dashi
- 1 tablespoon mirin
- 2 teaspoons light soy sauce
½ tablespoon cane sugar
1 tablespoon potato starch or cornstarch
Vegetable oil
- 7 ounces /200 g daikon (Japanese radish)
Soy sauce for serving

Make

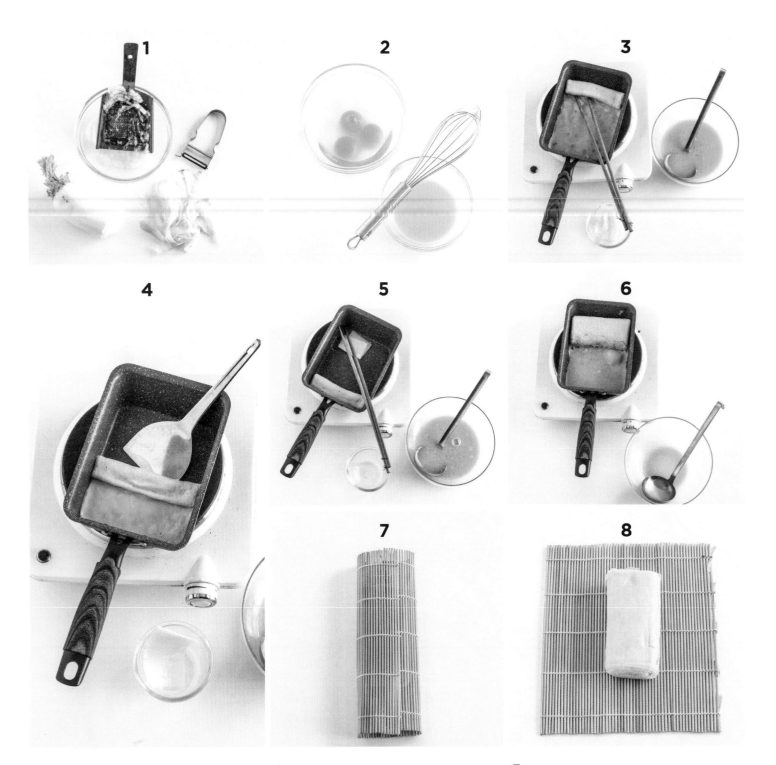

1   Wash, peel, and grate the daikon. Set aside.

2   Place the dashi (page 28), mirin, soy sauce, sugar, a little salt, and the starch in a bowl. Mix well with a whisk. Break the eggs into a larger bowl and stir with chopsticks (do not whisk). Add the dashi mixture and stir. Strain through a fine-mesh sieve.

3   Heat a non-stick skillet over medium heat and grease the pan using chopsticks with half of a folded paper towel and oil. When the skillet is hot enough, pour in about ⅕ of the egg mixture and spread it evenly around the skillet.

4   Using a spatula or chopsticks, fold the omelet over about 1¼ inches / 3 cm from the top. Fold it over on itself a second time. Roll it tightly towards the bottom of the skillet.

5   Re-grease the remaining part of the skillet. Slide the omelet towards the top of the skillet. Grease the uncovered lower section and pour in another ⅕ of the egg mixture.

6   Place the chopsticks under the top section, lifting it slightly while letting the omelet mixture pour underneath. Cook, then roll over twice. Repeat until all the mixture has been used.

7   When cooked, wrap the omelet in a makisu and leave it to rest for 3 to 4 minutes to allow the shape and internal heat to stabilize.

8   Cut into 5 or 6 portions and place on a plate. Serve immediately with the grated radish and soy sauce.

Understand

OKONOMIYAKI

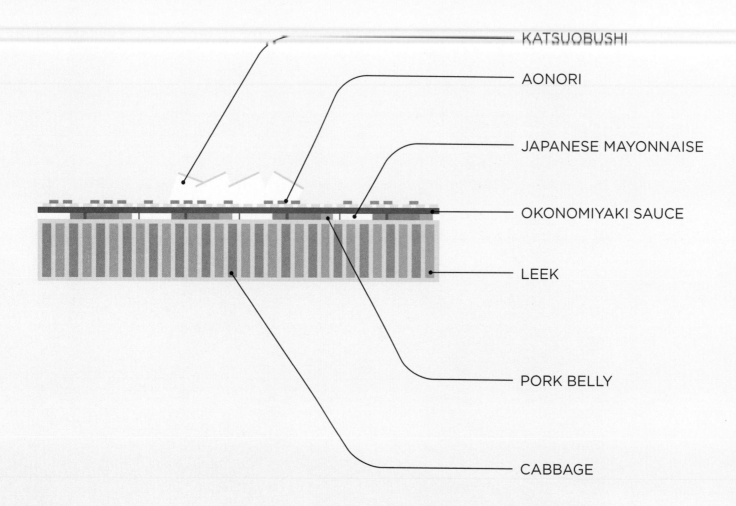

KATSUOBUSHI

AONORI

JAPANESE MAYONNAISE

OKONOMIYAKI SAUCE

LEEK

PORK BELLY

CABBAGE

WHAT IS IT?

A thick cabbage and leek pancake topped with pork belly slices, squid, and mayonnaise.

ORIGIN

Okonomi = how you like it; yaki = grilled: you can fill it and top it with whatever you like.

TOTAL TIME

Prep time: 15 minutes
Cook time: 10 minutes

EQUIPMENT

Piping bag
Spatula
10-inch / 25 cm skillet

TECHNIQUE TO MASTER

Preparing squid (page 39)

HOW TO ENJOY

Cook and eat as you go. Use a small portable stove to prepare it at the table.

VARIATION

Hiroshima-style Okonomiyaki: place the pancake on a bed of fried yakisoba noodles.

ADDITIONS AND SUBSTITUTIONS

- Add oysters, ground beef, mochi, etc.
- **Vegetarian:** replace the meat with mushrooms, corn, soybean sprouts, etc.
- **With barbecue sauce:** replace the okonomiyaki sauce with the same quantity of barbecue sauce.

Learn

JAPANESE MAYONNAISE

Try to find the Kewpie brand, available in Asian markets.

OKONOMIYAKI SAUCE

A thick, brown, salty-sweet sauce made with simmered vegetables and fruit, and seasoned with spices and vinegar. It is essential for a good okonomiyaki.

AONORI

Dried seaweed flakes, not to be confused with nori.

KATSUOBOSHI

Dried and smoked bonito shavings.

FOR 4 PEOPLE

BATTER

3⅓ cups / 400 g flour
4 eggs
1⅔ cups / 400 ml cold dashi (page 28)
Canola oil

FILLING

14 ounces / 400 g pointed cabbage or green cabbage
¼ of the white part of a leek
4 thin slices of pork belly
1 squid (about 10½ ounces / 300 g)

GARNISH

- 2 tablespoons aonori (seaweed flakes)
- 2 tablespoons katsuobushi (dried bonito shavings)
- Okonomiyaki sauce
- ¼ cup / 60 ml Japanese mayonnaise

1   Wash the cabbage and leek, then cut into thin strips.

2   Cut the slices of pork into 3 or 4 pieces. Clean the squid (page 39) and cut into small squares (1 inch / 2.5 cm).

3   To make the batter, place the flour in a bowl. Pour the cold broth and eggs into the center, stirring for 30 seconds. Add the cabbage and leek and toss to coat.

4   Heat a little oil in a skillet. Pour in the batter, then place the slices of pork and squid on top.

5   Cook over medium heat for about 5 minutes until golden brown, then flip with a spatula. Cook the other side for about 5 minutes. Slide onto a plate.

6   Fill a piping bag with the mayonnaise. Coat the pancake with okonomiyaki sauce, then draw a lattice pattern with the mayonnaise. Sprinkle with aonori powder and garnish with a little katsuobushi.

IWASHI NO
KABAYAKI

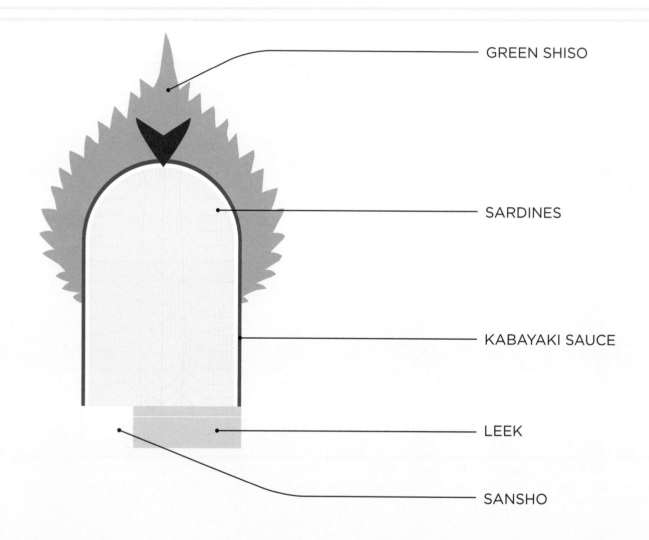

GREEN SHISO

SARDINES

KABAYAKI SAUCE

LEEK

SANSHO

WHAT IS IT?

Sardines sautéed in soy sauce, sake, and mirin (kabayaki).

ORIGIN

Kaba, which gives this recipe its name, is a plant (typha) that tastes similar to grilled flatfish.

TOTAL TIME

Prep time: 10 minutes
Cook time: 10 minutes

EQUIPMENT
10-inch / 25 cm nonstick skillet

HOW TO ENJOY
An everyday, easy-to-make, inexpensive dish that can be included in a bento and is most often served with rice (donburi).

TECHNIQUES TO MASTER
Preparing sardines (page 35)

TIP
Use very fresh whole sardines to prevent them from falling apart during cooking.

VARIATION
Donburi: place 2 sardines on top of a bowl of rice (page 180).

Learn

FOR 4 PEOPLE

8 sardines
1 tablespoon canola oil
¼ cup / 30 g flour

KABAYAKI SAUCE

3 tablespoons / 50 ml soy sauce
3 tablespoons / 50 ml mirin
3 tablespoons / 50 ml cooking sake
1 tablespoon raw cane sugar

FOR SERVING

1 leek
4 green shiso leaves
2 tablespoons toasted sesame seeds
1 teaspoon sansho powder

1   Cut the leeks into 2½-inch / 6.5 cm pieces, then cut them in half lengthwise. In a bowl, combine all sauce ingredients.

2   Clean the sardines (page 35). Dredge in flour, removing excess by hand.

3   Heat a little oil in a skillet. Place the sardines skin-side down and cook over medium heat. When the skin is golden brown, turn over and cook for a few moments, until the sardines are almost cooked through. Add the leeks, then the sauce mixture, and simmer over medium heat for another 2 minutes. When the sauce begins to thicken, reduce the heat to low and spoon the sauce over the fish.

4   Arrange 2 sardines per person on each plate, add leeks and shiso, and sprinkle with sesame seeds. Serve with sansho.

Understand
SAIKYO YAKI

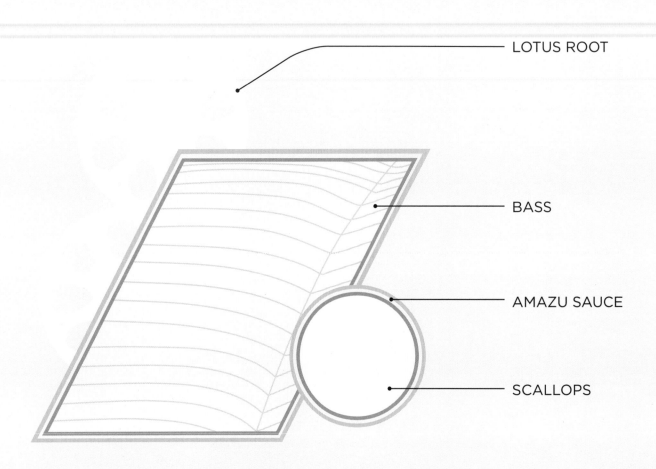

LOTUS ROOT

BASS

AMAZU SAUCE

SCALLOPS

WHAT IS IT?

Bass and scallops marinated in white miso then grilled and served with lotus root pickles.

ORIGIN

The dish is normally made with saikyo miso, a white miso with a sweet taste and very low salt content that is difficult to find outside of Japan. It is replaced by white miso here.

TOTAL TIME

Prep time: 30 minutes
Cook time: 20 minutes
Rest time: overnight

EQUIPMENT

Mandoline
Stainless steel cooling rack
Large airtight container
Freezer bag
Spatula

WHEN TO ENJOY

A very rich recipe made all year round, especially for entertaining. It is also served in traditional upscale restaurants (kaiseki) because of the products used: high-quality fish, scallops, and the special white miso.

TIP

The fish and scallops can be marinated for 4 to 5 days in an airtight bag in the refrigerator.

VARIATIONS

This dish can be made with squid or other types of fish, such as salmon, bass, turbot, and mackerel.

Learn

RICE VINEGAR

Pure rice vinegar with a smooth, mellow taste and a slightly amber hue.

LOTUS ROOT

The edible part of the lotus. It has a crunchy texture and tastes a little like a radish.

WHITE MISO

Soybean paste with very little fermentation (between 2 and 8 weeks). Mild and lightly salted.

FOR 4 PEOPLE

4 skin-on fillets of bass, 1-inch / 2.5 cm thick (about 1 pound 5 ounces / 600 g)
4 scallops
1 lime

PICKLES

3½ ounces / 100 g lotus root
• 1 teaspoon vinegar

AMAZU SAUCE

• 3 tablespoons / 50 ml rice or Japanese grain vinegar
5 teaspoons / 20 g sugar
½ teaspoon fine salt

MARINADE

• 1 heaping cup / 300 g white miso
2 tablespoons cooking sake
2 tablespoons mirin
2 tablespoons cane sugar

1

2

3

4

5

1 Prepare the scallops (page 40). Arrange the bass fillets and scallops on a stainless-steel rack in a deep tray or roasting pan. Sprinkle both sides lightly with salt to draw out excess water and soften. Let stand for 30 minutes in the refrigerator. Wipe away any moisture from the fish and scallops with paper towels.

2 To make the marinade, mix the miso, sake, mirin, and sugar in a bowl with a spatula. Pour into a large, airtight container. Place the fish and scallops in the marinade. Use a spatula to distribute the miso evenly on both sides. Cover with plastic wrap, close the container, and refrigerate overnight.

3 To make the pickles, peel the lotus root and slice thinly using a mandoline. Plunge the slices into cold water to prevent oxidation. Bring a pan of water and 1 teaspoon of vinegar to a boil and add the lotus slices. Cook for around 10 minutes, until translucent. Drain. Place the still-warm lotus root slices in an airtight freezer bag and add the rice vinegar, sugar, and salt. Close the bag, leave to cool at room temperature, and then place in the fridge. Marinate at least 2 hours (ideally 3 hours).

4 Preheat the oven to 350°F/ 180°C. Quickly rinse the fish and scallops and wipe dry.

5 Cook the fillets and scallops in the oven for 10 to 15 minutes, taking care not to burn them. You can also cook them in a skillet over medium heat. Arrange the saikyo yaki on each plate with the lotus pickles and ⅛ of a lime wedge.

Understand
DENGAKU

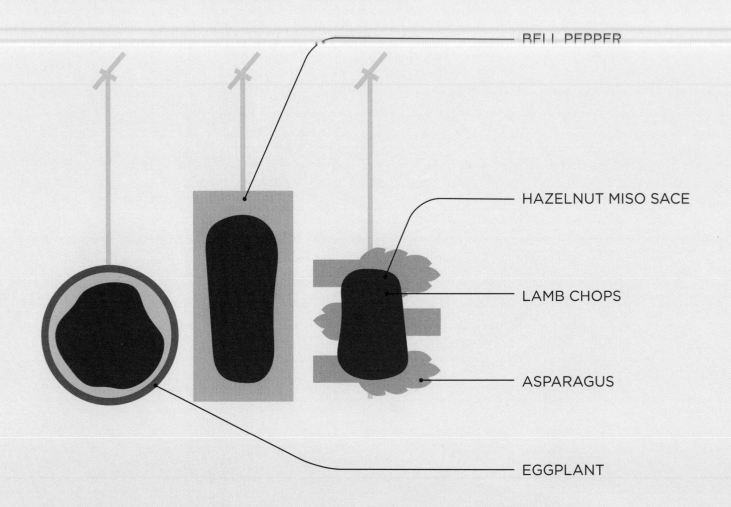

BELL PEPPER

HAZELNUT MISO SACE

LAMB CHOPS

ASPARAGUS

EGGPLANT

WHAT IS IT?
Grilled lamb chops and vegetable skewers topped with miso sauce.

ORIGIN
Miso dengaku is a specialty from Aichi prefecture. This traditional Japanese dish has been enjoyed for centuries.

TOTAL TIME
Prep time: 20 minutes
Cook time: 20 minutes

EQUIPMENT
Bamboo skewers (optional)

WHEN TO ENJOY
Dengaku is served in izakayas year-round and is also made at home, especially on weekends.

TIPS
- Cook miso for a short time over low heat to preserve its flavor.
- The miso sauce can be used in other recipes. For example, you could add vinegar and make a dressing for a wakame or soybean sprout salad.

VARIATION
Drizzle the sauce over onigiri, then grill them in a skillet (yaki onigiri).

SUBSTITUTIONS
- Replace hazelnut paste with tahini, almond butter, or peanut butter.
- Mirin can be replaced by apple juice
- Replace cane sugar with maple syrup, agave syrup, or honey.
- The lamb chops can be replaced by pork, beef, or even firm tofu for a vegetarian version.

Learn

SHISO

A highly aromatic plant, somewhere between mint and basil, sold in Asian markets.

HACHO MISO

Dark soy miso with a full-bodied flavor.

RED YUZU KOSHO

Fermented paste made from red chili pepper and yuzu peel and used as a condiment.

INAKA MISO

Light-colored wheat miso with a very mild flavor.

FOR 4 PEOPLE

4 lamp chops
1 eggplant
1 zucchini
1 red bell pepper
½ bunch of asparagus
4 chives
2 sprigs of cilantro
4 shiso leaves

HAZELNUT MISO SAUCE

2 teaspoons / 10 g hacho miso
2½ tablespoons / 40 g inaka miso
3 tablespoons / 50 ml hazelnut paste
3 tablespoons / 50 ml mirin
2 tablespoons cane sugar
3 tablespoons / 50 ml water

FOR SERVING

1 tablespoon toasted sesame seeds
1 tablespoon red yuzu kosho
2 tablespoons goji berries

Make

1   For the sauce, combine the water, hazelnut paste, misos, mirin, and cane sugar in a small saucepan. Heat over low heat, stirring constantly, until the sauce is smooth. Keep warm.

2   Wash the eggplant and cut into rounds about ½-inch / 15 mm thick (if the eggplant is large, cut it in half). Soak the slices in water for 5 minutes, then drain and place on a kitchen towel to dry. Wash the zucchini, remove the ends, and cut into rounds. Wash the bell pepper, cut in half, and remove the core and the seeds. Cut into 1 to 2-inch / 2.5 to 5 cm strips. Cut the asparagus into pieces about 2 inches / 5 cm long.

3   Heat the sesame oil in the skillet, add the eggplant rounds, and cook, turning regularly, for about 3 minutes. Transfer to a deep tray or plate.

4   In the same skillet, add a little oil and cook the zucchini. Repeat for the bell peppers and asparagus. All the vegetables should be cooked through and vibrant in color.

5   In the same skillet, grill the lamb chops for 2 minutes on each side over high heat.

6   Place vegetables on bamboo skewers. Coat vegetables and lamb chops with miso sauce. Garnish with sesame seeds, yuzu kosho, goji berries, and herbs.

Understand

YAKITORI

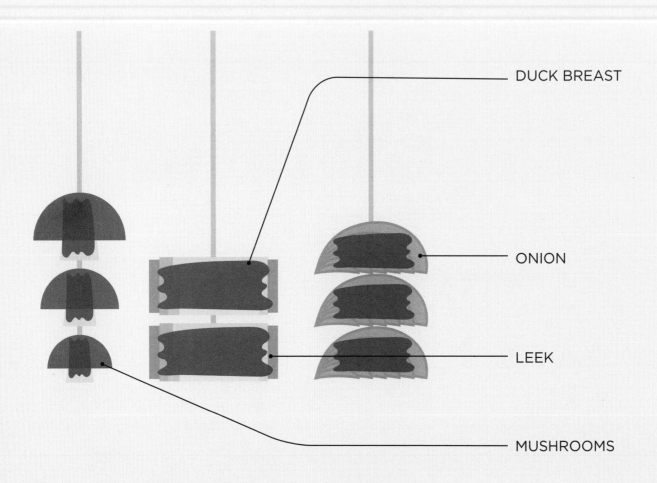

DUCK BREAST

ONION

LEEK

MUSHROOMS

WHAT IS IT?

Duck, leek, mushroom, and onion skewers brushed with a sake-mirin-soy sauce, then cooked in a skillet or on a grill.

ORIGIN

The first yakitori recipe is from the Edo period. The dish became increasingly known during the Meiji era in the 19th century, though it wasn't until the 1950s that its popularity became widespread, especially among Japanese salarymen, for its practicality as a meal that could be eaten on the go.

TOTAL TIME

Prep time: 20 minutes
Cook time: 20 minutes
Rest time: 30 minutes

EQUIPMENT

20 bamboo skewers

HOW TO ENJOY

There are 2 ways to season yakitori:
- Tare – with sauce
- Shio – with salt
Choose according to personal taste.

TIP

Soak the wooden skewers in cold water for 30 minutes before use to prevent them from burning on the grill.

VARIATIONS

- Add vegetables: bell pepper, spring onions, etc.
- Replace the homemade sauce with store-bought yakitori or teriyaki sauce.

Learn

COOKING
SAKE

Sake with added salt

MIRIN

A Japanese rice wine
used as a condiment;
it is sweeter than sake.

SANSHO

Powdered citronella-
like berries with minty
and woody notes.

WASABI
SALT

Salt mixed with wasabi
powder. Adds a bit of
heat and an element
of freshness to dishes.

FOR 4 PEOPLE

1 duck breast
1 leek
12 button mushrooms
1 onion

YAKITORI SAUCE

⅓ cup plus 4 teaspoons / 100 ml
    soy sauce
● ⅓ cup plus 4 teaspoons / 100 ml mirin
● ⅓ cup plus 4 teaspoons / 100 ml
    cooking sake
2 tablespoons raw cane sugar
1 garlic clove
1 piece of fresh ginger

FOR SERVING

● Sansho
● Wasabi salt

Make

1 Grate the garlic and ginger for the sauce. Add to a saucepan with the sugar, soy sauce, mirin, and sake. Bring to a boil, then cook over high heat until syrupy and reduced by half. Pour the hot sauce into a small bowl.

2 Wash the leeks and cut into 1-inch / 2.5 cm pieces. Peel and quarter onions. Remove mushroom stems. Make 4 skewers of onions and 4 of mushrooms.

3 Cut the duck breasts into 16 slices, each about ¼-inch / 5 mm thick. Wrap a slice of duck around a piece of leek. Repeat for the remaining 15 slices. Place 2 slices on each of the 8 skewers.

4 Heat a little oil in a skillet, add the mushroom and onion skewers, and cook for 2 minutes on each side over high heat.

5 Do the same for the duck and leek skewers, cooking for 3 minutes on each side over high heat.

6 Brush the duck and onion skewers with the sauce. Sprinkle the mushroom skewers with wasabi salt. Serve immediately with sansho pepper and wasabi salt.

Understand
GYOZA

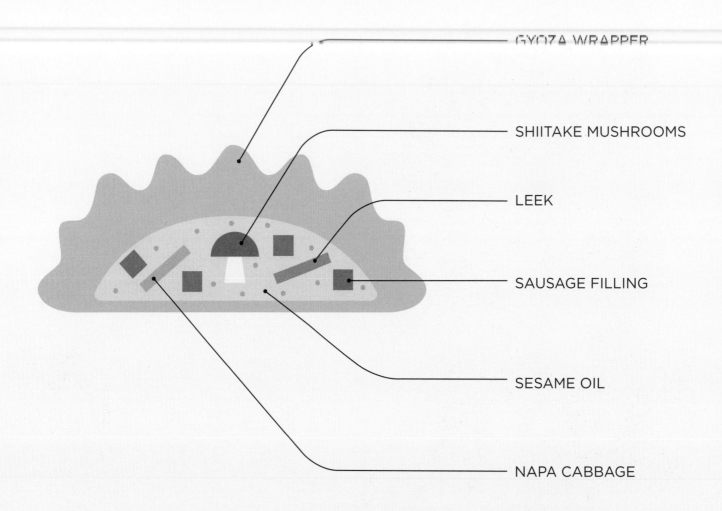

GYOZA WRAPPER

SHIITAKE MUSHROOMS

LEEK

SAUSAGE FILLING

SESAME OIL

NAPA CABBAGE

WHAT IS IT?

Grilled and steamed dumplings stuffed with pork and vegetables.

ORIGIN

Gyoza were imported from China in the 20th century, and then adapted to suit local preferences: the Japanese version contains more garlic and is wrapped in a thinner, lighter dough.

TOTAL TIME

Prep time: 45 minutes
Cook time: 15 minutes
Rest time: 1 hour 10 minutes

EQUIPMENT

Large nonstick skillet with a lid

HOW TO ENJOY

Serve with a little soy sauce and vinegar.

STORAGE

Uncooked gyoza will keep for several weeks in the freezer. Thaw before cooking.

VERSIONS

Gyoza can be boiled (sui gyoza) or steamed in a bamboo basket (mushi gyoza).

VARIATIONS

- Replace the sausage meat with ground beef, shrimp, squid, fish, etc.
- For a veggie version, use firm tofu.

Learn

SHIITAKES
Plump, fleshy mushrooms with a woody flavor.

RICE VINEGAR
Pure rice vinegar with a smooth, mellow taste and a slightly amber hue.

YUZU KOSHO
Fermented paste made from green chili peppers and yuzu peel and used as a condiment.

LAYU
Red chili oil

FOR 20 GYOZA

GYOZA WRAPPER
1 pinch of salt
6 tablespoons/ 90 ml warm water
1 cup / 130 g pastry flour
½ cup / 50 g all-purpose flour

FILLING
5¼ ounces / 150 g sausage meat
7 ounces / 200 g napa cabbage or pointed cabbage
½ teaspoon fine salt
1½ ounces / 40 g leek
- 1¾ ounces /50 g shiitake or button mushrooms
1 (1½-inch / 20 g) piece fresh ginger
- 1 teaspoon yuzu kosho
1 tablespoon toasted sesame oil
1 tablespoon soy sauce
1 tablespoon cooking sake (optional)
1 teaspoon cane sugar
Black pepper

FOR COOKING
2 tablespoons vegetable oil
½ cup plus 2 tablespoons / 150 ml hot water

FOR SERVING
Soy sauce
- Rice vinegar
- Layu (optional)

Make

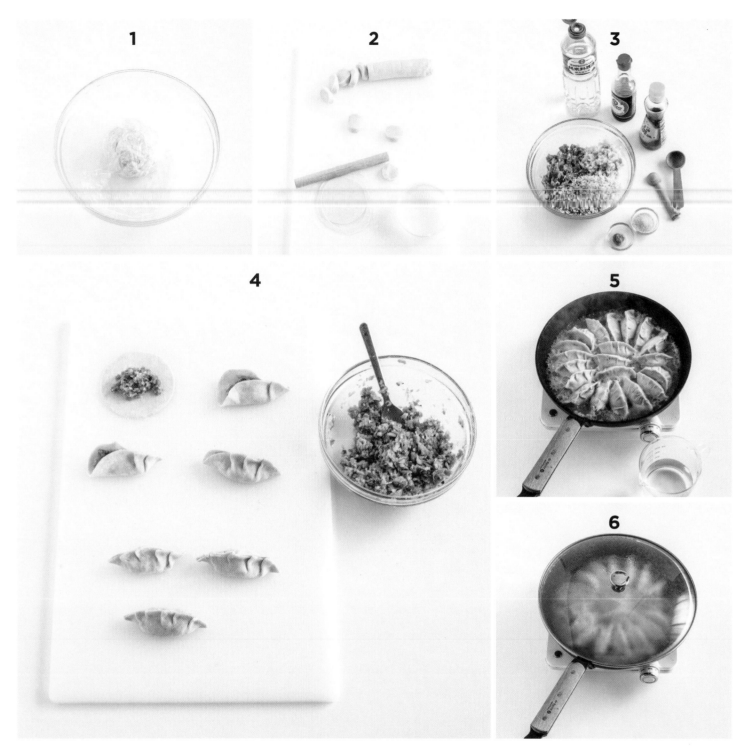

1 To make the dough, pour 6 tablespoons / 90 ml of warm water into a bowl, dissolve the salt in the water, and mix in the flours. Knead the dough until combined. Form into a ball, cover with plastic wrap, and leave to rest for 10 minutes at room temperature. Knead the dough for another 5 minutes, wrap it again, and leave to rest for a further 30 minutes at room temperature, or in the refrigerator if the weather is warm.

2 Shape the dough into a roll (1 inch / 2.5 cm in diameter), then cut into 20 slices. On a floured surface, roll out each piece to a thickness of 2 mm and cut out a 4-inch / 10 cm disk using a round cookie or pastry cutter. Cover the dough rounds with a kitchen towel to prevent them from drying out.

3 For the filling, finely dice the cabbage, sprinkle with ½ teaspoon salt, and leave to drain for 20 minutes. Rinse with water, drain, and pat dry. Mince the leek and mushrooms. Mix the chopped ginger, yuzu kosho, vegetables, and sausage, and add the soy sauce, sesame oil, sake, sugar, and black pepper.

4 To make the dumplings, place 1 tablespoon of filling in the center of a dough round and moisten the edge. Fold in half and seal, making 3 to 5 folds.

5 Heat a skillet with 1 tablespoon vegetable oil and brown the flat bottom of the gyoza for 2 to 3 minutes. Pour in ½ cup plus 2 tablespoons / 150 ml of hot water, cover, and cook for 10 minutes over medium heat. Remove the lid and allow all the water to evaporate.

6 Serve immediately with soy sauce, rice vinegar, and layu.

Understand

BUTA NO KAKUNI

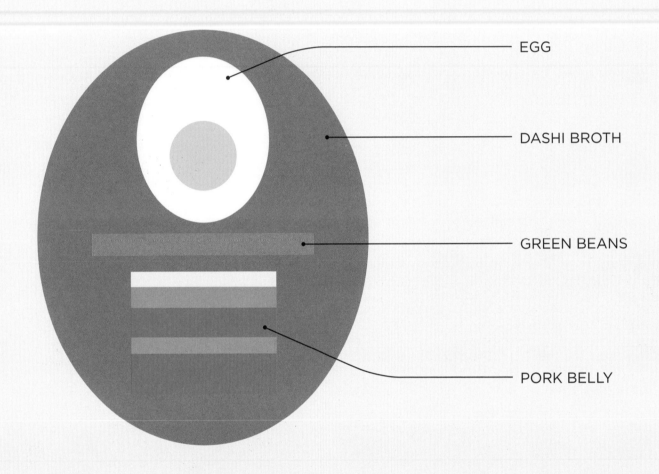

EGG

DASHI BROTH

GREEN BEANS

PORK BELLY

WHAT IS IT?

Large cubes of pork belly simmered with sake, soy sauce, mirin, and sugar.

ORIGIN

Buta = pork; kaku = cube; ni = simmered: simmered pork cubes or ribs.

TOTAL TIME

Prep time: 20 minutes
Cook time: 1 hour 45 minutes
Rest time: 3 to 6 hours

EQUIPMENT

Dutch oven (10 inches / 25 cm in diameter)

WHEN TO ENJOY

This is a winter dish. Slow cooking the meat makes it very tender, so it's a very popular home-cooked meal.

TIPS

- Covering the casserole with parchment paper keeps all the ingredients in the liquid and speeds up cooking.
- Browning the pork before simmering reduces excess fat.

SUBSTITUTION

Replace the soy sauce with 2 tablespoons of red miso.

Learn

COOKING
SAKE

Sake with added salt.

SOY SAUCE

Choose brands
with labels that say
"naturally brewed" or
"naturally fermented."

DEHYDRATED
DASHI

Kombu seaweed and
katsuobushi broth
sold as a powder.

FOR 4 PEOPLE

2.2 pounds / 1 kg pork belly
4 eggs
7 ounces / 200 g green beans
1 (1½-inch / 20 g) piece fresh ginger
2 garlic cloves
4 inches / 10 cm of the green part
    of a leek
Shichimi (optional)

BROTH

2½ to 3⅓ cups / 600 to 800 ml water
• ¾ cup plus 4 teaspoons / 200 ml
    cooking sake
• 5 teaspoons / 40 ml soy sauce
2 tablespoons raw cane sugar
• 1 teaspoon dehydrated dashi

1   Slice the unpeeled ginger into 3 mm-thick rounds. Peel garlic cloves and halve. Cut the pork belly into 2-inch / 5 cm squares.

2   Heat a skillet with a little oil and brown the pork over medium heat. Start fat side down and then brown all over to render the fat. Drain on paper towels.

3   Place the pork, garlic, ginger, and green leek in a Dutch oven. Pour in the water, sake, and dehydrated dashi. Bring to a boil and skim. Cover with a disk of parchment paper the same diameter as the pot. Simmer for about 20 minutes with the lid on. Remove from heat and leave the ingredients to cool in the stock for 3 to 6 hours.

4   Put the eggs one by one into a pan of boiling water and cook for 10 minutes. Rinse in cold water, then remove the shells and leave to cool. Trim and wash the green beans.

5   Use a spoon to remove the film of fat that has formed on the surface of the broth.

6   Return heat to high and add sugar and soy sauce to the pan. Bring to a boil and then simmer over low heat for about 50 minutes with a disc of parchment paper in place. Add the eggs and beans to the pot and cook for 10 more minutes. Place the meat and eggs in a serving dish, add the green beans, and pour over a little of the cooking juices. Add shichimi if desired.

Understand

NIKU JYAGA

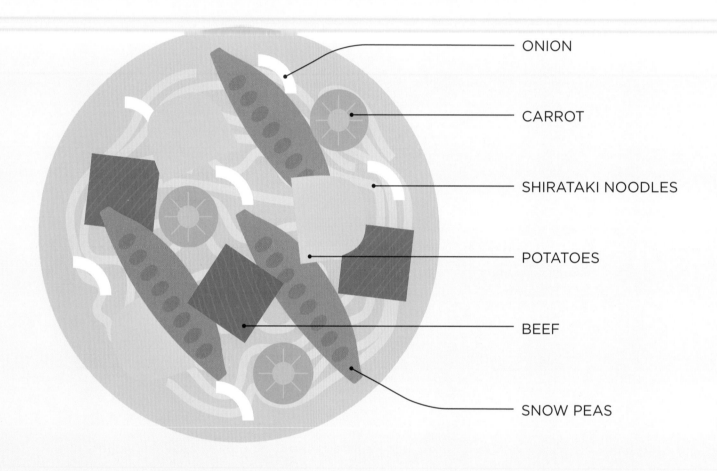

ONION

CARROT

SHIRATAKI NOODLES

POTATOES

BEEF

SNOW PEAS

WHAT IS IT?

Beef and vegetable stew.

ORIGIN

Niku = meat; jyaga = potatoes.

TOTAL TIME

Prep time: 20 minutes
Cook time: 25 minutes
Rest time: 30 minutes

EQUIPMENT
Dutch oven (10 inches / 25 cm in diameter)

TRADITION
Every household has its own recipe, handed down from generation to generation.

TECHNIQUE TO MASTER
Cutting vegetables (page 280)

TIPS
- This dish can be prepared in advance and kept for 3 days in the refrigerator.
- Plunging the cubed potatoes into cold water avoids discoloration.
- Covering the pan with parchment paper keeps the ingredients immersed in the broth, thus speeding up cooking.

VARIATIONS
With pork: replace the beef with the same quantity of pork belly.
With mushrooms: rehydrate a heaping cup / 40 g of dried shiitake mushrooms and add to the cooking broth.
Express: replace the homemade sauce with ¼ cup / 60 ml of teriyaki sauce.

Learn

MIRIN
A Japanese rice wine used as a condiment; it is sweeter than sake.

SHIRATAKI
Translucent, gelatinous noodles made from konjac starch.

DEHYDRATED DASHI
Kombu seaweed and katsuobushi broth sold as a powder.

FOR 4 PEOPLE
10½ ounces / 300 g beef (tenderloin or other tender cut)
1¾ pounds / 800 g waxy potatoes
2 carrots
1 onion
10 snow peas
1 packet of shirataki (konjac vermicelli noodles)
1 tablespoon vegetable oil
2½ cups / 600 ml water

SAUCE
½ teaspoon dehydrated dashi
2 tablespoons raw cane sugar
3 tablespoons / 50 ml sake
3 tablespoons / 50 ml mirin
3 tablespoons / 50 ml soy sauce

1   Wrap the meat in aluminum foil and set aside in the freezer for 30 minutes—it will be easier to cut. Cut the konjac vermicelli into pieces 4 inches (10 cm) long. Blanch in a large pot of boiling water for about 2 minutes and drain.

2   Peel the potatoes and cut into 1½-inch / 4 cm cubes. Place in cold water and leave to soak until ready to cook. Peel carrots and cut using the rangiri technique (page 281). Peel the onion, cut in half, and then into slices (¼-inch / 6 mm thick).

3   Remove the beef tenderloin from the freezer and cut into thin slices (¼-inch / 6 mm thick).

4   Heat the oil in a Dutch oven and saute the meat and onions over high heat for 3 minutes. Add the drained potatoes and carrots and pour in the water. Bring to a boil.

5   Skim, add the konjac vermicelli, then the sugar, soy sauce, mirin, sake, and dehydrated dashi. Mix with a spatula.

6   Cover with a disk of parchment paper the same diameter as the Dutch oven. Lower the heat and simmer with the lid on for about 20 minutes. Check that the potatoes are cooked by pricking them with a small knife (the blade should go in easily). Remove the parchment paper and simmer for another 5 minutes to allow the cooking water to evaporate. Add the snow peas and cook for 2 minutes. Ladle the meat, vegetables, and broth into bowls and serve hot.

KABOCHA
NO NIMONO

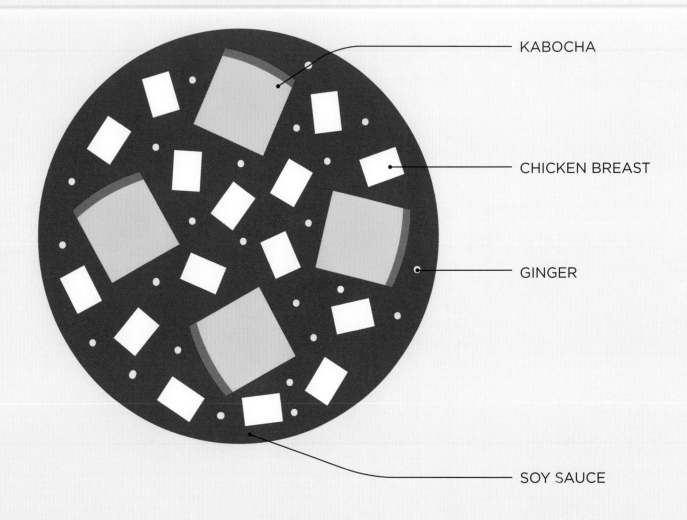

KABOCHA

CHICKEN BREAST

GINGER

SOY SAUCE

WHAT IS IT?

Simmered dish made with kabocha squash and chicken.

ORIGIN

Kabocha = winter squash; nimono = simmered: simmered winter squash

TOTAL TIME

Prep time: 20 minutes
Cook time: 20 minutes

EQUIPMENT
Dutch oven

TECHNIQUES TO MASTER
Hari-shouga (ginger matchsticks, page 281).

TIPS
- Kabocha is a very sweet variety of Japanese squash. It can be eaten with or without the skin.
- To test for doneness, simply insert the tip of a knife into a piece of kabocha: if it penetrates easily, it's done.
- Covering the pieces of kabocha with parchment paper keeps them submerged in the liquid, which speeds up cooking time.

VARIATIONS
- Replace the squash with white radish (daikon)
- Use the same amount of beef or pork instead of chicken (7 ounces / 200 g).

Learn

FOR 4 PEOPLE

1 pound 5 ounces / 600 g Japanese
    kabocha
7 ounces / 200 g chicken breast
1 (⅓-inch / 5 g) piece fresh ginger, minced
½ teaspoon canola oil

SAUCE

2 tablespoons soy sauce
2 tablespoons mirin
1 tablespoon cooking sake
1 tablespoon cane sugar
½ teaspoon salt
½ teaspoon dehydrated dashi
1¼ cups / 300 ml water

TO FINISH THE DISH

1 tablespoon cornstarch
2 tablespoons water
(1½-inch / 20 g) piece fresh ginger,
    julienned

1   Quarter the kabocha, then remove the
seeds with a spoon. Cut into 1½-inch /
4 cm cubes. Peel and finely chop the 5 g
of ginger using the hari-shouga technique
(page 281). Then chop the 20 g of ginger
separately in the same way and set aside.
Finely chop the chicken with a knife.

2   In a bowl, combine the sauce ingredients.
Pour the oil into a Dutch oven and heat over
medium heat. Add the 5 g ginger, saute

for 1 minute, then add the chicken. Cook
until the chicken turns white, then add the
sauce and 1¼ cups / 300 ml water. Cook
on high heat, stirring. Skim the surface.

3   Add the kabocha and cover with a
disk of parchment paper the same size as
the diameter of the Dutch oven. Simmer
for about 10 minutes with the lid on.

4   Remove the kabocha cubes with a
skimmer and place in a dish. In a small
bowl, combine the cornstarch and 2
tablespoons of water. Add to the squash
cooking juices and stir. Leave to cook,
stirring, and when the cooking juices
become transparent, remove from heat.
Pour the juice over the kabocha. Top
with the julienned ginger and serve.

Understand

CURRY RICE

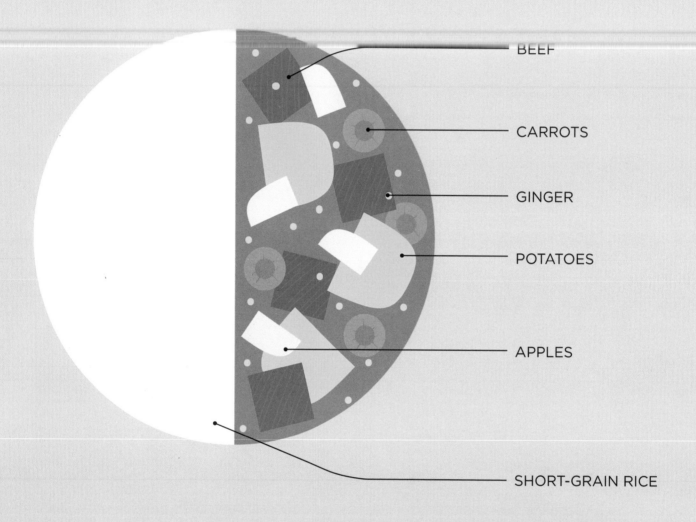

BEEF

CARROTS

GINGER

POTATOES

APPLES

SHORT-GRAIN RICE

WHAT IS IT?

A stew-like dish with vegetables and meat in a spicy curry sauce.

ORIGIN

Curry was first imported to Japan from India during the Meiji era in the 19th century and became popular in the 1960s.

TOTAL TIME

Prep time: 20 minutes
Cook time: 30 minutes

EQUIPMENT

Dutch oven or saucepan
Grater with large holes

TECHNIQUES TO MASTER

Cooking rice (page 11)

NOTE

Japanese curry recipes are made with either an instant curry sauce or a curry cube, which is added to the broth at the end of cooking to thicken the sauce. The sauce is brown and more or less spicy depending on the curry mix.

SUBSTITUTIONS

Replace the beef with pork or chicken.
- **Vegetarian:** replace the meat with firm tofu.

Learn

JAPANESE RICE

Oval (almost round) rice. Rich in starch, which gives it a sticky, glutinous texture when cooked.

FUKUSHIN-ZUKE

Pickled vegetables marinated in soy sauce. Used to accompany Japanese curries.

JAPANESE CURRY CUBE

A paste made from a curry roux. The blend of spices is similar to Indian curry and caramelized onion is added for a slightly sweeter taste. Available in mild and hot versions.

FOR 4 PEOPLE

- 2¼ cups / 450 g Japanese short-grain white rice
- 2½ cups / 600 ml water for cooking the rice
- 14 ounces / 400 g tender beef (tenderloin, rib eye, etc.)
- 2 medium potatoes
- 2 carrots
- 1 onion
- 1 (¾-inch / 10 g) piece fresh ginger
- 1 clove of garlic
- ½ apple
- 3⅓ cups / 800 ml water for the curry
- 3½ to 4 cubes (3½ ounces / 100 g) Japanese curry
- 1 tablespoon oil
- Salt
- Pepper

FOR SERVING

- ¼ cup / 40 g fukushin-zuke (Japanese pickles - optional)
- 2 tablespoons pickled white onions

1 Prepare and cook the rice (page 10).

2 Peel the potatoes and cut into medium-sized cubes. Place in a bowl of water and leave to soak until ready to cook. Peel and cut the carrots into ¾-inch / 2 cm pieces. Peel and halve the onion and cut each half into slices about 5 mm thick. Peel and grate ginger and garlic. Peel, core, and grate the apple using a grater with large holes.

3 Cut beef into pieces 1¼-inch / 3 cm thick, then into cubes. Season with salt and pepper.

4 Pour the oil into a Dutch oven, add the meat cubes, and saute over high heat. Add onions and sauté over medium heat for 3 minutes. Add the carrots, grated apple, and strained potato cubes, along with the garlic and ginger, and stir. Pour in water. Cover the pot, bring to a boil, then skim.

5 Lower the heat and cook for about 20 minutes. Cut the curry paste into small pieces. Turn off the heat and stir the pieces of curry paste into the broth; the sauce will change color and thicken.

6 Cook over low heat for 5 minutes. Divide the cooked rice between 4 plates. Add the curry mixture. Serve with pickles.

TEMPURA
SHRIMP & VEGETABLES

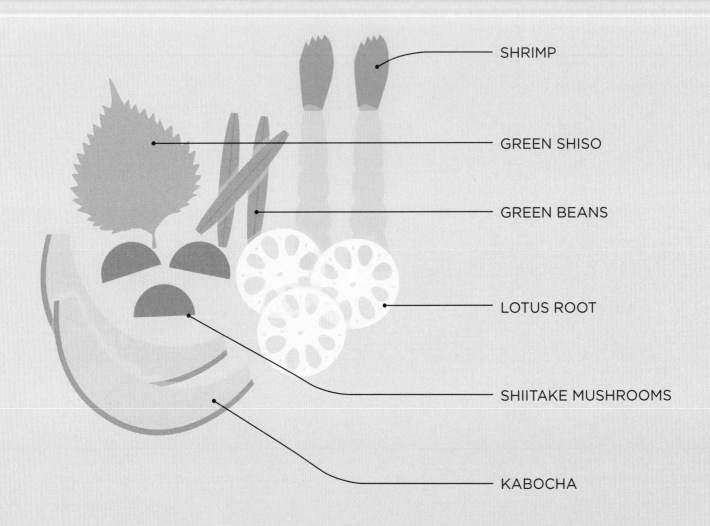

SHRIMP

GREEN SHISO

GREEN BEANS

LOTUS ROOT

SHIITAKE MUSHROOMS

KABOCHA

WHAT IS IT?

Battered and fried vegetables and seafood.

ORIGIN

A hallmark of Japanese cuisine, tempura originated in Europe, and was brought to Japan by the Portuguese during the Edo period (17th century). At the time, the dish was sold in small street stands.

TOTAL TIME

Prep time: 30 minutes
Cook time: 20 minutes

EQUIPMENT

Dutch oven, frying pan, or wok (10 inches / 25 cm)
Mandoline
Daikon oroshi

TECHNIQUES TO MASTER

Preparing daikon (page 281)
Cutting vegetables (page 280)
Preparing shrimp (page 36)
Preparing tempura batter (page 46)

TIPS

Frying seafood tends to discolor the oil, so the vegetables are fried first. Only 5 or 6 items can be fried at a time (about half the surface area of the oil). If there are too many ingredients, the oil temperature will be too low and the fritters won't be crispy. To check for doneness, watch and listen: as the frying progresses, the large bubbles formed on the surface become smaller; at the end of frying, the noisy bubbling of the oil slows down as the water in the ingredients has evaporated - it's ready.

HOW TO ENJOY

Tempura can be used to accompany and enhance other dishes like udon tempura, soba tempura, and tendon (tempura placed on a bowl of rice).

Learn

LOTUS ROOT

Edible part of the lotus. It has a crunchy texture and tastes a little bit like a radish.

SHISO

A highly aromatic plant, somewhere between mint and basil, sold in Asian markets.

KABOCHA

Orange-fleshed squash with a sweet flavor and a dense, starchy texture. Found in Asian grocery stores and some organic markets.

ERINGI MUSHROOMS

A member of the oyster mushroom family. Select mushrooms with white stems and smooth caps.

FOR 4 PEOPLE

8 raw shrimp
12 green beans
- 4 green shiso leaves
4 shiitake mushrooms
- 2 eringi mushrooms
- 3½ ounces / 100 g lotus root
- 7 ounces / 200 g kabocha

TEMPURA BATTER (PAGE 46)

Heaping ¾ cup / 100 g flour for dredging
2½ cups / 600 ml vegetable oil for frying
1 tablespoon toasted sesame oil

TEMPURA DIPPING SAUCE

¾ cup plus 4 teaspoons / 200 ml dashi (page 28)
3 tablespoons / 50 ml mirin
3 tablespoon / 50 ml soy sauce

FOR SERVING

7 ounces / 200 g daikon (top part)
1 (3-inch / 40 g) piece fresh ginger

Make

1   To make the sauce, pour the dashi, mirin, and soy sauce into a small saucepan. Bring to a boil, then remove from heat. Set aside and reheat just before serving. Peel the upper part of the daikon (page 28) and the ginger. Grate using a grater or a daikon oroshi (radish grater). Place in a bowl. Set aside. Wash and trim the green beans. Clean the shiitake mushrooms and remove the stems. Clean and slice the eringi mushrooms into pieces ¼-inch / 6 mm thick. Wash shiso leaves and drain on a kitchen towel. Cut the kabocha into quarters, then remove the seeds with a tablespoon. Cut into slices ¼-inch / 6 mm thick. Peel and slice lotus root into rounds ¼ inch / 6 mm thick using a mandoline.

Submerge them in water to prevent discoloration, then drain and pat dry with paper towels just before cooking. Prepare the shrimp (page 36). Prepare the tempura batter (page 46).

2   Lightly dust the ingredients with flour, then dip them in the tempura batter, holding them with chopsticks.

3   Heat the frying oil to 340°F / 170°C (page 284). For the kabocha, fry for about 3 minutes until the slices are crisp, turning occasionally. Drain excess oil by holding them vertically above a wire rack. Proceed in the same way for the lotus root slices and the green beans, allowing 1 minute for cooking.

4   Flour and batter one side only of the shiso leaves. Cook for 1 minute. For the shiitakes, flour and batter the inside of the caps. Cook for 2 minutes. Raise the oil temperature to 350°F / 180°C. Dip the shrimp in the batter (except for the tails) and fry for 1 to 2 minutes.

5   Reheat the sauce and divide into 4 bowls. Arrange tempura fritters on serving dishes. Place lightly drained grated radish and ginger on small plates. Dip the fritters into the sauce, mixing in the grated radish and ginger.

Understand

KAKIAGE

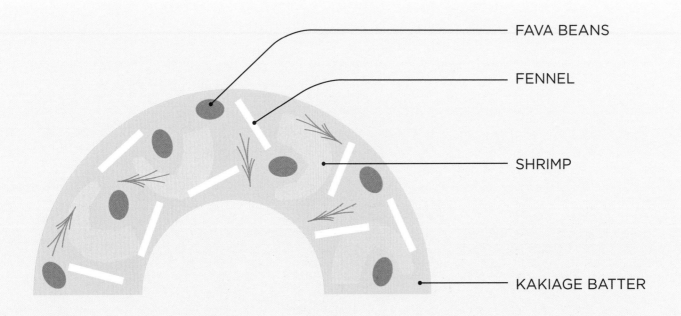

FAVA BEANS

FENNEL

SHRIMP

KAKIAGE BATTER

WHAT IS IT?

Pieces of shrimp, seafood, vegetables, etc. that are soaked in a batter (wheat flour, egg, and water) then fried.

ORIGIN

Kaki (kakimazeru) = mixed;
age = fried: mixed and fried.
Kakiage is a type of tempura.

TOTAL TIME

Prep time: 20 minutes
Cook time: 10 minutes

EQUIPMENT

Dutch oven, frying pan, or
wok (9 inches / 23 cm)
Mandoline

TECHNIQUE TO MASTER

Preparing the frying oil (page 284)

TIP

The ingredients are divided
into four portions so that each
fritter is the same size.

HOW TO ENJOY

Kakiage tempura is a very popular side dish that can be prepared in many ways. It can be served with rice (kakiage don), soba (kakiage soba), or udon (kakiage udon).

Learn

●

COOKING
SAKE

Sake with added salt.

●

YUZU
SALT

Salt subtly flavored
with powdered
yuzu peel.

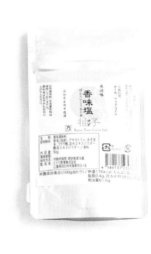

FOR 4 PEOPLE
(8 PIECES)

10½ ounces / 300 g raw shrimp
7 ounces / 200 g fennel with fronds
1¼ cups / 150 g shelled fava beans
● 1 tablespoon cooking sake
Vegetable oil for frying
● Yuzu salt

KAKIAGE BATTER

½ cup / 70 g pastry flour
⅓ cup plus 4 teaspoons / 100 ml
    cold water
1 egg

1 Place all the ingredients for the batter and the mixing bowls in the fridge for 30 minutes before use. Using a mandoline, slice the fennel into strips about 5 mm thick. Remove the thin skin from the fava beans.

2 Remove the heads from the shrimp and peel off the shells. Using a knife, make a small incision in the back and remove the vein. Cut the shrimp into small pieces (about 1 inch / 2.5 cm), place in a small bowl, and mix with 1 tablespoon of sake. Strain and set aside.

3 Sift the flour into a bowl. In another bowl, mix the egg with the cold water. Pour into the flour and mix quickly but gently with chopsticks or a fork.

4 In another bowl, place ¼ of each ingredient (fava beans, fennel, shrimp), add 1 teaspoon of flour, and mix.

5 Add 4 tablespoons of kakiage batter and mix.

6 Heat the frying oil to 340°F / 170°C (page 284). Using a spatula or ladle, form two small fritters from the batter mixture (approx. 4 inches) and, using chopsticks or a fork, slide them into the oil. Fry for around 2 minutes, turning, until the pastry is crisp. Remove the fritters and drain on a wire rack, then on an absorbent kitchen towel. Repeat the process three more times with the remaining ingredients. Transfer to plates. Serve immediately with yuzu salt.

KARAAGE
CHICKEN

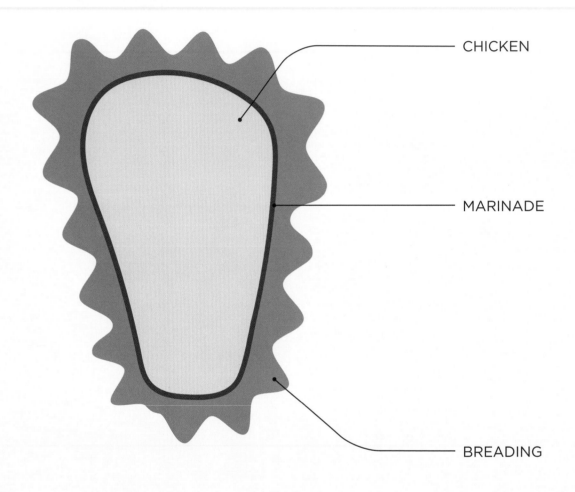

CHICKEN

MARINADE

BREADING

WHAT IS IT?

Fried marinated chicken.

ORIGIN

Kara = without batter; age = fried: it is fried without being coated in batter. This dish dates back to the Edo period and its history is linked to that of tempura. It became popular after the war with the development of intensive chicken farming. It is now a dish cooked by all Japanese home cooks.

TOTAL TIME

Prep time: 15 minutes
Cook time: 10 minutes
Rest time: 20 minutes

EQUIPMENT

Dutch oven or wok
Grater with small holes

WHERE AND WHEN TO ENJOY

A classic dish that you can find in any Japanese home, bento box, street stall, restaurant, or izakaya. It's served all year round and it is endlessly popular.

TECHNIQUES TO MASTER

Deboning chicken (page 42)
Preparing the frying oil (page 284)

TIP

Frying in two stages keeps the chicken juicy in the center and crispy on the outside.

VARIATIONS

There are many regional variations. Prawns, fish, octopus, and vegetables can also be used.

Learn

COOKING
SAKE

Sake with added salt.

SOY SAUCE

Choose brands
with labels that say
"naturally brewed" or
"naturally fermented."

TOASTED
SESAME OIL

Use pure sesame oil.

FOR 4 PEOPLE

4 skin-on boneless chicken thighs
      (about 2.6 pounds / 1.2 kg)
Salt
Pepper

MARINADE

- 3 tablespoons / 50 ml soy sauce
- 3 tablespoons / 50 ml cooking sake
- 1 teaspoon toasted sesame oil
  1 (2¼-inch / 30 g) piece fresh ginger
  1 clove of garlic

BREADING

1¼ cup / 150 g potato starch or cornstarch
2½ cups / 600 ml vegetable oil

FOR SERVING

1 lemon
¼ bunch of watercress

1   Debone the chicken thighs (page 42). Remove the nerves and the fat. Cut the chicken into 1½-inch / 4 cm pieces. Season with salt and pepper.

2   To make the marinade, pour the soy sauce, sesame oil, and sake into a bowl. Add the grated garlic and ginger and place the chicken in the marinade. Cover with plastic wrap and chill in the refrigerator for around 20 minutes.

3   In a Dutch oven or wok, heat the oil to 320°F / 155°C (page 284). Drain the marinated chicken pieces and then coat generously with the cornstarch.

4   Fry on each side for 1 minute and 30 seconds, turning only once. Remove and place on a rack, leaving the chicken to rest for 3 to 4 minutes. During this time, the chicken will continue to cook.

5   Raise the temperature slightly (to 355-375°F / 180 to 190°C). Return all the chicken pieces to the oil and fry for another 1 to 2 minutes, until golden and crispy. Drain on the grill, then on paper towels to absorb excess oil. Arrange on a serving dish and garnish with lemon wedges and watercress leaves.

Understand

NANBANZUKE

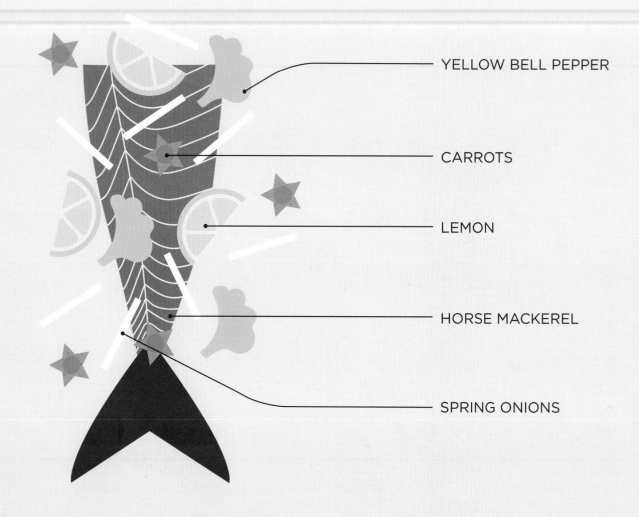

YELLOW BELL PEPPER

CARROTS

LEMON

HORSE MACKEREL

SPRING ONIONS

WHAT IS IT?

Marinated deep-fried horse mackerel served with aromatic vegetables.

ORIGIN

Nanban = Portuguese fry; zuke = marinated: marinated and fried, from Portugal.

TOTAL TIME

Prep time: 30 minutes
Cook time: 5 minutes
Rest time: 6 hours minimum

EQUIPMENT

Dutch oven or frying pan
Leaf-shaped cookie cutter (1-inch / 2.5 cm)
Mandoline

TECHNIQUES TO MASTER

Preparing the frying oil (page 284)
Preparing fish (page 282)

TIPS

Because the fish is fried in oil and then marinated overnight, the bones are soft; the entire fish can be eaten.

VARIATIONS

- The horse mackerel can be replaced by sardines.
- The mirin can be replaced by the same amount of apple juice.

WHEN TO ENJOY

This dish is made whenever fresh fish is available. Even though it is fried, the horse mackerel pairs perfectly with the marinade, which adds lightness and a sweet and salty touch.

Learn

MIRIN

A Japanese rice wine used as a condiment; it is sweeter than sake.

WHITE SOY SAUCE

This fermented condiment is the lightest of the soy sauces and has a delicate flavor.

RICE VINEGAR

Pure rice vinegar with a smooth, mellow taste and a slightly amber hue.

SHICHIMI TOGARASHI

Also known as Japanese seven spice, it contains red chili pepper, sesame and poppy seeds, nori, sansho, ginger, shiso, hemp seeds, and chenpi (mandarin peel).

FOR 4 PEOPLE

FISH

4 small horse mackerels
    (1 pound 5 ounces / 600 g)
⅓ cup (heaping) / 50 g potato
    starch or cornstarch
2 cups plus 4 teaspoons / 500 ml
    vegetable oil for frying

TOPPINGS

1 carrot
1 yellow bell pepper
½ fennel bulb
4 spring onions
½ lemon

MARINADE

1⅔ cups / 400 ml dashi (page 28)
- ⅓ cup plus 4 teaspoons / 100 ml
    rice vinegar
- ⅓ cup / 80 ml mirin
- ⅓ cup / 80 ml light or white soy sauce
1 teaspoon salt
2 tablespoons cane sugar

FOR SERVING

2 sprigs of shiso
Some chives
1 tablespoon toasted sesame seeds
- 1 pinch of shichimi togarashi

1   Place all the ingredients for the marinade in a small saucepan. Bring to a boil, then pour into a deep rectangular dish.

2   Wash and peel the carrot and slice into 2 mm-thick rounds using a mandoline. Cut the bell pepper in half. Use a cookie cutter to cut out carrot and bell pepper pieces. Thinly slice the fennel and onions using a mandoline. Slice the lemon into rounds and cut them in half.

3   Prepare the horse mackerel (page 33).

4   Dust the fish with the starch.

5   Fry the horse mackerel for 2 minutes, then drain on paper towels. Fry a second time, for 2 more minutes, then drain again.

6   Place the fried horse mackerel in the marinade. Add the vegetables and cover with plastic wrap. Leave to cool at room temperature, then chill in the fridge for at least 6 hours (ideally overnight). Arrange the fish on a plate and sprinkle with sesame seeds, shichimi togarashi, chopped chives, and shiso leaves.

Understand

AGEBITASHI

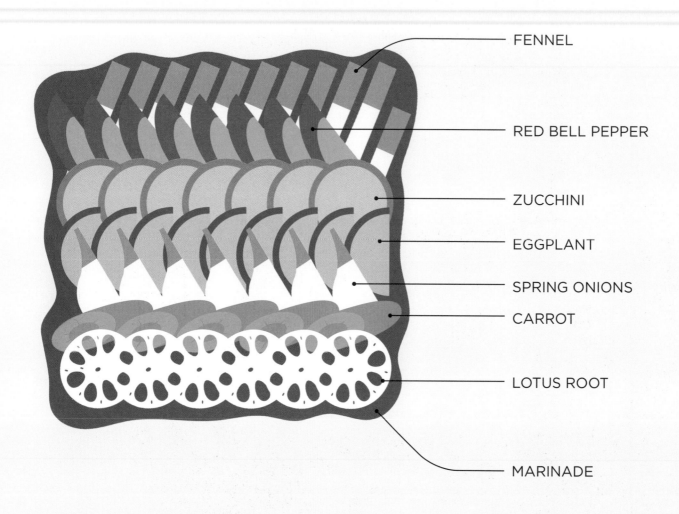

FENNEL

RED BELL PEPPER

ZUCCHINI

EGGPLANT

SPRING ONIONS

CARROT

LOTUS ROOT

MARINADE

WHAT IS IT?

Fried summer vegetables marinated in dashi.

ORIGIN

Age = fried; bitashi (hitashi) = marinated. This is a traditional dish made with seasonal vegetables that are fried in oil and then soaked in soup stock so that the flavors infuse.

TOTAL TIME

Prep time: 20 minutes
Cook time: 30 minutes
Storage: 3 days in the fridge

EQUIPMENT

Mandoline
Skillet (10 inches / 25 cm)
Baking dish

TIP

While cooking the vegetables, add oil if necessary, so that there is always a depth of 5 mm.

VARIATION

In winter, use root vegetables such as Jerusalem artichokes and turnips.

HOW AND WHEN TO ENJOY

Serve hot or cold, preferably in summer, with seasonal vegetables. Although the vegetables are fried, the marinade lightens this pleasant dish.

Learn

FOR 4 PEOPLE

1 zucchini
1 red bell pepper
1 lotus root
1 bunch of spring onions
1 eggplant
1 carrot
7 ounces / 200 g fennel
Vegetable oil for frying

MARINADE

1⅔ cups / 400 ml dashi
5 tablespoons / 80 ml soy sauce
1 tablespoon cane sugar
1 tablespoon mirin

FOR SERVING

1 lemon
1 sprig of cilantro
Yuzu shichimi

1 To make the marinade, pour the dashi, soy sauce, sugar, and mirin into a saucepan. Bring to a boil and pour into a baking dish.

2 Wash all the vegetables. Slice the zucchini into rounds ⅜-inch / 1 cm thick. Cut the bell pepper in half, remove the seeds and the white core, then cut vertically into eight strips. Peel the lotus root, slice into rounds ⅛-inch to ¼-inch / 3 to 6 mm thick using a mandoline, then plunge the rounds in water to prevent oxidation (drain just before

cooking). Cut the onions in half vertically. Slice the eggplant into 1 cm-thick slices, then cut them in half. Peel the carrot and slice on a diagonal (to about ¼-inch / 6 mm thick). Chop the fennel into small pieces.

3 Pour the oil into a skillet to a depth of ¼-inch / 6 mm and heat over high heat. Quickly cook all the vegetables. Remove and drain on a wire rack.

4 Add the vegetables to the marinade while still hot. Serve immediately with the yuzu, cilantro leaves, and lemon slices, or leave to rest for 2 to 4 hours in the fridge to allow the flavors to combine.

Understand
AGEDASHI TOFU

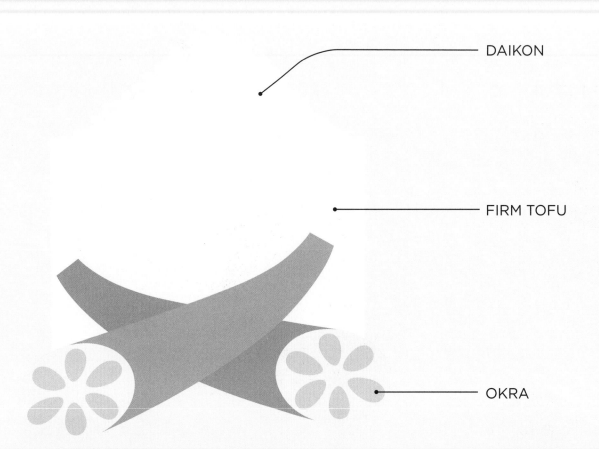

DAIKON

FIRM TOFU

OKRA

WHAT IS IT?
Fried tofu served in a sauce and topped with condiments.

ORIGIN
Age = fried: fried tofu in dashi broth. Agedashi dofu is a traditional dish from the Edo period cookbook *Tofu Hyakuchin* (100 Tofu Recipes).

TOTAL TIME
Prep time: 15 minutes
Cook time: 15 minutes

EQUIPMENT
Grater

HOW TO ENJOY
Agedashi tofu is an appetizer. The sauce adds a pleasant flavor to the somewhat neutral taste of the tofu.

TIPS
-The tofu is fried in oil at 320 to 340°F / 160 to 170°C. Tofu contains a lot of water, so it's best not to fry it at very high temperatures. If the tofu gets too hot, small air bubbles will form inside the cubes and they will lose their smooth texture.

- Squeeze excess water out of the grated daikon radish to avoid diluting the flavor of the sauce.

ADDITIONS AND SUBSTITUTIONS
- You can add nori flakes or bonito shavings on top.
- The okra can be replaced by bell peppers.

Learn

FOR 4 PEOPLE

2 blocks (about 1 pound 5 ounces / 600 g) momen (firm) tofu
8 okra pods
5¼ ounces / 150 g daikon
Ichimi togarashi (ground chili pepper)
Flour
Vegetable oil for frying

SAUCE

1 cup plus 2 teaspoons / 250 ml dashi
3 tablespoons / 50 ml soy sauce
3 tablespoons / 50 ml mirin

1   Cut the tofu blocks into 16 large cubes, then place on kitchen towels and leave to drain for around 10 minutes. Wash the okra pods and cut them in half on an angle. Wash and peel the daikon, then grate and set aside.

2   Pour the dashi, soy sauce, and mirin into a small saucepan. Bring to a boil, remove from heat, and set aside.

3   Heat the oil to between 320°F and 340°F / 160°C and 170°C. In a shallow dish, roll the tofu cubes in the flour, coating well. Shake off any excess flour with a brush or by hand.

4   Fry for 5 minutes, turning halfway through. Drain on paper towels.

5   Fry the okra in the same way.

6   While the sauce is still hot, pour it into 4 small soup plates, then add 4 fried tofu cubes and 4 fried okra pods to each. Add the grated radish in the middle and sprinkle with the ichimi togarashi.

Understand

TONKATSU

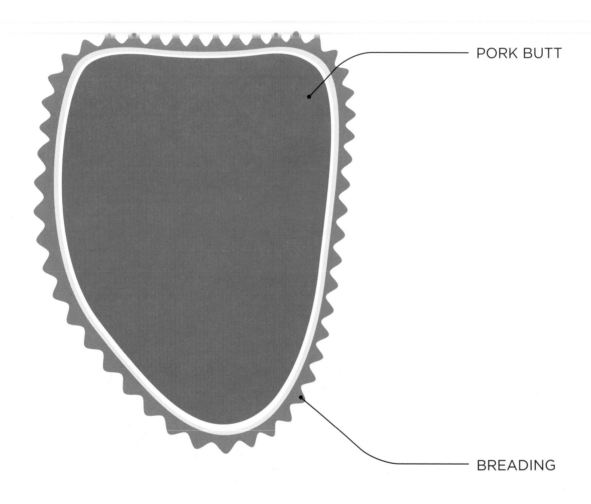

PORK BUTT

BREADING

WHAT IS IT?

Thick slices of pork loin or tenderloin coated in flour, whisked egg, and breadcrumbs, then fried.

ORIGIN

Tonkatsu is a very popular Japanese dish that appeared at the end of the nineteenth century (Meiji era) when an English-style breaded cutlet was served in a restaurant in Ginza. The English word "cutlet" was mispronounced by the Japanese as katsuretsu, later shortened to katsu. The ton in tonkatsu means pork.

TOTAL TIME

Prep time: 15 minutes
Cook time: 10 minutes
Rest time: 5 minutes

EQUIPMENT

Iron or cast-iron skillet (11 inches / 28 cm)
Mandoline

TECHNIQUES TO MASTER

Preparing the frying oil (page 284)

TIP

Choose a tender cut of pork that is not too dry, such as pork loin, pork chops, or pork tenderloin.

VARIATIONS

Katsu sando: a sandwich with sliced bread, thinly sliced cabbage, and tonkatsu cutlets topped with sauce.
Katsu don: a rice bowl with a beaten egg, a blend of soy sauce and mirin, and tonkatsu cutlets.

VARIATIONS

Keeping the same breading, replace the pork with prawns (ebi fry) or oysters (kaki fry).

HOW TO ENJOY

Tonkatsu is a very popular dish thanks to its special salty-sweet sauce.

Learn

PANKO

Breadcrumbs made from sliced bread. They are crispier and lighter than traditional breadcrumbs.

TONKATSU SAUCE

The Japanese version of Worcestershire sauce. Salty-sweet with a syrupy texture.

FOR 2 PEOPLE

2 slices of boneless pork butt (1 inch thick, about 13 ounces / 360 g)
⅓ cup / 40 g flour
Salt
Pepper

BREADING

⅓ cup plus 4 teaspoons / 50 g flour
1 egg
2 tablespoons water
● ⅔ cup / 50 g panko (Japanese breadcrumbs)

FOR SERVING

7 ounces / 200 g pointed cabbage
6 cherry tomatoes
1 lemon
● 4 to 6 tablespoons / 60 to 90 ml tonkatsu sauce

Make

1 Wash the cabbage, then slice thinly using a mandoline. Set aside.

2 Tap both sides of the meat lightly with the flat of a knife blade, then season with salt and pepper. Leave to rest for about 5 minutes at room temperature, then press with paper towels, wiping excess moisture from both sides.

3 Place the ⅓ cup / 40 g of flour in a shallow dish. In a bowl, whisk together the ⅓ cup plus 4 teaspoons / 50 g of flour, 1 egg, and 2 tablespoons of water. Pour into a second shallow dish. Put the Japanese breadcrumbs in a third dish. Dip the pork chops in the flour, then in the wet mix, and finally in the breadcrumbs.

4 Heat the frying oil to 320°F / 160°C (page 284). Fry the pork for 6 to 7 minutes on each side, turning occasionally until golden brown. During the last minute of cooking, increase the temperature to 355°F / 180°C.

5 Remove and drain, then place on a wire rack. Leave to rest for 4 to 5 minutes. During this time, the pork will continue to cook with the residual heat. Cut each piece of meat into 5 or 6 slices with a knife. Arrange the cabbage on each plate, place the pork chops on top, and add the cherry tomatoes and lemon wedges. Serve with the tonkatsu sauce.

Understand
CHAWANMUSHI

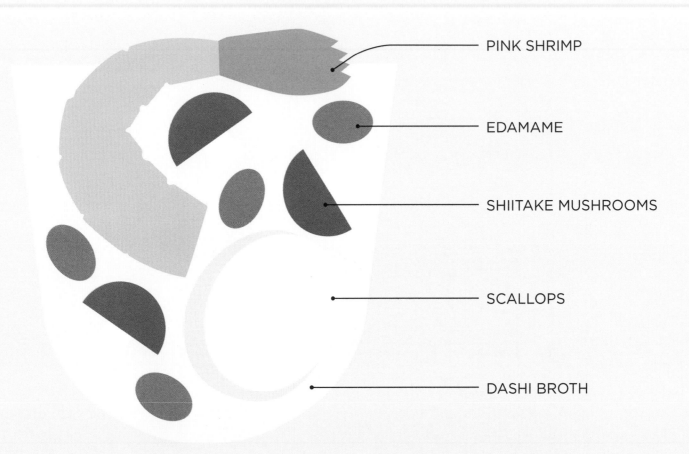

PINK SHRIMP

EDAMAME

SHIITAKE MUSHROOMS

SCALLOPS

DASHI BROTH

WHAT IS IT?

Egg and dashi custard with seafood and mushrooms.

ORIGIN

Chawan = bowl; mushi = steamed: literally a steamed bowl. This traditional dish originated in the busy port city of Nagasaki.

TOTAL TIME

Prep time: 25 minutes
Cook time: 35 minutes
Rest time: 1 hour

EQUIPMENT

Dutch oven with steamer basket or a saucepan with a lid (for a bain-marie)

TECHNIQUES TO MASTER

Rehydrating dashi (page 28)
Preparing shrimp (page 36)

TIPS

- Allow the dashi to cool before adding to the eggs so that they don't overcook.
- To check the custard for doneness, insert a bamboo skewer into the center. If a clear liquid emerges, the chawanmushi is ready. Otherwise, increase the heat slightly and steam for a few more minutes.

VARIATIONS

- The shiitake mushrooms can be replaced by button mushrooms.
- The scallops can be replaced by chicken fillets or surimi.

Learn

DASHI POWDER

Dehydrated kombu and katsuobushi broth.

WHITE SOY SAUCE

This fermented condiment is the lightest of the soy sauces and has a delicate flavor.

DRIED SHIITAKES

A good alternative to fresh shiitake mushrooms; they keep longer and still retain their fragrant flavor and rich nutrients.

FOR 4 PEOPLE

3 eggs
4 raw pink shrimp
4 scallops
8 small dried shiitakes
8 chives
Orange or yuzu zest
¼ cup / 40 g shelled edamame

DASHI BROTH

- 1¼ cups / 300 ml cold dashi (page 28)
  or 1 teaspoon dashi powder and
  1¼ cups / 300 ml water
- 2 teaspoons white soy sauce
- 1 teaspoon mirin
  ¼ teaspoon salt

Make

1   Soak the shiitake mushrooms in 5 ounces / 150 ml water for 1 hour. Keep the soaking water for the broth. Remove the stems and thinly slice the caps.

2   Prepare the shrimp. Remove the black vein from the back of the shrimp using a skewer. Remove the head and then shell the body (leave the tail intact). Cut the scallops in half horizontally.

3   Bring a pot of water to a boil and blanch the shrimp and scallops for 1 minute. Drain and set aside.

4   Break the eggs into a bowl and stir with chopsticks without whisking. Pour into the dashi bowl and mix. Add the shiitake soaking water (about 5 ounces / 150 ml), soy sauce, mirin, and salt.

5   Strain through a fine sieve.

6   Divide the shiitake mushrooms and scallops among small bowls arranged in a steamer basket. Set aside ¼ cup / 60 ml of the egg mixture and pour the rest into the bowls.

7   Pour 1⅔ cups / 400 ml of water into a pot and place the steamer basket in the pot. Bring to a boil over high heat, covered. Leave to cook for 3 minutes. Reduce heat to low and cook for 15 minutes. Pour 1 tablespoon of the reserved egg mixture over each bowl, along with 1 shrimp, and leave to cook for a further 5 minutes.

8   Remove the bowls from the heat and sprinkle a little orange zest over the custard for flavor. Scatter the chopped chives and edamame on top.

RED MULLET, TOFU
& SHIITAKE SAKAMUSHI

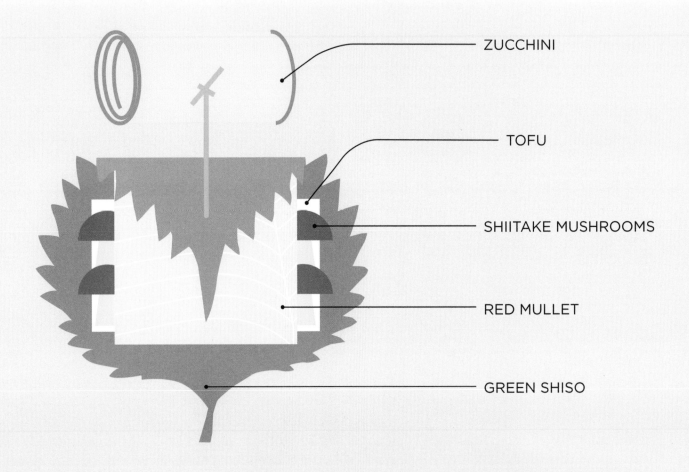

ZUCCHINI

TOFU

SHIITAKE MUSHROOMS

RED MULLET

GREEN SHISO

WHAT IS IT?

Red mullet, tofu, and shiitake marinated in sake and then steamed.

ORIGIN

Saka = sake; mushi = steamed: with sake and steamed. Sake softens the fish while steaming ensures that the flesh remains firm and flavorful.

TOTAL TIME

Prep time: 20 minutes
Cook time: 6 minutes
Rest time: 1 hour

EQUIPMENT

Steamer basket
Pot (11 to 13 inches / 28 to 32 cm)
Heat-resistant plate
Mandoline
2 bamboo skewers

TECHNIQUE TO MASTER

Preparing fish (page 33)

TIP

The sakamushi cooking technique requires the use of the freshest possible ingredients.

SUBSTITUTIONS

Replace red mullet with shellfish such as clams or abalone.

WHEN TO ENJOY

This is an autumn-winter dish. Sakamushi is popular in Japan because it is oil-free; allowing the quality of the ingredients to be appreciated and their nutritional value, tenderness, and delicacy to be preserved.

Learn

SHIITAKE MUSHROOMS

Plump, fleshy mushrooms with a woody flavor.

KOMBU SEAWEED

Giant seaweed with a briny taste from the genus Laminaria.

SHISO

A highly aromatic plant, somewhere between mint and basil, sold in Asian markets.

YUZU KOSHO

Fermented paste made from green chili and yuzu peel; used as a condiment.

FOR 2 PEOPLE

2 red mullet fillets (10½ ounces / 300 g)
1 block of firm tofu (5¼ ounces / 150 g)
- 4 fresh shiitake mushrooms
1 small zucchini
- 2 green shiso leaves
Zest of 1 orange (or 1 yuzu)
- 2 pieces of kombu (2 inches / 5 cm)

SAKA-SHIO

⅓ cup / 80 ml cooking sake
1 pinch of fine salt

SAUCE

⅓ cup plus 4 teaspoons / 100 ml ponzu, store-bought or homemade (page 51)
- 1 tablespoon yuzu kosho

1   Prepare the fish (page 33).

2   Mix the sake and salt in a bowl. Arrange the pieces of kombu in the bottom of a dish, place the fillets on top, then pour over the sake mixture. Cover with plastic wrap and chill in the fridge for around 1 hour.

3   Remove the shiitake stems and thinly slice the caps. Using a mandoline, slice the zucchini lengthwise into ribbons (1/16-inch / 2 mm thick). Slice the orange zest into narrow strips. Cut the tofu into 2¾ by 1½ by 1-inch / 7 by 4 by 2½ cm pieces.

4   Place a piece of kombu from the marinade in a shallow dish, and add 1 piece of tofu, some shiitake slices, and 1 fish fillet. Pierce the fish and tofu with a short skewer. Repeat the process with the other piece of tofu and the remaining ingredients.

5   Pour 1⅔ cups of water / 400 ml into a large saucepan and place the steamer basket on top. Set the plate in the basket and bring the water to a boil over medium heat. Cook for 3 minutes with the lid tightly closed.

6   Place the zucchini ribbons on the side and cook for a minute more. Arrange the fish on plates. Add the zucchini, place the shiso leaves on the folded fish, and sprinkle with the orange zest. Serve with ponzu and yuzu kosho.

SHIITAKES
STUFFED WITH COD

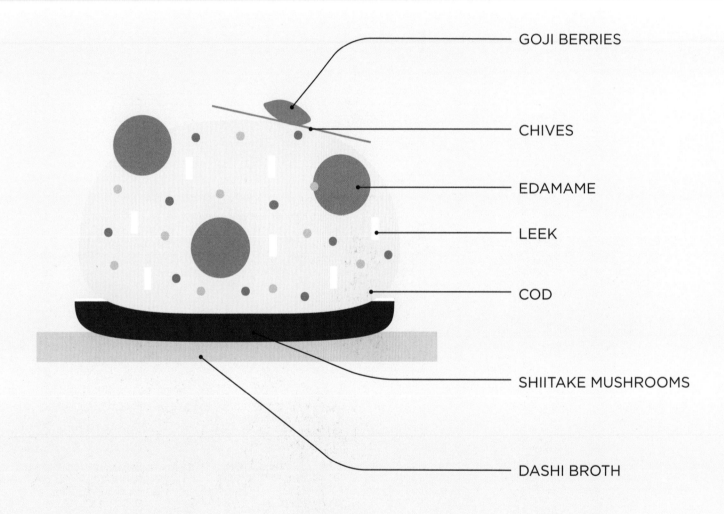

GOJI BERRIES

CHIVES

EDAMAME

LEEK

COD

SHIITAKE MUSHROOMS

DASHI BROTH

WHAT IS IT?

Shiitake mushrooms stuffed with cod then steamed and served with a dashi broth.

TOTAL TIME

Prep time: 20 minutes
Cook time: 10 minutes

EQUIPMENT

Dutch oven or other pot, with a steamer basket

WHEN TO ENJOY

This is a spring and autumn recipe tied to mushroom season. Its sophisticated presentation highlights the fish and mushrooms and makes it a popular dish for entertaining or for enjoying with the family on weekends.

TIP

Choose fresh shiitakes that are firm and plump.

VARIATION

You can also cook these in a skillet with a lid to keep in the steam.

SUBSTITUTIONS

- Replace the cod with pork, which also complements the ingredients nicely.
- For a fried version, replace the stuffing with shrimp or scallops.

Learn

WHITE SOY SAUCE
This fermented condiment is the lightest of the soy sauces and has a delicate flavor.

SHIITAKE MUSHROOMS
Plump, fleshy mushrooms with a woody flavor.

KUZU
A starch made from kuzu root; used for its binding abilities.

YUZU KOSHO
A fermented condiment made from green chili peppers and yuzu peel.

INAKA MISO
Light-colored wheat miso with a very mild flavor.

FOR 4 PEOPLE
- 12 shiitakes
- ⅓ cup / 50 g shelled edamame
- 1 to 2 tablespoons flour

STUFFING
- 14 ounces / 400 g cod
- 1½ ounces / 40 g leek (white part only)
- 1 (1½-inch) piece / 20 g ginger
- 2 tablespoons cooking sake
- 1 tablespoon white miso
- 1 tablespoon potato starch or cornstarch
- 1 teaspoon white soy sauce
- 1 egg white

BROTH
- ½ cup plus 2 tablespoons / 150 ml water
- ½ teaspoon dashi powder
- 2 tablespoons mirin
- 1 teaspoon white soy sauce
- 1 pinch of fine salt
- 1 teaspoon toasted sesame oil

TO FINISH THE SAUCE
- 1 tablespoon kuzu
- 1 tablespoon water

FOR SERVING
- ½ bunch of chives
- 1 teaspoon goji berries
- 1 teaspoon yuzu kosho

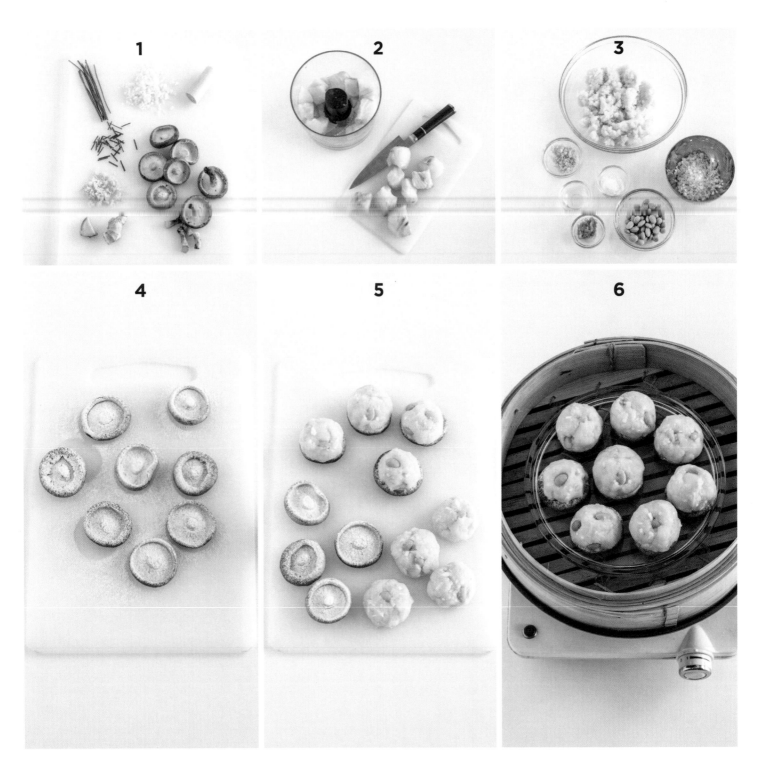

1 Cut off the stems of the shiitake mushrooms and lightly rub the caps to remove any impurities. Chop the white part of the leek and the peeled ginger. Cut the chives and set aside for serving.

2 Chop the cod into pieces and blend until soft.

3 Place the cod in a bowl with the leek, ginger, sake, white miso, egg white, and starch. Mix well with your hands and divide into 12 equal parts.

4 Sprinkle the inside of the shiitake mushroom caps with flour and tap lightly to distribute the flour into a thin layer.

5 Form a small ball of stuffing and gently press it into one of the mushroom caps. Repeat for the other shiitake mushrooms.

6 Arrange the stuffed mushrooms on a heatproof plate and place in a steamer basket. Steam for about 6 minutes. Pour all the broth ingredients into a saucepan. Heat over medium heat. In a small bowl, combine the kuzu and 1 tablespoon of water, then add to the saucepan and stir. Leave to cook, stirring, and remove when the stock becomes transparent. Arrange the stuffed caps on a soup plate and drizzle with the hot stock. Sprinkle with chopped chives, goji berries, and edamame. Serve with yuzu kosho.

TOFU HIYAYAKKO

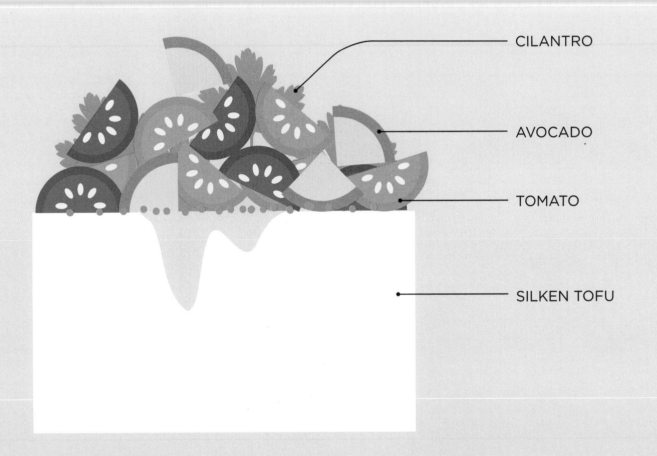

CILANTRO

AVOCADO

TOMATO

SILKEN TOFU

WHAT IS IT?

Tofu appetizer or side dish with spring onions and green shiso.

ORIGIN

Hiya = cold; yakko = square, which refers to the square shape of tofu.

TOTAL TIME

Prep time: 5 minutes
Rest time: 10 minutes

EQUIPMENT
Mandoline

TECHNIQUE TO MASTER
Shiraga Negi (page 280)
- cutting technique

TIP
The tofu is essential to this recipe: make sure you drain it well (for 2 to 3 minutes) because silken tofu contains more liquid than firm tofu. Once drained, its flavor will be stronger and richer.

WHEN TO ENJOY
This simple summer dish is refreshing thanks to the creamy texture of the tofu. It is served as a starter or side dish and pairs well with edamame and sake. Serve with ginger, shiso leaves, and bonito shavings.

Learn

TAMARI SOY SAUCE

Has a more intense flavor and a lower salt content than conventional soy sauce.

WASABI

A condiment similar to strong mustard. Select wasabi made from wasabi rather than horseradish, which isn't as fragrant or flavorful.

YUZU KOSHO

Fermented paste made from green chili peppers and yuzu peel; used as a condiment.

SILKEN TOFU

Very supple, smooth, and soft tofu made from coagulated, undrained, and unpressed soy milk. Its texture is similar to that of yogurt.

LAYU

Red chili oil.

FOR 4 PEOPLE

VERSION 1

- 2 blocks silken tofu (1¾ pounds / 800 g)
  16 cherry tomatoes
  1 avocado
- 1 tablespoon soy sauce
  1 tablespoon white sesame oil
- 1 teaspoon wasabi
  2 sprigs of cilantro

VERSION 2

2 blocks silken tofu (1¾ pounds / 800 g)
2 small cucumbers
1 pinch of fine salt
1 tablespoon soy sauce
1 tablespoon sesame oil
- 2 drops layu (red chili oil)
¼ bunch of chives
1 tablespoon toasted sesame seeds
1 (2¼-inch / 30g) piece fresh ginger

VERSION 3

2 blocks silken tofu (1¾ pounds / 800 g)
1 leek (white part only)
¼ cup / 25 g cooked edamame
2 tablespoons tamari soy sauce
1 tablespoon grape seed oil
- ½ teaspoon yuzu kosho
1 tablespoon dried wakame

VERSION 4

2 blocks silken tofu (1¾ pounds / 800 g)
1 bunch of spring onions
4 green shiso leaves
1 tablespoon toasted sesame seeds
4 teaspoons soy sauce
4 teaspoons sesame oil
4 cloves black garlic

Make

1

2

3

4

VERSION 1

Cut the tofu into 4 pieces and drain. Place on 4 plates. Cube the tomato and avocado. In a bowl, mix the soy sauce, sesame oil, and wasabi. Divide the tomato and avocado cubes onto the tofu pieces. Drizzle with the sauce and sprinkle with the chopped cilantro.

VERSION 2

Cut the tofu into quarters and drain. Place on 4 plates. Cut the cucumbers into thin slices (2 mm) using a mandoline. Add a pinch of fine salt and leave to drain in a colander for 10 minutes, then squeeze dry. Season with the soy sauce, sesame oil, and layu. Sprinkle with the chives and 1 tablespoon toasted sesame seeds. Grate the ginger. Arrange the cucumber and ginger over the tofu.

VERSION 3

Chop the leek using the shiraga negi technique (page 280). Spread over the tofu and edamame. Mix the soy sauce, grape seed oil, and yuzu kosho. Divide the sauce into each plate. Soak the wakame for 10 minutes. Drain, then place on the tofu pieces.

VERSION 4

Finely slice the spring onion using a mandoline (1 mm thick). Plunge in cold water for about 10 minutes, then drain in a colander. Blot excess water with a kitchen towel. Cut the shiso leaves into thin strips. Cut the tofu into 4 pieces, add the shiso, and sprinkle with the sesame seeds and black garlic. Add 1 teaspoon of soy sauce and 1 teaspoon of sesame oil to each plate.

Understand

GOMAE

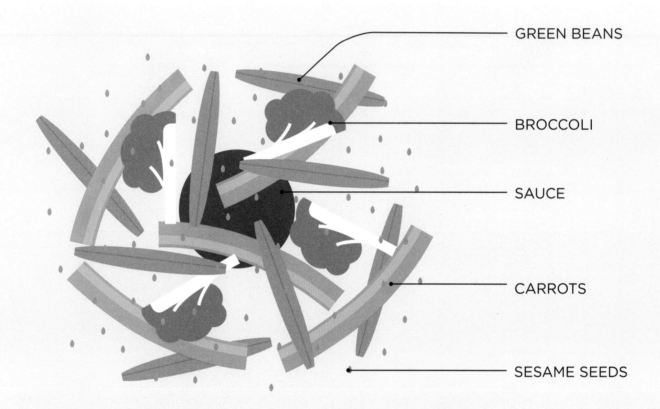

GREEN BEANS

BROCCOLI

SAUCE

CARROTS

SESAME SEEDS

WHAT IS IT?

Green bean and broccoli salad with sesame sauce.

ORIGIN

Goma = sesame; ae = to mix. This recipe is popular throughout Japan.

TOTAL TIME

Prep time: 10 minutes
Cook time: 10 minutes

EQUIPMENT
Suribachi or blender

WHEN TO ENJOY
A very popular and traditional accompaniment to everyday meals.

TECHNIQUES TO MASTER
Toasting seeds (page 283)
Okaage (page 284) – resting technique

TIPS
- Gomae can also be enjoyed as an appetizer.
- It will keep in the refrigerator for 2 to 3 days.

SUBSTITUTIONS
Horenso gomae: the green beans and broccoli can be replaced by another seasonal green vegetable such as spinach.

VARIATION
The sesame seeds can be replaced by 2⅔ tablespoons / 40 g of tahini or hazelnut paste to vary the flavor.

Learn

FOR 4 PEOPLE

7 ounces / 200 g green beans
½ head of broccoli
1 carrot
2 tablespoons dried goji berries

SAUCE

¼ cup / 60 g white sesame seeds
2 tablespoons soy sauce
2 teaspoons cane sugar

1 For the sauce, toast the sesame seeds in a skillet (see page 283), then crush them in the suribachi.

2 Add the soy sauce, sugar, and 1 tablespoon of water. Mix well and set aside.

3 Wash and trim the green beans. Cut into pieces 1½ inches / 4 cm long. Wash the broccoli, separate into florets, and cut into small pieces.

4 Steam the green beans for about 2 minutes, then add the broccoli and cook for a further 3 minutes, ensuring they remain crisp. Drain. Leave to cool (okaage technique, page 284).

5 Peel the carrot, then slice it into thin ribbons using a vegetable peeler. Mix the vegetables with the sauce.

6 Divide into bowls and sprinkle with goji berries.

KIMIZU AE

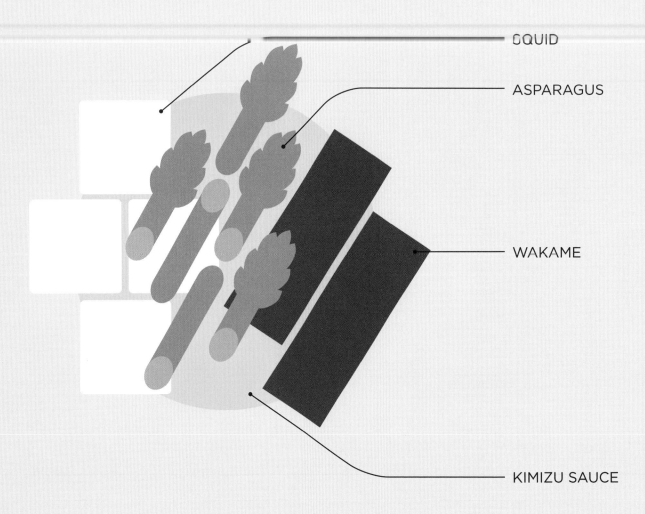

SQUID

ASPARAGUS

WAKAME

KIMIZU SAUCE

WHAT IS IT?

Asparagus, squid, and wakame salad with a kimizu sauce (Japanese dressing).

ORIGIN

Kimi = egg yolk; su = vinegar.

TOTAL TIME

Prep time: 20 minutes
Cook time: 5 minutes

HOW TO ENJOY

Kimizu ae is a popular sauce because it contains no fat, unlike ordinary dressing with oil or mayonnaise. It has a refreshing taste and goes well with seafood and vegetables. It's perfect as an appetizer or starter.

TECHNIQUES TO MASTER

Okaage (page 284) – resting technique
Rehydrating wakame (page 283)
Cleaning squid (page 39)

TIP

To make a good kimizu sauce, the temperature of the bain-marie should be 140°F / 60°C. Lumps will form if the temperature is too high.

ADDITIONS

Miso sauce: add 1 teaspoon of white miso
Goma su miso sauce: add 1 tablespoon of white sesame paste or tahini
Karashi su miso sauce: add 1 teaspoon of karashi (Japanese mustard)

Learn

FOR 4 PEOPLE

SQUID

1 squid (7 to 9 ounces /200 to 250 g)
3 tablespoons / 50 ml cooking sake
1 pinch of fine salt

VEGETABLES

1 bunch of green asparagus
2 tablespoons dried wakame
2 sprigs of chervil

SAUCE

½ cup / 120 g kimizu sauce (page 48)

1 Rehydrate the wakame (page 283).
Wash the asparagus and peel the bottom
2 inches / 5 cm. In a saucepan, boil the
asparagus with 1 teaspoon of salt for
about 3 minutes. Drain and leave to
cool in a basket or colander (okaage
technique, page 284). Slice the asparagus
diagonally in 2-inch / 5 cm pieces.

2 Clean the squid (page 39) and cut it
into small squares (1¼ inches / 3 cm).

3 Pour the sake and salt into a saucepan,
bring to a boil, and add the squid. Cook
for 1 to 2 minutes (the squid should turn
white). Drain and leave to cool. Divide
into 4 bowls, add the wakame and
asparagus, drizzle with the kimizu sauce,
and garnish with the chervil leaves.

Understand

TAKO SU

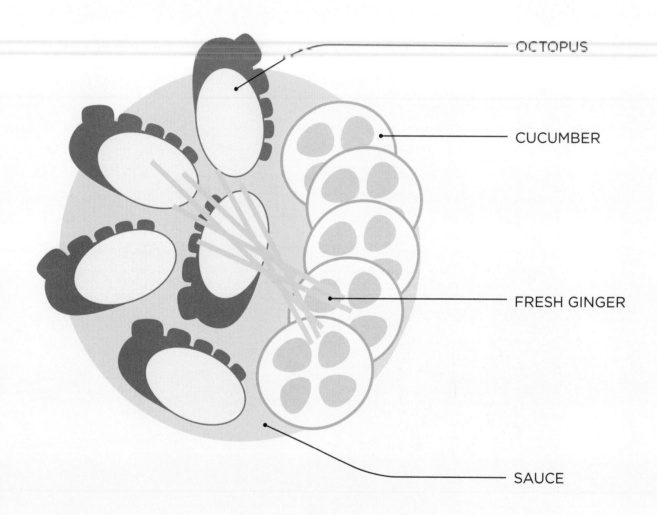

OCTOPUS

CUCUMBER

FRESH GINGER

SAUCE

WHAT IS IT?

A cold dish containing octopus, cucumber, and wakame dressed with a traditional sanbaizu sauce.

ORIGIN

Su = vinegar; dako or tako = octopus: octopus with vinegar.

TOTAL TIME

Prep time: 20 minutes
Cook time: 5 minutes

EQUIPMENT
Skimmer
Wooden chopsticks

TECHNIQUES TO MASTER
Tate shio (page 282) – soaking technique
Hari-shouga (ginger matchsticks - page 281)

TIPS
- To ensure the freshness of cooked octopus, check the skin is dark purple and the flesh white.
- Cooked octopus is available in Japanese and Korean markets.

SUBSTITUTIONS
Replace the sanbaizu with kimizu (page 48) or ponzu sauce.

FOR 4 PEOPLE

OCTOPUS

7 ounces / 200 g cooked octopus tentacles (see preparing octopus, page 38)

SALAD

4 small cucumbers
1 teaspoon fine salt
2 tablespoons dried wakame
1 (1½-inch / 20 g) piece fresh ginger

TATE SHIO

2 teaspoons fine salt

Learn

DRESSING

½ cup / 120 ml sanbaizu sauce or
store-bought or homemade
ponzu sauce (page 49)

1   Rehydrate the wakame (page 283).

2   Cut the ginger into matchsticks (hari-shouga, page 281). Set aside for serving.

3   Bring a pan of water to a boil and turn off the heat. Prepare a bowl of cold water. Place the cucumbers on a cutting board, sprinkle with 1 teaspoon of fine salt, then massage to distribute the salt evenly.

4   Using a skimmer, quickly rinse the cucumbers in hot water and then drain. Plunge into cold water and drain again.

5   Place a cucumber between two wooden chopsticks on a board and make parallel cuts every 1 mm. Turn the cucumber over and cut the other side in the same way. Cut into 1-inch / 2.5 cm lengths. Prepare the tate shio (page 282) by pouring 1⅔ cups / 400 ml of water and 2 teaspoons of fine salt into a dish. Soak the cucumbers in the tate shio for around 10 minutes, then drain and gently press dry.

6   Cut 3 to 4 mm-thick slices of octopus. Prepare the sanbaizu dressing (page 49). Divide the wakame, cucumber, and octopus into bowls. Drizzle 2 tablespoons of dressing over each bowl and top with the ginger matchsticks.

ONIGIRI
& TSUKEMONO

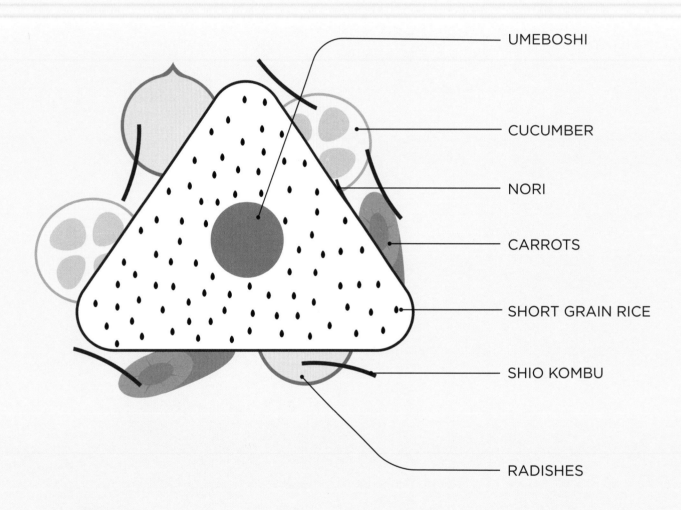

UMEBOSHI

CUCUMBER

NORI

CARROTS

SHORT GRAIN RICE

SHIO KOMBU

RADISHES

WHAT IS IT?

Rice balls filled with fish, seaweed, or condiments, served with tsukemono (Japanese pickles).

ORIGIN

These rice balls are derived from the verb nigiru, which means to hold in one's hands. Rice balls are very old (Nara period, 7th century); the triangular shape came later, during the Heian period.

TOTAL TIME

Prep time: 30 minutes

EQUIPMENT
Onigiri mold
Airtight freezer bag

WHEN AND WHERE TO ENJOY
Onigiri are deeply rooted in Japanese culture. They can be eaten at any time of day, as a quick snack at work, when traveling, on picnics, or as part of a bento box. They are a staple of Japanese cuisine.

TECHNIQUES TO MASTER
Cutting vegetables (page 280)
Preparing rice (page 10)

VARIATIONS
There are a variety of filling options to satisfy any craving: tuna mayonnaise, sausage, omelet, etc.

VERSIONS
Onigiri come in a variety of forms: balls, triangles, wrapped in a sheet of nori, shiso, or kombu. They are as versatile as they are practical and healthy.

Learn

JAPANESE RICE

Oval (almost round) rice. Rich in starch, which gives it a sticky, glutinous texture when cooked.

YUKARI

Salted purple-red shiso leaves, dried and ground into a powder.

SHIO KOMBU

Kombu seaweed cooked in soy sauce with salt and sugar, finely dried, then cut into strips.

KURO GOMA SHIO

Toasted and salted black sesame seeds.

UMÉBOSHI

A variety of Japanese plum that has been pickled and then dried; it has an acidic, salty flavor.

FOR 10 PIECES

- 3 cups / 600 g Japanese short-grain white rice
  3⅓ cups / 800 ml water
  Fine salt
  4 sheets of nori

WITH SHISO

- 1 teaspoon yukari
  2 green shiso leaves

WITH KOMBU

1 tablespoon shio kombu (salted kombu confit)
1 teaspoon white sesame

WITH SALMON

1 ounces / 30 g salted grilled salmon (salmon maze gohan, page 206)

WITH BONITO

2 tablespoons katsuobushi (dried bonito shavings)
1 teaspoon toasted white sesame
1 teaspoon soy sauce
½ teaspoon sesame oil

WITH UMEBOSHI

- 2 umeboshi
- Kuro goma shio for sprinkling

TSUKEMONO

½ bunch of radishes
2 mini cucumbers
1 carrot
- 1 teaspoon shio kombu
1 teaspoon salt
½ teaspoon sugar
1 teaspoon orange zest
1 tablespoon water

1   To make the pickles, wash and peel the carrot and wash the cucumber. Chop the vegetables (rangiri technique, page 281). Trim, wash, and halve the radishes. Place the vegetables in a freezer bag, add the salt, sugar, orange zest, shio kombu, and 1 tablespoon of water. Seal the bag and toss to distribute the marinade evenly. Set aside for 1 hour at room temperature.

2   Cook the rice (page 10). In a bowl, combine the ingredients of your chosen onigiri version. Crumble the salmon and tear the umeboshi plums in half by hand.

3   Use the rice while it is still hot. Fill an onigiri mold halfway with rice, place half the filling in the center, then cover with rice.

4   Press each side of the mold by hand to perfect the triangular shape. Unmold and sprinkle lightly with a little salt. Repeat for 1 more piece.

5   Garnish the top of the 2 onigiris with the unused filling. For the umeboshi onigiri, sprinkle with black sesame seeds.

6   Cut the sheets of nori horizontally into 3 strips. Wrap the middle of each onigiri and fold over the edges. Arrange them attractively on a serving dish with the drained tsukemono.

ONIGIRAZU

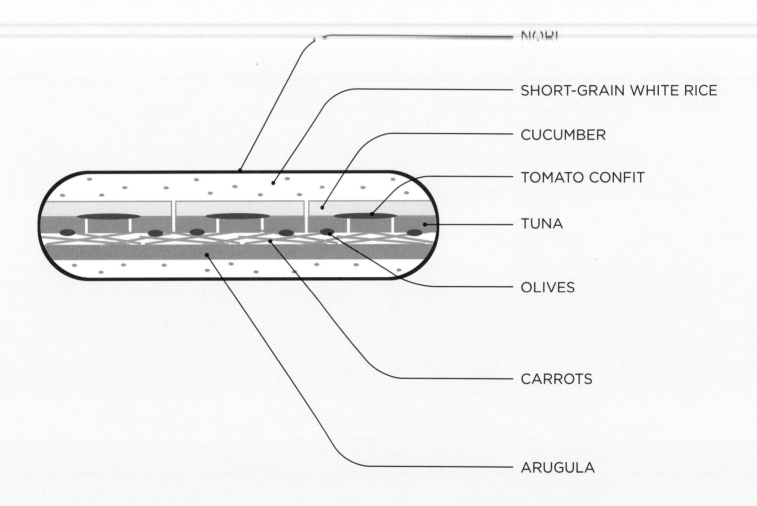

NORI

SHORT-GRAIN WHITE RICE

CUCUMBER

TOMATO CONFIT

TUNA

OLIVES

CARROTS

ARUGULA

WHAT IS IT?

Nori-wrapped rice sandwich filled with your choice of ingredients.

ORIGIN

Onigirazu was invented in the Japanese manga series *Cooking Papa*, which depicted a father making onigirazu for his son. The cartoonist created the series 30 years ago, and it is still very popular throughout Japan today.

TOTAL TIME

Prep time: 20 minutes
Cook time: 15 minutes

WHERE TO ENJOY

Onigirazu is a homemade snack that's easy to make, tasty, and beautiful. It can be enjoyed on a picnic, in a bento box, at a party, for brunch, for lunch, etc.

TIP

Leave the onigirazu to rest before cutting so that the rice and nori come together well; this will prevent it from falling apart.

VARIATIONS

Make with sliced ham, cheese, eggs, vegetables, or even Italian-style with mozzarella and Parma ham, or Indian-style with a little leftover curry, etc.

Learn

FOR 4 ONIGIRAZU

1½ cups / 300 g Japanese short-grain
    white rice
1⅔ cups / 400 ml water
7 ounces / 200 g oil-packed solid tuna
1 tablespoon Japanese mayonnaise
1 teaspoon soy sauce
¼ cucumber
1 carrot
3½ ounces / 100 g tomato confit (in oil)
8 pitted olives
1 ounces / 30 g arugula
1 tablespoon white sesame seeds
4 nori sheets
Fine salt

1 Prepare the rice (page 10). Drain the tuna
and mix with mayonnaise and soy sauce
in a small bowl. Thinly slice the cucumber.
Chop the olives, drain the tomatoes, and
cut into halves or thirds. Wash and drain
the arugula. Peel the carrot, then slice into
thin ribbons using a vegetable peeler.

2 Place a nori sheet on a cutting board
with one of the corners facing you. Arrange
the rice in a square about 4 inches / 10 cm
wide and a little less than ½-inch thick.
Salt the rice very lightly.

3 Add the filling.

4 Cover with rice, sprinkling a little
more salt over the top. Fold over the
nori like an envelope and close.

5 Wrap in cling wrap. Leave to rest
for 10 minutes. Cut in half and serve.

Understand
TAKIKOMI GOHAN

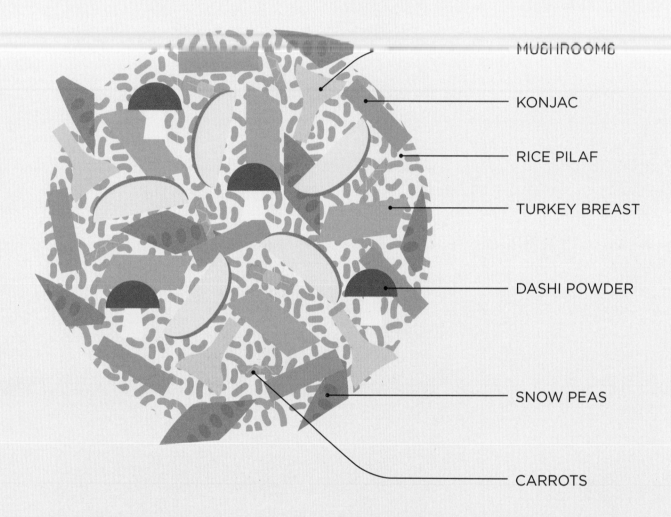

MUSHROOMS

KONJAC

RICE PILAF

TURKEY BREAST

DASHI POWDER

SNOW PEAS

CARROTS

WHAT IS IT?

Japanese rice pilaf, cooked with dashi and topped with simmered and seasoned turkey and mushrooms.

ORIGIN

Takikomi gohan dates back to the Nara period (710 to 794) when rice was mixed with awa (millet) to increase its volume; the blend was known as awa-gohan. Rice was expensive at the time, so other ingredients were mixed in to economize.

TOTAL TIME

Prep time: 20 minutes

Cook time: 20 minutes
Rest time: 1 hour 15 minutes

EQUIPMENT
Dutch oven

WHEN AND WHERE TO ENJOY
This all-season dish is cooked primarily at home; ingredients vary according to the region (octopus and oysters in Hiroshima, scallops in Hokkaido, chicken and leeks seasoned with miso in the Tokyo region).

TECHNIQUE TO MASTER
Preparing rice (page 10).

TIPS
- For the best broth, use dried shiitake mushrooms.
- The leftover rice can be used to make onigiri (page 170).

OTHER USES
Takikomi gohan can be used to make delicious onigiri.

VARIATION
- Replace the chicken with 10½ ounces / 300 g of clams. Cook them with the vegetables until they open, then set aside for serving
- For a zestier version, add minced fresh ginger (from a 1-inch / 2.5 cm piece).

176

Learn

DRIED SHIITAKES

A good alternative to fresh shiitake mushrooms, they keep longer and still retain their fragrant flavor and rich nutrients.

KONJAC

Konyakku is a jelly made from konjac, a root vegetable native to south-east Asia. It is very neutral and takes on the flavor of other foods.

DASHI POWDER

Dehydrated kombu and katsuobushi broth.

FOR 4 PEOPLE

RICE PILAF

2¼ cups / 450 g Japanese short-grain white rice
- 1 teaspoon dashi powder for cooking

TURKEY AND VEGETABLES

10½ ounces / 300 g turkey breast
1 carrot
3½ ounces / 100 g snow peas
- 5¼ ounces / 150 g mushrooms (chanterelle, porcini, or button mushrooms)
- 4 dried shiitake mushrooms
- 1 packet of konnyaku (konjac)

SEASONING

3 tablespoons / 50 ml soy sauce
3 tablespoons / 50 ml cooking sake
3 tablespoons / 50 ml mirin
1 pinch of salt
1 tablespoon sesame oil

1   Soak the dried shiitake mushrooms in 1 cup / 240 ml of water for 1 hour. When they are soft, remove the stems and thinly slice the caps. Reserve the soaking water. To wash the rice (page 10), place it in a bowl and add cold water. Stir with your hand, then quickly discard the water. Repeat until the water runs clear. Leave to stand for about 1 hour so that the rice changes from translucent to white.

2   Wash and trim the snow peas Cut them at an angle. Remove the mushroom stems and slice the caps thinly. Cut the carrot into small strips.

3   Cut the konjac into small pieces. Blanch in a pan of boiling water for about 2 minutes and drain.

4   Cut the turkey into small ½-inch pieces, then saute in sesame oil in a skillet. When the turkey starts to brown, add the carrots, shiitake mushrooms, and konjac. Pour in the shiitake soaking water, soy sauce, mirin, sake, and salt. Bring to a boil, then reduce the heat. Simmer for around 10 minutes.

5   Add the mushrooms and snow peas and cook for a further 5 minutes. Strain through a sieve to separate the ingredients and cooking juices.

6   Add water to the cooking juices to make 2½ cups / 600 ml of liquid. Place the drained rice and the liquid in a saucepan. Cook over high heat, covered, and boil for about 3 minutes. Turn the heat to low and simmer for 10 minutes. Remove the

pan from heat and leave to stand for 10 minutes with the lid on to allow the rice to finish cooking in its own steam.

7   Place the vegetables on top of the rice and cover. Leave to rest for a further 5 minutes. Divide into bowls.

DONBURI

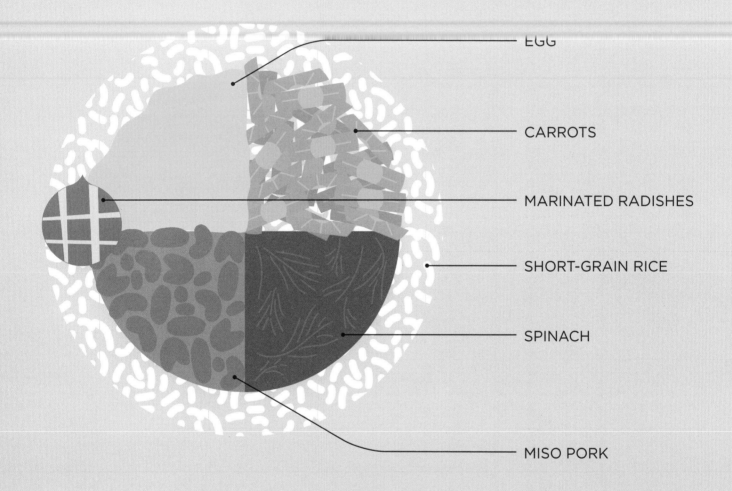

EGG

CARROTS

MARINATED RADISHES

SHORT-GRAIN RICE

SPINACH

MISO PORK

WHAT IS IT?

A bowl of rice topped with minced miso pork, scrambled egg, and seasoned root vegetables.

ORIGIN

Donburi = ceramic bowl; don = a bowl of rice with toppings.

TOTAL TIME

Prep time: 40 minutes
Cook time: 30 minutes

EQUIPMENT

Mandoline

HOW TO ENJOY

This everyday dish can also be served in a bento lunch.

TECHNIQUE TO MASTER

Preparing rice (page 10)

VARIATIONS

Donburi can be made with different bases and toppings according to the season:
- Mackerel and marinated grilled vegetables (yakibitashi don)
- Spicy grilled chicken (spicy tori don)
- Chicken meatballs and asparagus (tsukune don)
- Minced pork, eggplant, and miso sauce (mabo nasu don)

- Grilled salmon and fava beans (salmon and soramame don)
- With raw fish (kaisen don)
- With tempura (ten don)
- Vegetarian (yasai don)
- With a bulgur, semolina, barley, or brown rice base

SUBSTITUTIONS

No pork: replace with ground beef or chicken
No miso: replace with 2 tablespoons of soy sauce
No spinach: replace with watercress, chopped snow peas, or chopped green beans.

Learn

SESAME OIL

Choose pure
sesame oil.

JAPANESE RICE

Oval (almost round)
rice. Rich in starch,
which gives it a sticky,
glutinous texture
when cooked.

DASHI POWDER

Dehydrated kombu
and katsuobushi broth.

RED MISO

Soybean paste
fermented for at least
1 year; it has a very
strong, salty taste.

FOR 4 PEOPLE

RICE

- 2¼ cups / 450 g short-grain white rice

MISO PORK

10½ ounces / 300 g sausage meat
    or unseasoned ground pork
1 (1½-inch / 20 g) piece fresh ginger
- 2 tablespoons red miso
2 tablespoons cooking sake
1 tablespoon cane sugar
- 1 tablespoon sesame oil
2 tablespoons water

SCRAMBLED EGGS

2 eggs
1 teaspoon sugar
1 pinch of salt
1 tablespoon cooking sake

CARROT KINPIRA

2 carrots
1 tablespoon soy sauce
1 tablespoon mirin
1 teaspoon cane sugar
- ¼ teaspoon dashi powder
1 tablespoon sesame oil

SPINACH SALAD

10½ ounces / 300 g fresh spinach
1 tablespoon olive oil
½ garlic clove, grated
Salt

MARINATED RADISH

8 small radishes
½ teaspoon salt
1 tablespoon sugar
1 tablespoon water

FOR SERVING

2 tablespoons white sesame seeds
2 tablespoons goji berries

Make

1

2

3

4

5

8

6

7

1 Prepare the rice (page 10). Wash and trim the radishes. Place a radish between two wooden chopsticks on a cutting board and make parallel cuts 1 mm thick. Turn the radish 90° and score at right angles to the first cuts.

2 Place the radishes in a freezer bag and marinate with the salt, sugar, and water for 1 to 2 hours.

3 Whisk the eggs in a bowl with the sugar and salt. Pour into a saucepan and cook over low heat, breaking up the mixture with 4 chopsticks to get small pieces, like you would for scrambled eggs. When the eggs are almost cooked, remove from the heat and keep stirring for a moment. Set aside.

4 For the miso pork, saute the minced ginger in a skillet with the sesame oil, then add the pork and cook for 5 minutes, stirring occasionally.

5 Add the red miso, sake, cane sugar, and water and cook for 3 minutes while stirring.

6 To make the salad, wash the spinach and microwave or steam for 2 or 3 minutes. Rinse, squeeze dry by hand, and chop coarsely. Place in a bowl and pour over the oil. Add the grated garlic and salt, then mix.

7 To make the kinpira, wash and peel the carrots and slice them into thin strips. Saute for 3 minutes in sesame oil in a skillet. Add the soy sauce, mirin, cane sugar, dashi powder, and a little water, and cook for a few minutes. The carrots should remain crisp.

8 Divide the rice into 4 bowls. Arrange the toppings evenly and sprinkle with the goji berries and sesame seeds. Drain the pickled radishes and add to each bowl.

TAI CHAZUKE

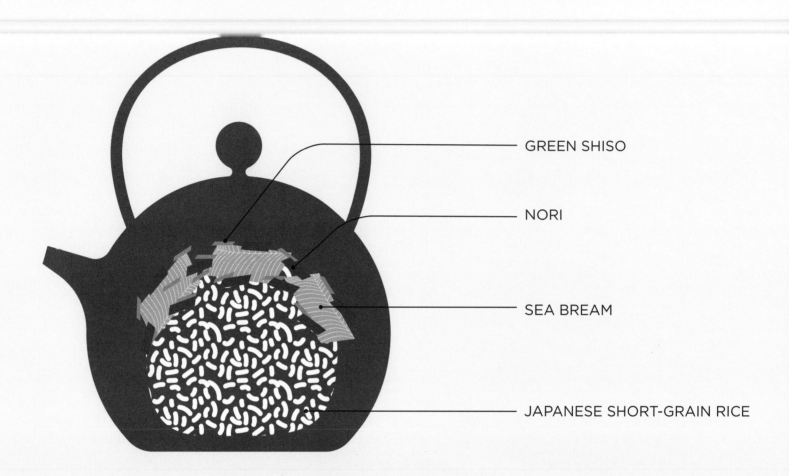

GREEN SHISO

NORI

SEA BREAM

JAPANESE SHORT-GRAIN RICE

WHAT IS IT?

A bowl of rice topped with sea bream sashimi marinated in sesame sauce and then submerged in hot tea.

TOTAL TIME

Prep time: 30 minutes
Cook time: 5 minutes

EQUIPMENT

Suribachi (a grooved ceramic mortar for crushing sesame seeds)
Surikogi (wooden pestle)
Teapot

HOW TO ENJOY

Raw: without the hot tea
Cooked: pour a little tea over the sashimi; it will become white and slightly cooked.

TECHNIQUES TO MASTER

Preparing rice (page 10)
Preparing fish (page 34)
Slicing sashimi (page 282)
Roasting seeds (page 283)

TIPS

- A blender can be used instead of a mortar and pestle.
- Sea bream is very mild; it's important to boil the mirin so its flavor doesn't dominate.

SUBSTITUTION

Replace roasted tea with the same amount of green tea or dashi.

Learn

FOR 4 PEOPLE

RICE

2¼ cups / 450 g Japanese short-grain
 white rice

SASHIMI

2 sea bream fillets (about 7 ounces /
 200 g)

SESAME SAUCE

¼ cup / 65 g white sesame seeds
3 tablespoons / 50 ml soy sauce
1 tablespoon mirin
1 tablespoon sake

FOR SERVING

1 nori sheet
1 tablespoon wasabi
4 green shiso leaves or
 ¼ bunch of chives (optional)
Roasted tea or green tea or dashi

1 Cook the rice (page 10). To make
the sauce, place the mirin and sake
in a heatproof container and heat in
the microwave at 600 W for 50 to 60
seconds to eliminate the alcohol smell
and bitter taste. Leave to cool. Put the
sesame seeds in a small hot skillet and
roast over low heat for 2 to 3 minutes.

2 Transfer the seeds to a mortar and
crush them. Gradually stir in the soy
sauce, sake, and mirin. Set aside.

3 Tear the nori into small pieces and place
in a bowl. Thinly slice the shiso leaves.

4 Cut the sea bream into slices
2¾-inch / 7 mm thick for the sashimi
(page 282). Pour the sesame sauce over
the sea bream slices, gently stir, and leave
for 1 minute to allow the flavors to infuse.

5 Divide the rice into bowls. Arrange
the sea bream sashimi on the rice and
sprinkle with the nori, wasabi, and shiso.
Place the pot of tea next to the rice.

TAIMESHI

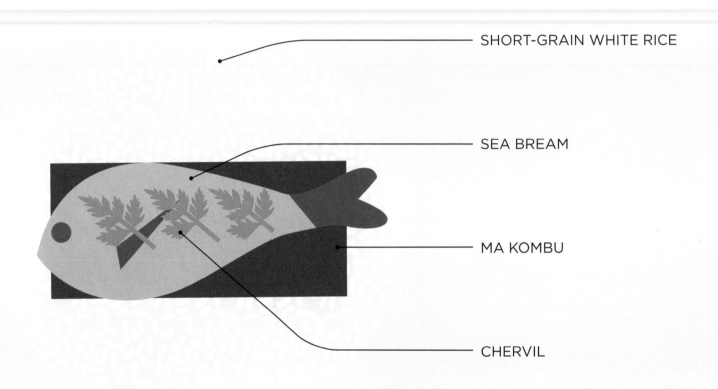

SHORT-GRAIN WHITE RICE

SEA BREAM

MA KOMBU

CHERVIL

WHAT IS IT?

Whole sea bream cooked in rice
on a sheet of ma kombu.

ORIGIN

The sea bream is pre-cooked to eliminate
odors and bring out its aroma, and the
rice is seasoned with soy sauce, salt,
sake, mirin, and kombu broth. This dish is
particularly delicious because the umami
of the grilled sea bream soaks into the
rice. Tai = sea bream, meshi = rice.

TOTAL TIME

Prep time: 30 minutes
Cook time: 30 minutes
Rest time: 1 hour

EQUIPMENT

Clay pot or Dutch oven with a lid
Wooden spatula

TECHNIQUES TO MASTER

Rehydrating kombu (page 283).
Preparing rice (page 10)
Preparing fish (page 34)

TIPS

For enhanced flavor, add some
finely sliced shiso leaves, sesame
seeds, and a little yuzu juice.

SUBSTITUTIONS

Replace the sea bream with a delicate
fish such as sea bass or mullet.

OTHER USES

Leftover taimeshi is a delicious
filling for onigiri.

Learn

JAPANESE RICE

Oval (almost round) rice. Rich in starch, which gives it a sticky, glutinous texture when cooked.

COOKING SAKE

Sake with added salt.

WHITE SOY SAUCE

This fermented condiment is the lightest of the soy sauces and has a delicate flavor.

MA KOMBU

From Hokkaido near Hakodate. It makes for a high-quality, clear dashi.

FOR 4 PEOPLE

SEA BREAM

1 sea bream (about 10½ ounces / 300 g)
1 teaspoon fine salt

RICE

- ¼ cups / 450 g Japanese short-grain white rice
  2¾ cups / 660 ml water for cooking the rice
- 2 (4 inch / 10 cm) square pieces / 20 g ma kombu
- 2 tablespoons cooking sake
- 2 tablespoons soy sauce
  ½ teaspoon salt

FOR SERVING

A few springs of chervil

1   Rehydrate the kombu (page 283) in 2¾ cups / 660 ml of water. Reserve the soaking water. Prepare the rice (page 10).

2   Preheat the oven to 425°F / 220°C. Prepare and clean the sea bream (page 34). Sprinkle 1 teaspoon of salt on the sea bream and leave to rest on a cooling rack for about 15 minutes in the refrigerator, then remove any excess liquid with a kitchen towel.

3   Place the sea bream on a sheet of parchment paper on the oven rack. Grill for 15 to 20 minutes, flipping over halfway through.

4   Place the drained rice in a pot, pour over the soaking water from the kombu, add the sake, soy sauce, and salt, then stir. Set the kombu in the center and the sea bream on top.

5   Cover and cook over medium heat until boiling. Count 3 minutes from boiling then reduce heat to low and continue cooking for 12 minutes. Turn off the heat and leave the pot closed for 10 minutes so that the fish continues cooking in its steam.

6   Discard the kombu and carefully remove the sea bream bones. Separate the flesh from the fish, mix it into the rice with a damp wooden spatula, and divide into bowls. Sprinkle with chervil leaves.

HOSOMAKI

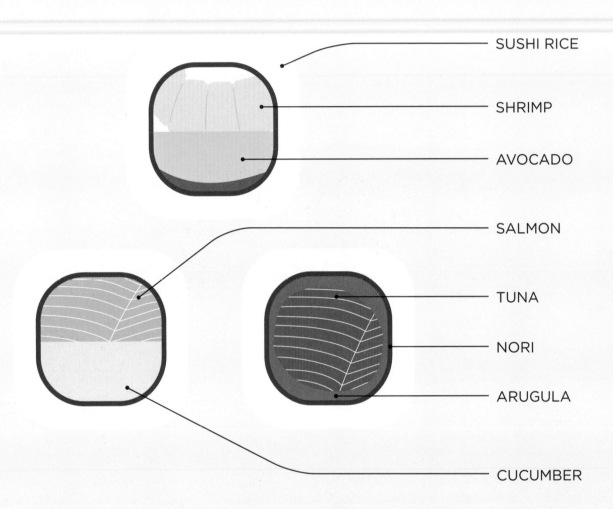

SUSHI RICE

SHRIMP

AVOCADO

SALMON

TUNA

NORI

ARUGULA

CUCUMBER

WHAT IS IT?

A roll made with seasoned rice, a variety of fillings, and nori.

ORIGIN

Maki = roll; hoso comes from hosoi which means thin: thin roll. This is the classic maki.

TOTAL TIME

Prep time: 20 minutes

EQUIPMENT
Makisu (sushi mat)

TECHNIQUES TO MASTER
Preparing sushi rice (page 12).
Preparing shrimp (pages 37)
Preparing tezu (page 283)

TIPS
- When using the makisu, wrap the entire surface in plastic wrap to prevent the rice from sticking.
- The tezu reduces hand temperature, prevents the rice from sticking, and thanks to the vinegar, it has an antibacterial effect.

VERSIONS
You can make hosomaki in an endless variety of ways, using your preferred ingredients: bluefin tuna, salmon, albacore tuna, crabmeat, grilled chicken, beef, etc.

HOW TO ENJOY
Since hosomaki are small, they are great as an appetizer. They can also be added to a bento box.

Learn

JAPANESE RICE

Oval (almost round) rice. Rich in starch, which gives it a sticky, glutinous texture when cooked

NORI

Very thin sheets of dried seaweed; sold in packs of 5 or 10.

TAMARI SOY SAUCE

Has a more intense flavor and a lower salt content than conventional soy sauce.

WASABI

A condiment similar to strong mustard. Select wasabi made from wasabi rather than horseradish, which isn't as fragrant or flavorful.

FOR 6 MAKIS OF EACH

RICE

- 1½ cups / 300 g Japanese short-grain white rice
  1⅔ cups / 400 ml water
- 3 sheets nori
  Tezu (page 283):
  ¾ cup plus 4 teaspoons / 200 ml cold water
  1 tablespoon white vinegar

SUSHI VINEGAR

¼ cup plus 1 teaspoon / 65 ml rice vinegar or Japanese grain vinegar
1⅔ tablespoons / 20 g granulated sugar
1 teaspoon fine salt

SHRIMP MAKI

6 pink shrimp
½ avocado
2 tablespoons toasted sesame seeds

TUNA MAKI

3½ ounces / 100 g bluefin tuna
10 chives
1 ounces / 30 g arugula
2 tablespoons pink peppercorns

SALMON MAKI

3½ ounces / 100 g salmon
1 small cucumber
1 ounce / 30 g arugula

FOR SERVING

- Tamari soy sauce
- Wasabi

Make

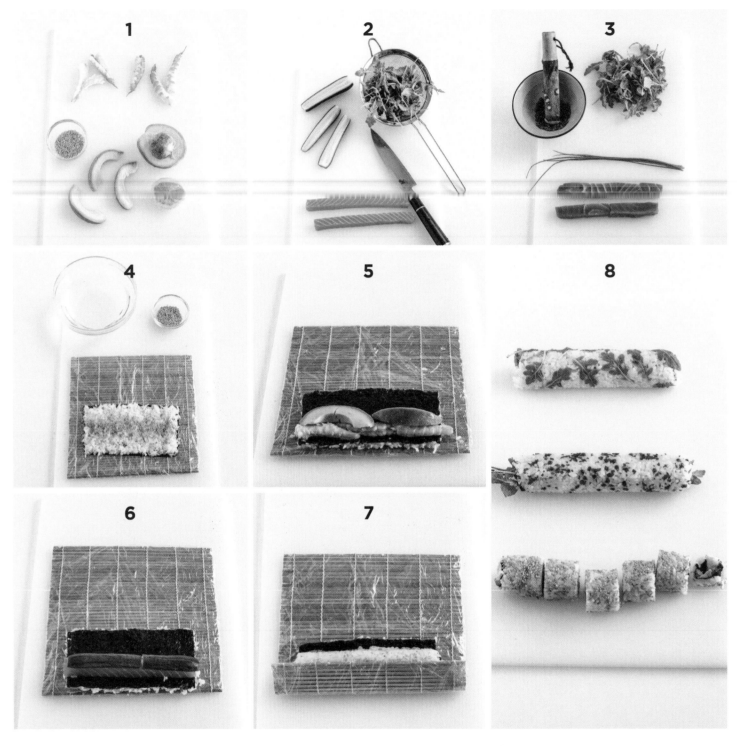

1 Prepare the sushi rice (page 12). Prepare the shrimp (page 37). Peel the avocados, cut into halves, then lengthwise into 6 slices.

2 Cut the bluefin tuna and the salmon into 1-inch / 2.5 cm thick sticks, the same length as the nori sheet. Wash the chives and arugula. Crush the pink peppercorns. Cut the cucumber lengthwise into 4 pieces.

3 Cover the entire sushi mat (makisu) with plastic wrap. Cut the nori horizontally in half.

4 Place half sheet of nori on the mat, shiny side down. Prepare the tezu by mixing the water and white vinegar. Use the tezu mixture to moisten your hands. Spread the rice over the entire surface of the nori sheet, a little less than ½-inch / 1.3 cm thick, and sprinkle with toasted sesame seeds for the shrimp maki, pink peppercorns for the tuna maki, or arugula for the salmon maki.

5 Turn the sheet over and place your chosen ingredients at the bottom: shrimp and avocado; tuna, chives, and half the arugula; or salmon and cucumber.

6 Align the bottom of the nori sheet with the bottom of the mat and place it in front of you.

7 Roll the mat, holding the ingredients in place with your fingertips towards the inside. As you roll, press the maki firmly several times along its length. Unroll the makisu and roll again until you reach the top of the nori sheet.

8 On a cutting board, slice the maki into 5 or 6 pieces with a sharp knife. Between each cut, wipe the blade with a damp cloth. Serve with the soy sauce and wasabi on the side.

FUTOMAKI

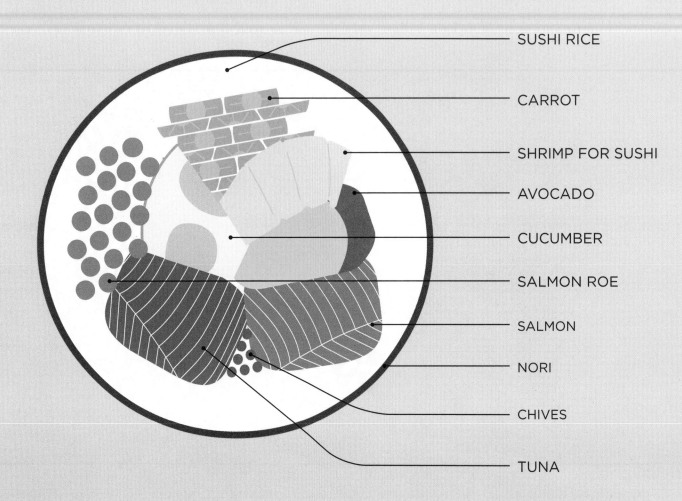

SUSHI RICE

CARROT

SHRIMP FOR SUSHI

AVOCADO

CUCUMBER

SALMON ROE

SALMON

NORI

CHIVES

TUNA

WHAT IS IT?

A large rice roll filled with colorful ingredients and wrapped in a sheet of nori.

ORIGIN

Maki = roll; futo comes from futoi, which means wide: wide sushi roll.

TOTAL TIME

Prep time: 20 minutes

EQUIPMENT

Makisu (sushi mat)
Sujikiri sashimi knife

WHEN TO ENJOY

Futomaki are served during traditional celebrations, such as New Year's Eve, graduation ceremonies, and birthdays.

TECHNIQUES TO MASTER

Preparing sushi rice (page 12)
Preparing shrimp (page 36)
Preparing the tezu (page 283)

TIP

You don't need to wrap the makisu in plastic wrap because the nori on the outside of the roll won't stick to the mat. Place the shiny surface of the nori sheet on the makisu.

VERSIONS

There are plenty of ways to make futomaki, with between 5 and 10 possible ingredients per roll (tamagoyaki, simmered shiitakes, vegetables, pickles, etc.).

Learn

RICE VINEGAR

Pure rice vinegar with a smooth, mellow taste and a slightly amber hue.

SHISO

A highly aromatic plant, somewhere between mint and basil, sold in Asian markets.

NORI SEAWEED

Very thin sheets of dried seaweed, sold in packs of 5 or 10.

WASABI

A condiment similar to strong mustard. Select wasabi made from wasabi rather than horseradish, which isn't as fragrant or flavorful.

GARI

Ginger pickles. Avoid pink gari, which contains artificial colors.

 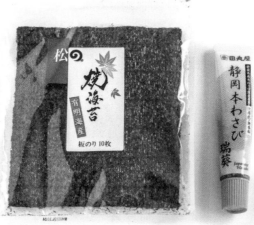 

FOR 2 LARGE MAKI

- 2 nori sheets
  1 tablespoon sesame seeds

PLAIN RICE

1 cup plus 2 tablespoons / 230 g Japanese short-grain white rice
1¼ cups / 300 ml water

Tezu (page 283):
¾ cup plus 4 teaspoons / 200 ml cold water
1 tablespoon white vinegar

SUSHI VINEGAR

- 3 tablespoons / 50 ml rice or Japanese grain vinegar
  1 tablespoon granulated sugar
  1 teaspoon fine salt

FILLINGS

3½ ounces / 100 g bluefin tuna
3½ ounces / 100 g salmon
6 shrimp, already prepared for sushi
¼ cup / 50 g salmon roe
½ avocado
1 carrot
2 small cucumbers
- 4 shiso leaves
  ¼ bunch of chives

FOR SERVING

Tamari soy sauce
- Wasabi
- 2 tablespoons / 30 g gari (page 55)

1   Prepare the sushi rice (page 12). Peel the carrots, then slice them into thin strips with a vegetable peeler. Peel the avocado, cut in half, and then into 6 slices. Quarter the cucumber lengthwise. Halve the shiso leaf. Wash and drain the chives.

2   Prepare the shrimp (page 37). Remove the tails and cut them in half lengthwise. Cut the bluefin tuna and salmon into sticks that are 1-inch / 2.5 cm thick and the same length as the nori sheet.

3   Spread a sheet of nori on the mat, shiny side down. Prepare the tezu by mixing the water and white vinegar. Use this mixture to moisten your hands as you spread the rice over the surface of the nori sheet. It should be a little less than ½-inch / 1.3 cm thick. Leave an empty strip at the top (about ¾ inch / 2 cm).

4   Align the bottom of the nori sheet with the bottom of the mat and place it in front of you. Set all the filling ingredients in the middle of the nori sheet.

5   Roll the mat, holding the ingredients in place with your fingertips towards the inside. While rolling, press the maki firmly several times along its length. Unroll the makisu and roll again, going all the way to the top of the nori sheet.

6   On a cutting board, cut the maki into 8 pieces with a sharp knife. Between each cut, wipe the blade with a damp cloth. Serve with the soy sauce, gari, and wasabi on the side.

TAZUNA SUSHI

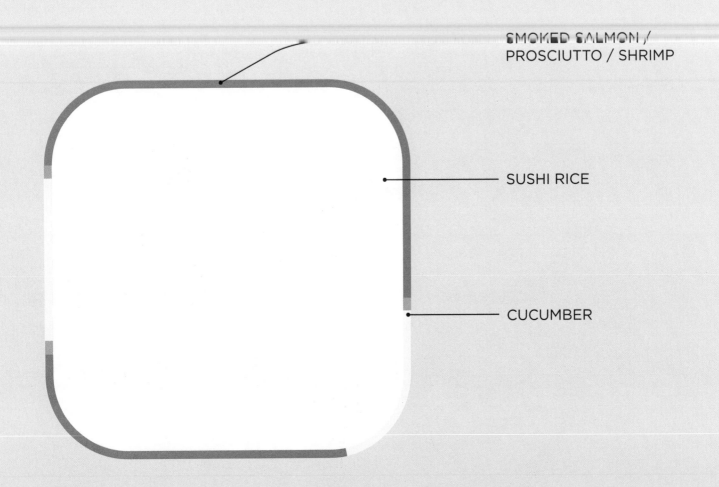

SMOKED SALMON /
PROSCIUTTO / SHRIMP

SUSHI RICE

CUCUMBER

WHAT IS IT?

Vinegar-seasoned rice wrapped in strips of fish. Other ingredients such as shrimp can be used in place of the fish.

ORIGIN

Tazuna = strip, cord: roll of sushi wrapped with ingredients (fish, meat or vegetables).

TOTAL TIME

Prep time: 45 minutes

EQUIPMENT

Makisu (sushi mat)
Mandoline

TECHNIQUES TO MASTER

Preparing sushi rice (page 12)
Cutting vegetables (page 281)
Preparing shrimp (page 37)
Preparing the tezu (page 283)

TIP

Between each cut, wipe the knife blade with a damp cloth or run it under water to facilitate slicing the maki.

VERSIONS

Tazuna sushi comes in a variety of forms: with thinly sliced raw fish, cold meats (beef tataki), etc.

Learn

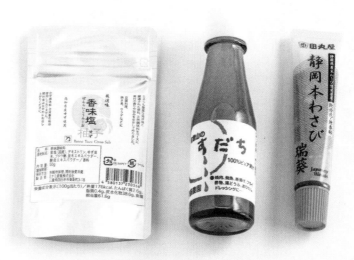

JAPANESE RICE

Oval (almost round) rice. Rich in starch, which gives it a sticky, glutinous texture when cooked.

RICE VINEGAR

Pure rice vinegar with a smooth, mellow taste and a slightly amber hue.

YUZU SALT

Salt subtly flavored with powdered yuzu peel.

SUDACHI JUICE

Juice of the sudachi citrus fruit; sweeter than lemon juice.

WASABI

A condiment similar to strong mustard. Select wasabi made from wasabi rather than horseradish, which isn't as fragrant or flavorful.

FOR 30 PIECES

SUSHI RICE

- ¼ cups / 450 g Japanese short-grain white rice

2½ cups / 600 ml water

Tezu (page 283):
¾ cup plus 4 teaspoons / 200 ml cold water
1 tablespoon white vinegar

SUSHI VINEGAR

- ⅓ cup plus 2 teaspoons / 90 ml rice vinegar (or other grain vinegar)
7 teaspoons / 30 g cane sugar
- 2 teaspoons / 10 g yuzu salt

FILLING

1 cucumber
2 slices of smoked salmon
2 slices of prosciutto
6 shrimp
- 2 tablespoons sudachi or yuzu juice

GARNISH

1 lime
1 lemon
⅛ bunch of chives
⅛ bunch of chervil
1 tablespoon pink peppercorns

FOR SERVING

- Wasabi

Make

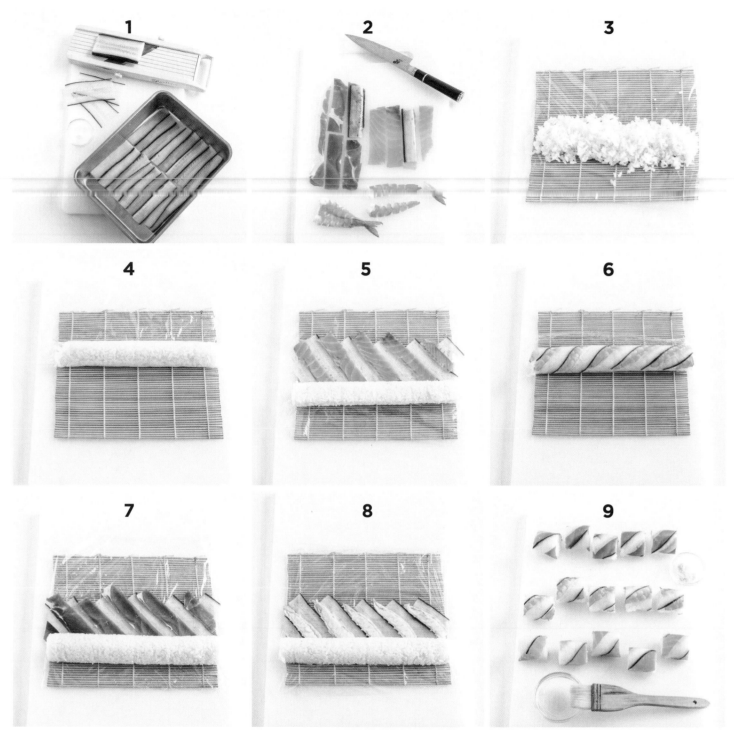

1   Prepare the sushi rice (page 12). Cut the cucumber into 4-inch / 10 cm sections, slice thinly lengthwise using a mandoline, then cut into 1-inch / 2.5 cm wide rectangles. Spread them on a plate and sprinkle lightly with salt to draw out moisture.

2   Prepare the shrimp for sushi (page 37). Remove the tails and cut the shrimp in half lengthwise. Cut the salmon and prosciutto into 1-inch / 2.5 cm wide rectangles.

3   Place plastic wrap over the makisu. Make the tezu with the water and white vinegar and use it to moisten your hands. Spread ⅙ of the rice on the makisu.

4   Roll the makisu tightly to form a stick of rice. Unroll and set the stick aside.

5   Place the cucumbers and salmon slices alternately at an angle in the middle of the makisu. Set the rice stick on top of the slices. Wrap with cling wrap and then roll up the maki using the makisu.

6   Wait about 10 minutes to allow the maki to take shape, then cut into 5 or 6 pieces using a sharp, wet knife. Remove the plastic wrap.

7   Repeat with the prosciutto and cucumber slices. Then repeat with the shrimp.

8   Brush some sudachi juice over the top of the makis. Garnish the salmon maki with chives and crushed pink peppercorns, the prosciutto maki with small slices of lime, and the shrimp maki with chervil and lemon zest.

CHIRASHI

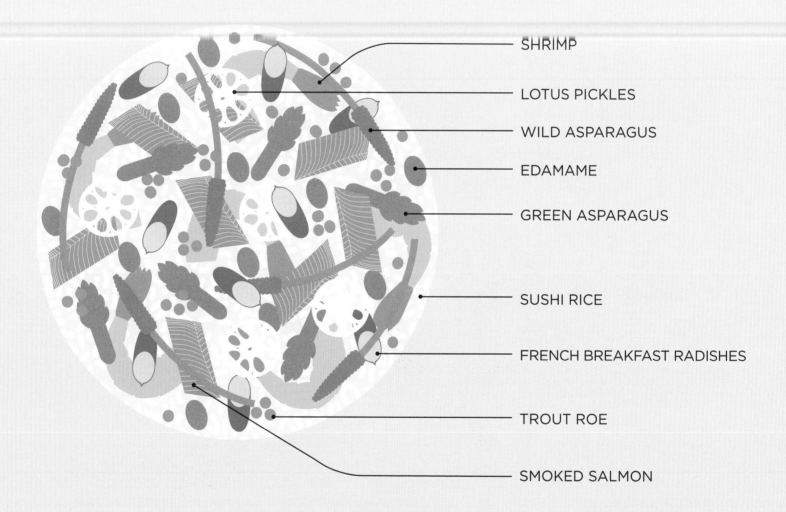

SHRIMP

LOTUS PICKLES

WILD ASPARAGUS

EDAMAME

GREEN ASPARAGUS

SUSHI RICE

FRENCH BREAKFAST RADISHES

TROUT ROE

SMOKED SALMON

WHAT IS IT?

Vegetables and sliced fish on a bed of rice.

ORIGIN

Chirashi comes from chirasu = to scatter: ingredients scattered over rice.

TOTAL TIME

Prep time: 40 minutes
Cook time: 15 minutes
Rest time: 1 hour

EQUIPMENT

Mandoline
Airtight freezer bag

WHEN TO ENJOY

Chirashi is a traditional dish commonly served during celebrations and festivals such as Hina matsuri (the festival of dolls, dedicated to young girls).

TECHNIQUES TO MASTER

Preparing shrimp (page 37)
Cutting vegetables (page 281)

TIP

Chirashi calls for some preparation. To simplify the process, you can replace the slices of fish with smoked salmon or shrimp.

VERSIONS

Nama chirashi: chirashi with sashimi only.

Learn

JAPANESE RICE

Oval (almost round) rice. Rich in starch, which gives it a sticky, glutinous texture when cooked.

KOMBU SEAWEED

Giant seaweed with a briny taste from the genus Laminaria.

SUSHI VINEGARI

Ready-to-use condiment made with rice vinegar, sugar, and salt.

LOTUS ROOT

The edible part of the lotus. It has a crunchy texture and tastes a little like a radish.

FOR 4 PEOPLE

SUSHI RICE

- 2¼ cups / 450 g Japanese short-grain white rice
  2½ cups / 600 ml water
- ¼ cup / 60 ml sushi vinegar

TOPPINGS

3½ ounces / 100 g green asparagus
2 ounces / 60 g wild asparagus, green beans, or snow peas
½ bunch of French breakfast radishes
- 2 (6 by 8 inch / 15 by 20 cm) pieces of kombu
¼ cup / 40 g shelled edamame
20 pink shrimp (cooked)
4 slices of smoked salmon
½ lemon
⅓ cup / 80 g trout roe
1 ounce / 30 g arugula
1 tablespoon white sesame seeds

LOTUS PICKLES

- 13½ ounces / 100 g lotus root
2 tablespoons sushi vinegar
1 teaspoon Japanese grain vinegar

SLICED OMELET

3 eggs
1 teaspoon cane sugar
Salt

Make

1 Prepare the rice (page 12). For the lotus pickles, peel the lotus root, slice thinly using a mandoline, then soak the slices in water to prevent discoloration. Boil with 1 teaspoon of Japanese grain vinegar for about 5 minutes. When the lotus slices become translucent, they are cooked. Drain. Place the lotus slices in a freezer bag while they are still hot and add 2 tablespoons of sushi vinegar. Close the bag, leave to cool to room temperature, and then refrigerate. Leave to marinate for about 30 minutes.

2 For the omelet slices, beat the egg, then add 1 teaspoon of sugar and a pinch of salt. Pour into a hot nonstick skillet and spread into a thin layer like a crepe.

3 Roll the egg and slice into thin strips.

4 Peel the shrimp except for the tails. Slit the back and remove the black vein. Cut the smoked salmon into small pieces.

5 Wash the radishes and cut in half lengthwise. Wash the asparagus and cut in half diagonally (page 281). Place in a heatproof bowl with 1 tablespoon of water, add the wild asparagus, and cover with plastic wrap. Cook in the microwave at 600 W for 1 minute, or in boiling water for 2 minutes. Drain and leave to cool.

6 Line a deep tray with plastic wrap. Cut 2 pieces of kombu slightly smaller than the size of the tray. Quickly rinse in cold water and place one piece on the plastic wrap. Arrange the vegetables on top of the kombu and sprinkle with salt. Cover with

the other piece of seaweed and wrap in plastic wrap. Place another tray on top so that the seaweed is in contact with all the ingredients. Place in the fridge for 1 hour.

7 Distribute the rice among 4 plates or onto a wooden sushi tray, then place the omelet, shrimp, salmon, vegetables, lemon slices, and trout roe on top. Sprinkle with arugula and sesame seeds.

GRILLED SALMON
MAZE GOHAN

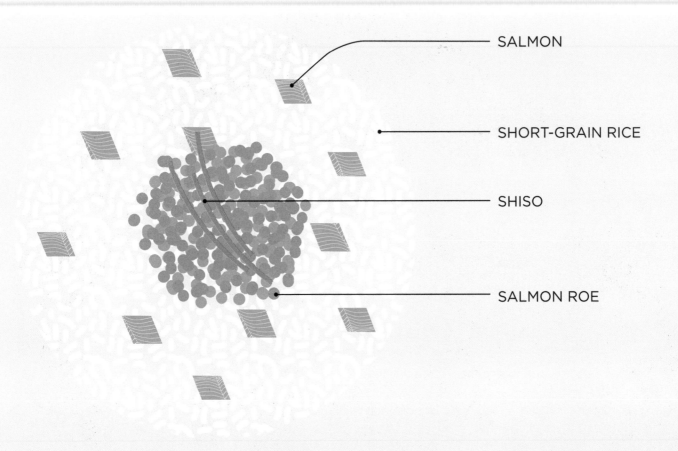

SALMON

SHORT-GRAIN RICE

SHISO

SALMON ROE

WHAT IS IT?

Plain rice mixed with salt-marinated, grilled salmon and sprinkled with chopped shiso leaves and salmon roe.

TOTAL TIME

Prep time: 15 minutes (overnight for salty salmon)
Cook time: 20 minutes

EQUIPMENT

Airtight freezer bag

WHEN AND HOW TO ENJOY

This dish is based on seasonal vegetables, such as carrots, mushrooms, edamame, and lotus root. Cooking in a clay pot will add depth and richness.

TECHNIQUE TO MASTER

Cooking rice (page 11)

OTHER WAYS TO ENJOY

Maze gohan can also be used to make onigiri.

VARIATIONS

Express version: season the salmon with plenty of salt and leave in the fridge for around 30 minutes, then rinse and dry.
- This recipe can be made with sushi rice (page 12).
- You can add pieces of seaweed or shredded nori.
- In the spring, you could use fava beans or peas.
- Pour hot tea onto the finished dish to make ochazuke (page 184).

Learn

FOR 4 PEOPLE

2¼ cups / 450 g Japanese short-grain rice
2 salmon fillets (about 14 ounces / 400 g)

SALT MARINADE

¾ cup plus 4 teaspoons / 200 ml water
2 tablespoons fine salt
1 tablespoon sugar

TOPPINGS

⅓ cup / 100 g salmon or trout roe
1 teaspoon white soy sauce
4 shiso leaves
2 tablespoons toasted white
     sesame seeds
Chives, for garnish

1   Cut the salmon fillets down the middle lengthwise and place in an airtight bag. Add the salt, sugar, and water. Leave to marinate in the fridge overnight.

2   Slice the shiso leaves into thin strips.

3   Cook the plain rice (page 11). Pour 1 teaspoon of soy sauce into the salmon roe and mix well, set aside in the refrigerator.

4   Pat the salmon dry with paper towels, then grill in the oven or cook over high heat in a lightly oiled skillet.

5   After cooking, remove the skin and bones, then separate the flesh into large flakes with a fork. In a large bowl, combine the hot rice, flaked salmon, and toasted sesame seeds. Divide the rice into serving bowls. Place the salmon roe in the center. Sprinkle with chopped chives.

SABA NO BOU ZUSHI

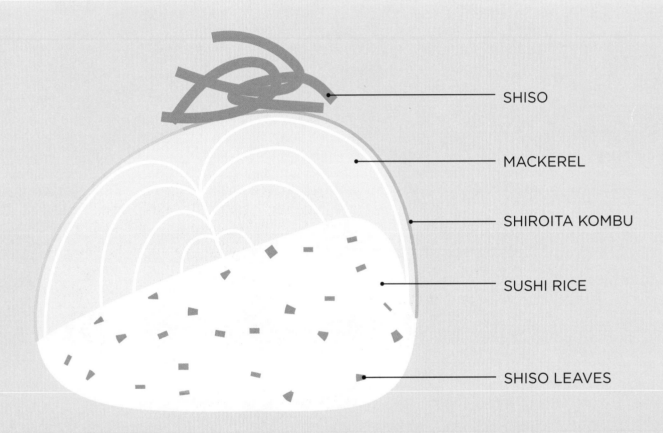

SHISO

MACKEREL

SHIROITA KOMBU

SUSHI RICE

SHISO LEAVES

WHAT IS IT?

A mackerel fillet rolled over seasoned rice, covered with shiroita kombu, then cut into sections and garnished

ORIGIN

Saba = mackerel; bou = stick; zushi = sushi: mackerel sushi rolled into a stick. The recipe originated in Kyoto, where mackerel, which spoils quickly, was pickled in salt and transported along the coast of the mackerel route (saba kaido) to the capital (Kyoto at the time) and then used to prepare saba zushi.

TOTAL TIME

Prep time: 20 minutes
Cook time: 15 minutes
Rest time : 2 hours

EQUIPMENT
Makisu (sushi mat)

WHERE TO ENJOY
This sushi is a specialty of Kyoto and remains a signature dish of the old capital. It is appreciated across Japan for its light-colored, umami-rich flesh.

TECHNIQUES TO MASTER
Preparing sushi rice (page 12)
Preparing mackerel (page 33)
Preparing the tezu (page 283)

TIP
Don't leave the mackerel to marinate too long, otherwise the skin may be damaged.

SUBSTITUTIONS
Use marinated salmon, sea bream, shrimp, or horse mackerel instead of mackerel.

Learn

RICE VINEGAR
Pure rice vinegar with a smooth, mellow taste and a slightly amber hue.

TAMARI SOY SAUCE
Has a more intense flavor and a lower salt content than conventional soy sauce.

SHIROITA KOMBU
The surface is smoothed with a knife blade, then the kombu is macerated in white vinegar for 1 day.

SHISO
A highly aromatic plant, somewhere between mint and basil, sold in Asian markets.

FOR 3 STICKS

MARINATED MACKEREL
3 mackerel fillets (page 33)
½ cup / 150 g fine salt
¾ cup plus 4 teaspoons / 200 ml Japanese grain vinegar
¾ cup plus 4 teaspoons / 200 ml cold water
1 tablespoon raw cane sugar

SUSHI RICE
1 cup plus 2⅓ tablespoons / 230 g Japanese short-grain white rice
1¼ cups / 300 ml water for cooking
1 heaping tablespoon / 20 g gari
2 green shiso leaves
1 lemon

Tezu (page 283)
¾ cup plus 4 teaspoons / 200 ml cold water
1 tablespoon white vinegar

SUSHI VINEGAR
3 tablespoons / 50 ml Japanese grain vinegar
1 teaspoon granulated sugar
1 teaspoon fine salt

SHIROITA KOMBU
6 shiroita kombu sheets
3 tablespoons / 50 ml Japanese grain vinegar
3 tablespoons / 50 ml water

1 tablespoon granulated sugar
½ teaspoon fine salt

FOR SERVING
2 tablespoons toasted white sesame seeds
2 tablespoons / 30 g gari (page 55)
Tamari soy sauce

209

Make

1 To make the shiroita kombu, place the grain vinegar, water, sugar, and salt in a small saucepan. Bring to a boil and add the shiroita kombu. Remove and leave to cool at room temperature.

2 Spread 2½ tablespoons / 40 g of salt in the bottom of a dish the size of the mackerel fillets. Place the mackerel, skin side down, on top of the salt. Sprinkle the rest of the salt over the top and leave for 1 hour in the fridge to draw out excess moisture. Rinse under running water and pat dry with paper towels. Rinse the dish and wipe dry.

3 Place the mackerel in the clean dish and cover with ¾ cup plus 4 teaspoons / 200 ml Japanese grain vinegar, ¾ cup plus 4 teaspoons / 200 ml cold water, and 1 tablespoon of sugar. Leave to marinate in the fridge for 1 hour.

4 Drain the fillets, place them on a cutting board, and carefully remove the thin translucent film covering the skin. Set aside.

5 Prepare the sushi rice (page 12). Divide the rice into 3 bowls. Place 2 teaspoons of finely minced gari in the first bowl (A), 1 thinly sliced shiso leaf in the second (B), and the lemon zest in the third (C).

6 Place plastic wrap on the makisu. Set a mackerel fillet in the center. Prepare the tezu (page 283) to moisten your hands. Put the rice from bowl A on the mat, and sprinkle with sesame seeds.

7 Roll the makisu to make a stick of rice. Pull back the plastic wrap, and place 2 shiroita kombu sheets on the mackerel, then close. Do the same thing with the remaining bowls of rice.

8 Cut the still-wrapped sushi into 6 or 8 slices. Remove the plastic wrap and place the remaining decorative elements on each sushi: 2 teaspoons of chopped gari, 1 chopped shiso leaf, and the zest of 1 lemon. Serve with gari and soy sauce.

Understand

TEMARI SUSHI

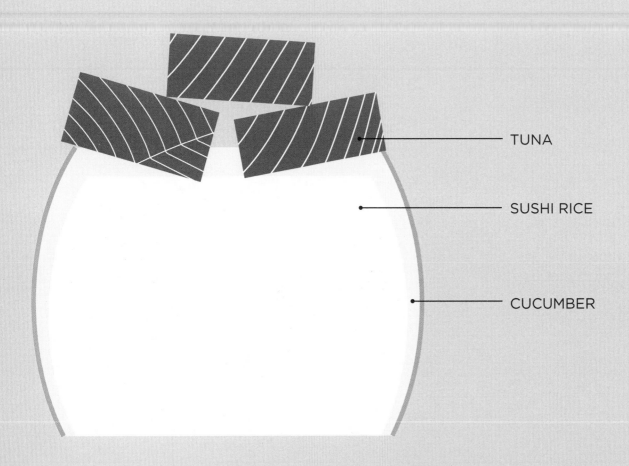

TUNA

SUSHI RICE

CUCUMBER

WHAT IS IT?

A bite-sized ball of vinegared rice topped with colorful fillings, such as sliced fish, pickles, marinated vegetables, and shiso leaves.

ORIGIN

Temari = embroidered playing ball; temari sushi = ball-shaped sushi.

TOTAL TIME

Prep time: 40 minutes
Cook time: 20 minutes
Rest time: 1 hour

TECHNIQUE TO MASTER

Preparing sushi rice (page 12)

TIP

To prepare the rice balls, place plastic wrap on a scale and weigh out 1 ounce / 30 g (2 tablespoons) of rice. Wrap with the plastic wrap and place on a damp cloth to prevent the rice from drying out.

WHEN TO ENJOY

This round sushi is prepared for festive occasions (like Christmas and New Year's) or to accompany ceremonial meals for celebrations such as Hinamatsuri (Girls' Day) in Japan.

FOR 2 PEOPLE

PLAIN RICE

1½ cups / 300 g short-grain white rice
14 ounces / 400 g water

SUSHI VINEGAR

¼ cup plus 1 teaspoon / 65 ml rice
    vinegar or Japanese grain vinegar
5 teaspoons / 20 g granulated sugar
1 teaspoon fine salt

Learn

WASABI SALT

Salt mixed with wasabi powder. Adds a bit of heat and an element of freshness to dishes.

UME SU

The brine from pickling umeboshi plums with red shiso leaves. It is acidic and can be used like vinegar. Be careful how much salt you use.

YUZU SALT

Salt subtly flavored with powdered yuzu peel.

VERSION A

2 slices of pickled lotus root
• 1 teaspoon ume su

VERSION B

4 slices of salmon
2 slices of pickled lotus root

VERSION C

2 radishes
2 tablespoons salmon roe

VERSION D

2 ounces / 60 g bluefin tuna
2 chives
• 1 pinch of wasabi salt

VERSION E

2 ounces / 60 g sea bream
1 kumquat
½ teaspoon white sesame oil
• 1 pinch of yuzu salt
6 slices of cucumber

VERSION F

2 scallops, along with their frills
1 shiso leaf
1 teaspoon salmon roe

VERSION G

1 egg
1 tablespoon cooking sake
½ teaspoon sugar
1 pinch of salt
Radish sprouts

VERSION H

2 cooked pink shrimp
Lime zest
½ avocado

A-G-H   **C-D-E**

B   **F**

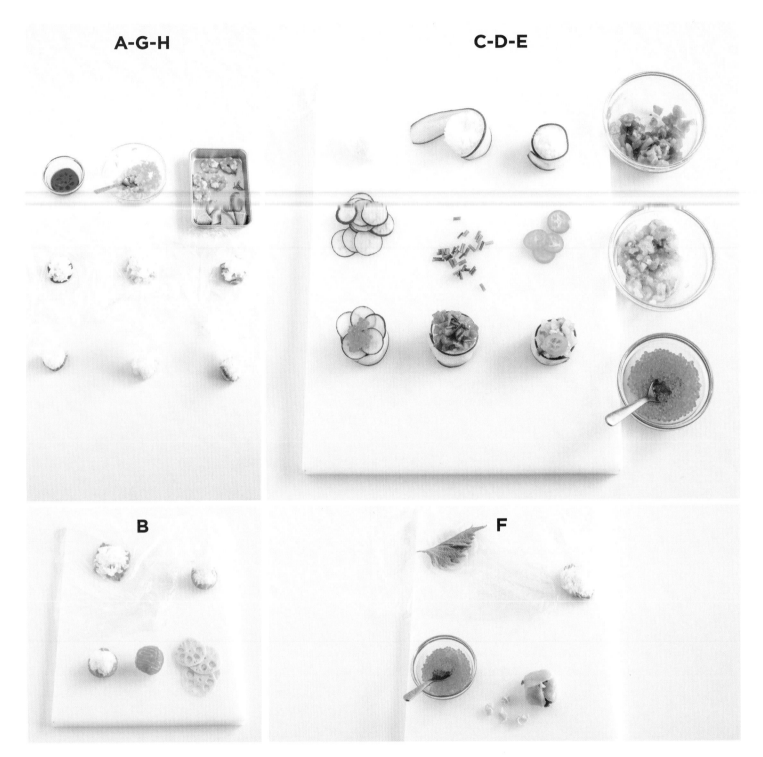

1 Prepare the sushi rice (page 12). Lightly salt the cucumber slices. Cut the lime zest into thin slices and the kumquat into rounds. Mince the chives. Slice the radish. Thinly slice the shiso leaf. **Version G:** mix 1 egg, the sake, sugar, and salt. Cover and microwave at 600 W for 20 to 30 seconds, then stir. Cook for a further 20 seconds. Leave to cool. **Version F:** prepare a bowl of ice water. Place the scallops and their frills in boiling water for 2 to 3 seconds, remove with a skimmer, and cool in the ice water. Drain on a kitchen towel. Cut the scallops into thirds and slice the frills thinly. **Version H:** slice the avocado. Prepare the shrimp by removing the shells (except for the tails), then slice along the back and remove the black vein. **Version E:** dice the sea bream and mix with ½ teaspoon of white sesame

oil and yuzu salt. **Version D:** dice the tuna and mix in wasabi salt and minced chives.

2 Cut out an 8-inch / 20 cm square of plastic wrap. Place 2½ tablespoons / 30 g of rice in the middle, wrap the plastic around the rice, and twist the top. Press on each side with your hand to form a ball shape. Remove the plastic wrap. Make 16 sushi balls in this way. Cut 16 6-inch /15 cm squares of plastic wrap. **Version H:** place 2 shrimp and 2 slices of avocado flat on the plastic wrap in a circle, place 1 ball of rice on top, wrap in the plastic, and twist the top. Shape the ball. Remove the plastic and add a lime zest strip. **Version B:** place 2 pieces of salmon on the plastic wrap, then 1 scoop of rice, and shape into a ball. Place the lotus root on top of the salmon. **Version F:** Arrange 3

scallop slices in the form of a flower, and top with 1 shiso leaf and 1 scoop of rice. Shape into a ball. Place the salmon roe and scallop frills on top. **Version G:** Spread a little scrambled egg in the center of the plastic wrap. Place 1 ball of rice on top. Shape the ball. Place the radish sprouts on top of the eggs. **Version A:** Place the pickled lotus root and ume su in the center of the plastic wrap. Place 1 rice ball on top. Shape the ball. **Version E:** surround the rice ball with a cucumber slice and place the sea bream mixture and kumquat on top. **Versions D and C:** surround the rice ball with a slice of cucumber and place the tuna mixture on top. Add the chives **(D)** or 5 slices of radish and the salmon roe in the center **(C)**.

COLD UDON NOODLES
WITH CHICKEN & VEGETABLES

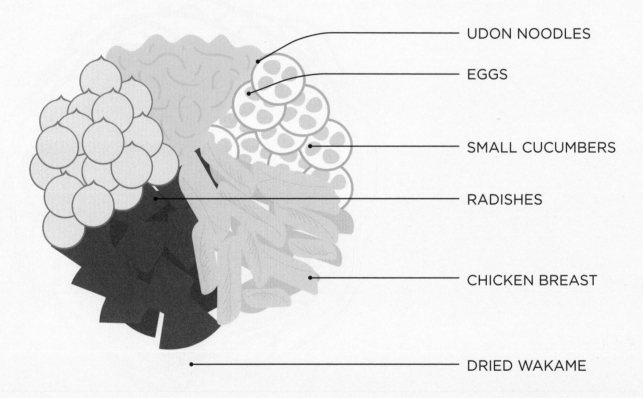

UDON NOODLES

EGGS

SMALL CUCUMBERS

RADISHES

CHICKEN BREAST

DRIED WAKAME

WHAT IS IT?

Cold wheat flour noodles, cooked then cooled, served with chicken, wakame seaweed, cucumber, and thinly sliced omelet.

ORIGIN

Udon noodles are more typical of Japanese cuisine than ramen, even though their manufacturing process shares the same centuries-old roots.

TOTAL TIME

Prep time: 20 minutes
Cook time: 25 minutes
Rest time: 30 minutes

TECHNIQUE TO MASTER
Roasting seeds (page 283).

EQUIPMENT
10-inch / 25 cm nonstick skillet
Freezer bag
Heat-resistant plastic wrap

TIP
Leave the chicken to cool in the plastic wrap after cooking, otherwise it will become very dry.

SUBSTITUTIONS
Many variations are possible, especially for the sauce, which can be replaced by goma dare or sesame sauce.

WHEN TO ENJOY
In Japan, cold udon noodles are very popular during summer.

Learn

COOKING SAKE

Sake with added salt.

DRIED UDON NOODLES

Noodles made from wheat flour.

DRIED WAKAME

Once opened, store in an airtight container in a cool place.

MENTSUYU

A sauce composed of dashi, soy sauce, mirin (or sake), and sugar.

FOR 4 PEOPLE

- 12 ounces / 350 g dried udon noodles (4 portions)

BROTH

- ⅓ cup plus 4 teaspoons / 100 ml mentsuyu, store-bought or homemade (page 23)
  ⅓ cup / 100 ml cold water

TOPPINGS

10½ ounces / 300 g chicken breast
- 2 tablespoons cooking sake
  1 pinch of salt
  7 ounces / 200 g small cucumbers
  8 radishes
  A few chives
  1 tablespoon toasted sesame seeds
- 2 tablespoons dried wakame

EGGS

3 eggs
1 teaspoon sugar
1 pinch of salt

1   Place the chicken breast, salt, and sake in an airtight bag. Close the bag securely and leave the ingredients to marinate in the fridge for 30 minutes. Toast the sesame seeds and set aside (page 283).

2   Soak the wakame in warm water for 10 minutes, then drain. Wash the cucumbers and slice thinly using a mandoline. Place them in a colander, sprinkle with a little fine salt and leave for 10 minutes, then drain. Slice 4 radishes into thin rounds using a mandoline.

3   Place the chicken in a shallow dish with the marinade and cover with heat-resistant plastic wrap. Cook for 2 minutes in the microwave at 600 W. Remove the plastic wrap, flip the chicken over, cover again, and cook for a further 3 minutes. Leave to cool at room temperature without removing the plastic wrap, then place in the fridge.

4   Beat the eggs, then add the sugar and a little salt. Pour into a hot non-stick skillet and tilt the skillet to distribute the egg mixture into a thin, even layer. Leave to cook for 2 minutes without turning, ensuring it does not brown.

5   Slide onto a plate, roll up, and cut into thin strips with a knife.

6   Cook the noodles in plenty of water. Drain, rinse under cold water, and drain again. Divide among 4 bowls.

7   Tear the chicken into pieces and spread over the noodles. Add the wakame, cucumbers, radishes, and thinly sliced omelet. Sprinkle with sesame seeds and chives. Mix the mentsuyu sauce with ⅓ cup plus 4 teaspoons / 100 ml cold water, then pour into the bowls.

NABEYAKI UDON

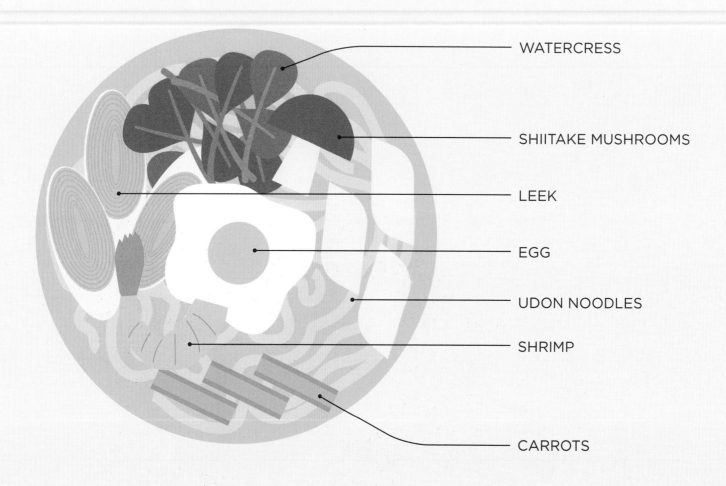

WATERCRESS

SHIITAKE MUSHROOMS

LEEK

EGG

UDON NOODLES

SHRIMP

CARROTS

WHAT IS IT?

Udon noodle soup simmered in a dashi broth and served in a clay pot.

ORIGIN

Nabeyaki first appeared in Osaka just before the start of the Meiji Restoration at the end of the 19th century. Nabe = pot; yaki = cooked: cooked in a pot. Nabeyaki is unique because it is usually served in a clay pot (donabe).

TOTAL TIME

Prep time: 30 minutes
Cook time: 10 minutes

EQUIPMENT

4 small clay or cast-iron pots
Flower-shaped cookie cutter
Toothpick

TECHNIQUE TO MASTER

Cutting vegetables (page 280)

TIP

Homemade udon noodles can be replaced by frozen, which are just as tasty and quicker to prepare.

VARIATIONS

Many modifications are possible depending on the ingredients available: add shrimp tempura or mochi, replace the shrimp with surimi, replace the watercress with spinach, etc. For a family version, make the recipe in a large pot.

WHEN TO ENJOY

This soup is served in winter.

Learn

UDON NOODLES

Soft noodles (2 to 4 mm thick) made from wheat flour. Use fresh pasta for this recipe.

DRIED SHIITAKES

A good alternative to fresh shiitake mushrooms; they keep longer and still retain their fragrant flavor and rich nutrients.

MIRIN

A Japanese rice wine used as a condiment; it is sweeter than sake.

SHICHIMI TOGARASHI

Also known as Japanese seven spice, it contains red chili pepper, sesame and poppy seeds, nori, sansho, ginger, shiso, hemp seeds, and chenpi (mandarin peel).

FOR 4 PEOPLE

- 4 portions of homemade (page 14), frozen, or dried udon noodles
- 7 ounces / 200 g chicken breasts
- 4 raw shrimp
- 4 eggs
- 1¾ ounces / 50 g watercress
- 1 carrot
- 4 dried (or fresh) shiitake mushrooms
- ½ leek
- Shichimi togarashi

BROTH

- 6 cups / 1.4 L dashi
- ⅓ cup / 80 ml soy sauce
- ⅓ cup / 80 ml mirin

1 Soak the shiitake mushrooms in a bowl of water (1 cup) for 1 hour. When they become soft, remove the stems. Measure out the soaking water and top off with dashi to make 7 cups / 1.6 L of liquid. Peel the carrots and cut into slices about 5 mm thick. Use a cookie cutter to cut the carrots into flower-shaped pieces. Slice the remaining carrot into strips. Slice the leek diagonally into rings 3⁄8 inch / 1 cm thick. Wash and coarsely chop the watercress. Set aside.

2 Thinly slice the chicken. Prepare the shrimp: remove the head and then shell the body (except for the tail). With a skewer, remove the black vein along the back.

3 Bring water to a boil in a large pot, then add the udon noodles. Stir occasionally with chopsticks and leave to cook for around 5 minutes. Drain the noodles in a colander and rinse in cold water.

4 Add the mirin and soy sauce to the dashi broth. Stir and set aside.

5 Divide the cooked udon noodles into 4 small clay pots. Add the carrots, leek, chicken, shiitake mushrooms, and shrimp. Pour 1⅔ cups / 400 ml of dashi broth into each pot. Bring to a boil and skim. Simmer over low heat for around 5 minutes, until the vegetables and meat are cooked.

6 At the end of cooking, in each pot, make a small nest in the center of the noodles and crack 1 egg into it. Add the watercress and shrimp. Cover the pots and cook for 1 or 2 minutes. Remove from heat and set aside for 1 or 2 minutes, covered. Sprinkle with the shichimi togarashi and serve immediately.

Understand

RAMEN

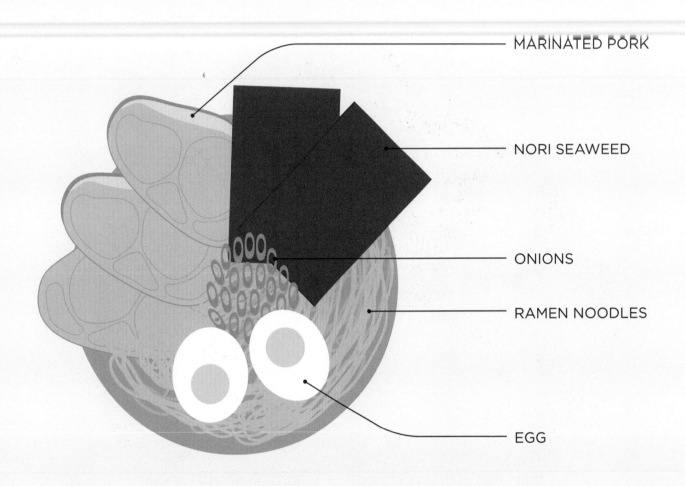

MARINATED PORK

NORI SEAWEED

ONIONS

RAMEN NOODLES

EGG

WHAT IS IT?

A hearty soup made from a broth of cooked and marinated slices of roast pork and noodles.

ORIGIN

Ramen, literally meaning "pulled noodles," is a veritable institution in Japan. The noodles made from wheat flour, eggs, and alkaline water. Ramen first appeared in Yokohama's Chinatown at the beginning of the 20th century.

TOTAL TIME

Prep time: 15 minutes
Cook time: 1 hours
Rest time: 2 hours

EQUIPMENT

Fine-mesh strainer
Airtight freezer bag

TECHNIQUE TO MASTER

Rehydrating kombu (page 283)

TIP

Start by cooking the pork butt and then marinating it. The pork's cooking juices are used to make the broth.

VERSIONS

Ramen noodles can be served in a variety of broths: shoyu (soy sauce), shio (savory broth), or miso.

HOW TO ENJOY

Ramen is most often served hot, but hiyashi ramen with ponzu sauce or goma dare (sesame sauce) can be served cold in summer.

Learn

RAMEN NOODLES

These yellow noodles of varying shapes and sizes are made of wheat flour and are sold fresh or dried.

SESAME OIL

Choose pure sesame oil.

KOMBU

Giant seaweed with a briny taste from the genus Laminaria.

NORI

Very thin sheets of dried seaweed, sold in packs of 5 or 10.

FOR 4 PEOPLE

- 4 portions of ramen noodles

PORK

1¾ pounds / 800 g pork butt, boned and tied
1 onion
1 carrot
1 (1½-inch / 20 g) piece fresh ginger
2 cloves of garlic
- 2 4x4 inch pieces / 20 g kombu
7⅔ cups / 1.8 L water
1 tablespoon canola oil
- 4 teaspoons sesame oil

MARINADE

⅓ cup plus 4 teaspoons / 100 ml soy sauce
3 tablespoons / 45 ml sake
3 tablespoons / 45 ml mirin
6 teaspoons / 20 g sugar
1 (1½-inch / 20 g) piece fresh ginger
1 garlic clove, grated

GARNISH

4 eggs
4 green onions or ¼ bunch of spring onions (green part only)
- 2 sheets of nori

1   Rehydrate the kombu. Crush 2 garlic cloves and slice 10 g (a ¾-inch piece) of ginger into thin rounds, leaving the skin on. Peel and halve the onion. Peel and slice the carrot into rounds.

2   Heat the oil in a large pot and brown the pork on all sides.

3   Add the aromatics: onion, carrot, ginger, and garlic. Pour in 7⅔ cups / 1.8 L of water, then add the kombu and its soaking water. Cook over medium heat and bring to a boil. Reduce the heat to low, cover and cook, skimming regularly, for around 50 minutes.

4   Remove the cooked pork. Finish by straining the broth through a fine mesh sieve. Set aside. Prepare the marinade: place all the ingredients in a small saucepan. Bring to a boil and simmer for around 3 minutes, then remove from heat. Pour the marinade into an airtight freezer bag. Add the still-warm pork and allow to cool to room temperature, then place in the fridge. Leave to marinate for 1 to 2 hours.

5   Cook the eggs in boiling water for 7 minutes. Rinse in cold water, then shell and leave to cool. Cut in half with a string or knife. Finely slice the spring onions into rounds. Cut the nori into quarters. Slice the marinated pork.

6   Heat the pork broth in a saucepan. Meanwhile, bring a large quantity of water to a boil in a saucepan and cook the noodles. Heat 4 bowls by pouring hot water into each, then emptying. Add 2 tablespoons of marinade and 1 teaspoon of sesame oil to each bowl. When the broth is hot, plunge the noodles into the pot of boiling water and cook them for a few minutes until they are neither too firm nor too tender. Drain the noodles, divide into the 4 bowls, and add the hot broth. Proceed quickly to maintain the noodles' doneness. In each bowl, arrange 3 slices of pork, an egg, some sliced leek, and a quarter of the nori. Sprinkle with the green onion and some sesame seeds.

COLD SOMEN

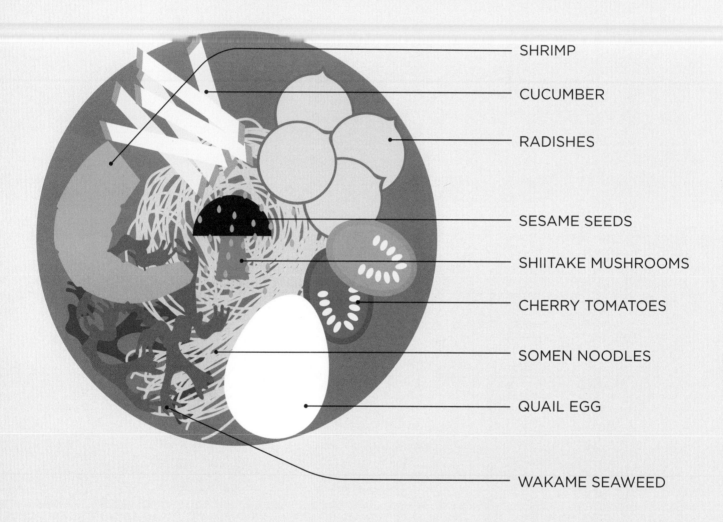

SHRIMP

CUCUMBER

RADISHES

SESAME SEEDS

SHIITAKE MUSHROOMS

CHERRY TOMATOES

SOMEN NOODLES

QUAIL EGG

WAKAME SEAWEED

WHAT IS IT?

Thin Japanese noodles served cold with grated ginger, green onions, vegetables, and mentsuyu sauce.

ORIGIN

Somen noodles arrived from China with the Buddhist monks and were soon manufactured throughout Japan, particularly in the south in the Kansai region.

TOTAL TIME

Prep time: 30 minutes
Cook time: 15 minutes

EQUIPMENT

Mandoline

WHEN AND HOW TO ENJOY

Served mainly in summer, these light, fresh noodles are simply dipped in mentsuyu sauce mixed with green onions, grated ginger, a little wasabi, or sesame seeds.

TECHNIQUE TO MASTER

Cutting vegetables (page 280)

TIPS

Because the noodles are served cold, it's best not to cook them al dente.

VARIATIONS

Hot somen: serve with vegetables in a hot dashi broth with soy sauce and mirin.
Sauteed somen: saute in vegetable oil, season with salt, and sprinkle with chopped green onions.

Learn

MENTSUYU

A sauce made from dashi, soy sauce, mirin (or sake), and sugar.

SHISO

A highly aromatic plant, somewhere between mint and basil, sold in Asian markets.

SOMEN NOODLES

Very thin wheat flour noodles (1.3 mm thick). They are available dried.

YUZU SHICHIMI

A blend of yuzu powder, chili pepper, sesame seeds, poppy seeds, and sansho. It is used as a spice in marinades.

FOR 4 PEOPLE

- 8 bundles (14 ounces / 400 g) dried somen noodles

FOR THE SAUCE

- ¾ cup plus 4 teaspoons / 200 ml mentsuyu sauce, store-bought or homemade (page 23)
  ¾ cup plus 4 teaspoons / 200 ml ice water

INGREDIENTS

7 ounces / 200 g small cooked pink shrimp
½ cup / 20 g dried shiitakes
1 tablespoon mirin
1 tablespoon soy sauce
3 tablespoons / 45 ml shiitake soaking water
½ cucumber
12 cherry tomatoes (mixed colors)
12 quail eggs
12 radishes
¼ bunch of spring onions
1 (3-inch / 40 g) piece fresh ginger
- Shiso leaves
Toasted sesame seeds
- Yuzu shichimi

Make

1   Place the quail eggs in a saucepan and add water until the eggs are covered. Bring to a boil, turn down the heat, and cook for 3 minutes. Cool in cold water, then remove the shells.

2   Prepare the shrimp: remove the head and shell. Make an incision in the back to remove the black vein.

3   Slice the cucumber on the diagonal (page 281) to a thickness of ¼-inch / 7 mm and then slice into thin strips. Halve the tomatoes. Thinly slice the radishes lengthwise using a mandoline. Trim the shiitakes then soak in water for 30 minutes. Put them in a saucepan and add the mirin, soy sauce, and 3 tablespoons / 45 ml of

the shiitake soaking water. Cook for 5 minutes over a medium heat. Place in a bowl and set aside. For the sauce, thinly slice the spring onions, grate the ginger, and set aside in separate bowls. Slice shiso leaves into thin strips and place in a bowl. Pour the sesame seeds into another small bowl. Arrange the ingredients on a shared basket (or plate). Cover with plastic wrap and place in the fridge.

4   Heat water in a large saucepan. When it starts to boil, add the somen noodles. Stir occasionally with chopsticks and cook for about 2 minutes or according to package directions. Drain. Rinse in cold water and drain again.

5   Mix the mentsuyu sauce (page 23) with the ice water in a small bowl.

6   Divide the noodles into several heaps on a large sharing basket. Place all the ingredients on the table. Divide the sauce into 4 individual bowls so that each person can add garnishes and toppings of their choosing. To eat, dip the noodles into the sauce.

Understand

SUDACHI SOBA

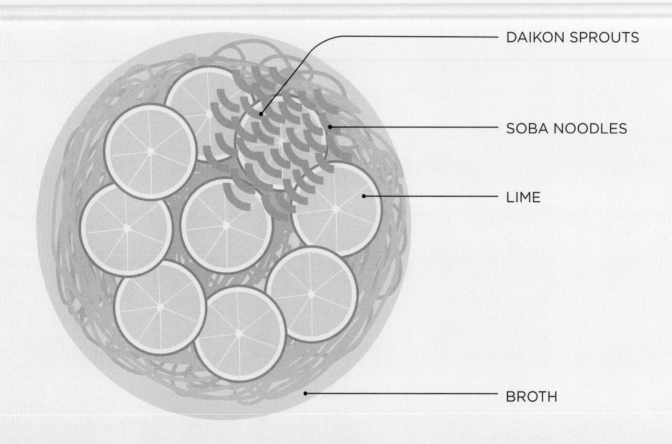

DAIKON SPROUTS

SOBA NOODLES

LIME

BROTH

WHAT IS IT?

Cold soba noodles (made from
buckwheat flour) in a cold lime broth.

ORIGIN

This dish originated in Tokushima, the
region where the majority of sudachi
fruit production takes place.

TOTAL TIME

Prep time: 10 minutes
Cook time: 3 minutes

WHEN TO ENJOY

Swimming in a cold broth of shiro dashi,
white soy sauce, and sudachi juice, these
cold soba noodles with lime bring a
refreshing touch to a hot summer's day.

TIPS

- Make the same amount of dashi (7 cups /
1.6 L) and chill. Add the same amount
of clear or white soy sauce and salt.
- Sudachi is a green Japanese citrus fruit.
Difficult to find outside of Japan, it is
replaced here by lime.

SUBSTITUTIONS

- Replace the soba noodles with somen.
- Replace the limes with lemons.
- Replace the sudachi juice with yuzu juice.

232

Learn

FOR 4 PEOPLE

BROTH

7 cups / 1.6 liters ice water
¼ cup / 60 ml shiro dashi
3 tablespoons / 50 ml light soy sauce
½ teaspoon fine salt
2 tablespoons sudachi (or lime) juice

INGREDIENTS

11 ounces / 320 g dried soba noodles
4 limes
1½ ounces / 40 g daikon (Japanese
    radish) sprouts
1 tablespoon white sesame seeds

1   Combine all the broth ingredients in
a bowl.

2   Thinly slice 4 limes into rounds with a
knife. Wash the sprouts and trim the stems.

3   Cook the noodles in plenty of
water. Drain, rinse in cold water, and
drain again. Divide into 4 bowls.

4   Pour the cold broth over the noodles,
add the lime slices and radish sprouts.
Add the sesame seeds and serve.

SHABU SHABU

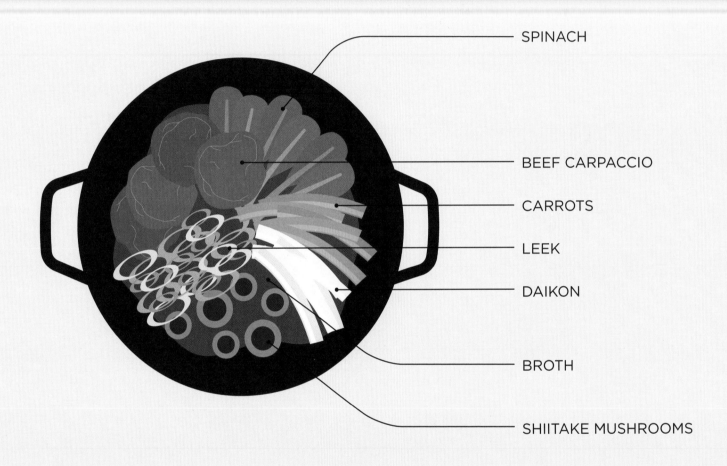

SPINACH

BEEF CARPACCIO

CARROTS

LEEK

DAIKON

BROTH

SHIITAKE MUSHROOMS

WHAT IS IT?

Beef and vegetables dipped into hot broth; served with a sauce on the side.

ORIGIN

Chef Chuichi Miyake created this recipe and named it shabu-shabu (a Japanese onomatopoetic phrase that means 'to wash in water') after seeing his waiter rinse a napkin in water.

TOTAL TIME

Prep time: 30 minutes
Cook time: 10 minutes

EQUIPMENT

Pot or wok
Portable gas or electric stove
Mandoline

TECHNIQUES TO MASTER

Rehydrating kombu (page 283)
Cutting vegetables (page 280)

TIPS

You can use a fondue set.
- To slice the meat, roll it up, wrap the roll in aluminum foil, and freeze for 30 minutes before slicing.
- If the water boils too vigorously, the meat will become tough and lose its umami, so keep it at a gentle boil on low heat.

SUBSTITUTIONS AND ADDITIONS

Replace the goma dare sauce with ponzu sauce (page 51)
With pork: replace the beef with thin slices of pork belly.
With fish: replace the beef with a carpaccio of white fish (like sea bream or bass).
With tofu: add chopped tofu.

Learn

SHIITAKE MUSHROOM	YUZU KOSHO	RAUSU KOMBU	SHICHIMI TOGARASHI
Plump, fleshy mushrooms with a woody flavor.	Fermented paste made from green chilis and yuzu peel; used as a condiment.	A very fragrant seaweed that produces a slightly cloudy broth with an intense flavor.	Also known as Japanese seven spice, it contains red chili pepper, sesame and poppy seeds, nori, sansho, ginger, shiso, hemp seeds, and chenpi (mandarin peel).

FOR 4 PEOPLE

1 pound 5 ounces / 600 g beef
    carpaccio
14 ounces / 400 g daikon
    (Japanese radish)
7 ounces / 200 g soybean sprouts
3½ ounces / 100 g spinach
3½ ounces / 100 g shiitake mushrooms
2 carrots
1 leek

BROTH

4¼ cups / 1 L water
⅓ cup plus 4 teaspoons / 100 ml
    cooking sake
8 inches / 20 cm rausu kombu

FOR SERVING

Goma dare sauce
1 bunch ofchives
Shichimi togarashi
Yuzu kosho

1 Rehydrate the kombu (page 283) with 4½ cups / 1 L of cold water and the sake. Remove the meat from the refrigerator and leave to rest at room temperature for 15 to 20 minutes.

2 Peel and wash the carrots and radishes. Cut the radishes into 2⅓-inch / 6 cm segments. Using a peeler, slice the carrots and radishes into thin ribbons. Wash the leek and cut into thin slices at an angle (page 280). Wash the spinach. Rinse the bean sprouts and drain. Cut off the stems of the shiitake mushrooms. Finely chop the chives and set aside in a small dish.

FOR SERVING

Arrange the vegetables on a platter and the carpaccio on a separate plate. Divide the sauces into bowls. Place the pot on a gas or electric stove on the table. Arrange the ingredients on the table. Heat the water in the pot over low heat with the kombu. When the water boils, remove the seaweed. Add the chosen ingredients (vegetables, mushrooms, noodles, meat) as you go, dipping them into the stock with chopsticks and cooking to taste. The beef is ready when it turns cherry-red. Skim from time to time if necessary and add water as the stock evaporates.

Dip the cooked ingredients into the bowl of sauce topped with spices (yuzu kosho, shichimi togarashi) and chopped chives.

Understand

TORI NABE

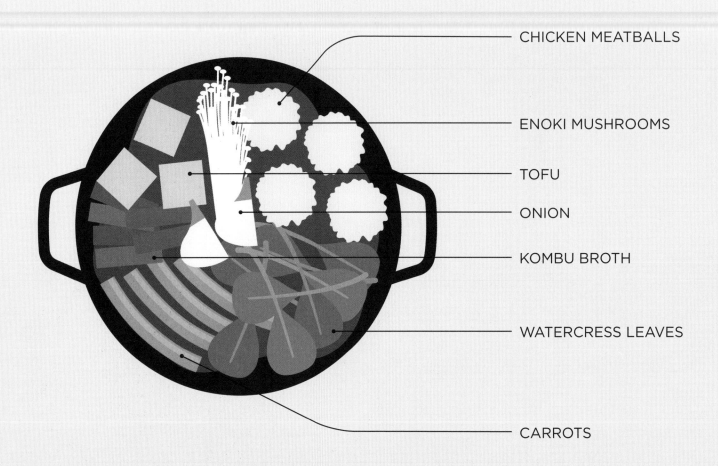

CHICKEN MEATBALLS

ENOKI MUSHROOMS

TOFU

ONION

KOMBU BROTH

WATERCRESS LEAVES

CARROTS

WHAT IS IT?

Chicken meatball hot pot with seasonal vegetables, tofu, and other ingredients simmered in seaweed broth; served with ponzu sauce and spices.

ORIGIN

Tori = chicken; nabe = hot pot: chicken hot pot. This dish is a specialty of the Fukuoka region (Kyushu).

TOTAL TIME

Prep time: 1 hour
Cook time: 1 hour
Rest time: 1 hour

EQUIPMENT

Food processor
Clay pot or wok
Gas or electric portable stove
10-inch / 25 cm pot

WHEN TO ENJOY

Perfect for winter, tori nabe can be cooked family-style directly in a clay pot (donabe) placed on the table. Add ingredients as you go.

TECHNIQUES TO MASTER

Rehydrating kombu (page 283)
Deboning chicken thighs (page 42)
Preparing daikon (page 281)

TIP

When there are no more ingredients left, dip cooked udon noodles into the stock. Season with a little soy sauce or miso and enjoy.

VARIATION

You can cook the chicken meatballs in a skillet like yakitori.

ADDITION

Season the stock with 2 tablespoons of miso.

Learn

•

KUZUKIRI

Vermicelli made
from kuzu starch.

•

ERINGI
MUSHROOMS

A member of the
oyster mushroom
family, also called
king trumpet
or king oyster
mushrooms. Select
mushrooms with
white stems and
smooth caps.

•

ENOKI
MUSHROOMS

Bundles of white
mushrooms with
very thin stems.

FOR 4 PEOPLE

MEATBALLS

4 chicken thighs
1 egg
2 tablespoons potato starch or cornstarch
1 tablespoon soy sauce
1 tablespoon sake
1 tablespoon toasted sesame oil
1 tablespoon grated fresh ginger
1 tablespoon toasted sesame seeds
A little ground white pepper
¼ teaspoon fine salt

BROTH

5-inch square piece / 15 g kombu
⅓ cup plus 4 teaspoons / 100 ml
   cooking sake

INGREDIENTS

9 ounces / 250 g silken tofu
½ daikon (Japanese radish)
1 carrot
1 bunch of watercress
1 bunch of spring onions
● 2 eringi mushrooms
● 1 bundle of enoki mushrooms
2 tablespoons dried wakame
● 3½ ounces / 100 g kuzukiri

FOR SERVING

¾ cup plus 4 teaspoons / 200 ml
   ponzu sauce
Shichimi togarashi
Yuzu kosho (green chili and yuzu paste)

Make

1 Rehydrate the kombu with 6½ cups / 1.5 L of water (page 283). Debone the chicken thighs (page 42).

2 Cut the chicken thighs into cubes (1¼ inch / 3 cm).

3 Grind them in a food processor along with all the ingredients for the meatballs, then mix well.

4 Place in a bowl, cover, and refrigerate.

5 Soak the wakame in warm water for about 10 minutes, then drain and set aside. Place the vermicelli in a bowl and pour in hot water until the noodles are covered. Leave to stand for 2 to 3 minutes, drain and set aside. Cut the tofu into 8 squares and set aside.

6 Cut off the tops of the onions, then halve them. Thinly slice 4 onion stalks and set aside. Slice the remaining stalks into approximately 2-inch / 5 cm lengths. Trim the base of the enokis and slice the eringis. Wash the watercress. Wash and peel the radish and carrot, then slice into thin strips using a vegetable peeler.

FOR SERVING

Divide the ponzu sauce between 4 bowls. Place the pot on the table over a gas or electric stove. Pour in the kombu, its soaking water, and the sake. Heat the pot, bring to a boil, and reduce to a gentle simmer. Place several meatballs in the broth along with the vegetables and cook simultaneously. Skim from time to time if necessary and add water as the stock evaporates. Serve by dipping a meatball or some vegetables into the bowl of ponzu sauce. Top with spices (yuzu kosho and shichimi togarashi) and chopped chives to taste.

KAMO NABE
SUKIYAKI

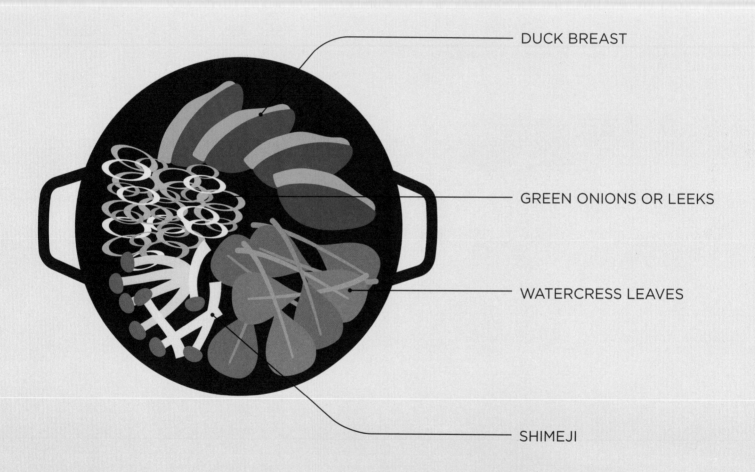

DUCK BREAST

GREEN ONIONS OR LEEKS

WATERCRESS LEAVES

SHIMEJI

WHAT IS IT?

Meat or other ingredients grilled or boiled in a cast-iron pot.

ORIGIN

There are several types of sukiyaki. The style used in this recipe comes from a traditional duck restaurant in downtown Tokyo. It's simple and flavorful. Sukiyaki is generally seasoned with "warishita," which is a combination of soy sauce, sugar, sake, and mirin. To eat, the meat is dipped in a raw beaten egg.

TOTAL TIME

Prep time: 20 minutes

EQUIPMENT

Pot or cast-iron skillet
Daikon oroshi or large-hole grater
Gas or electric portable stove
Gyuto-style knife for cutting meat

WHEN TO ENJOY

This is a warming winter dish.

TECHNIQUE TO MASTER

Preparing daikon (page 281)

TIP

Be careful not to overcook the duck or it will become tough.

SUBSTITUTIONS AND ADDITIONS

- Replace the soy sauce with ponzu sauce (page 51).
- Replace the watercress with edible chrysanthemums.
- Replace the duck meat with game meat.
Warishita (sukiyaki sauce): mix ⅓ cup plus 4 teaspoons / 100 ml soy sauce, ⅓ cup plus 4 teaspoons / 100 ml sake, ⅓ cup plus 4 teaspoons / 100 ml mirin and 2 tablespoons raw cane sugar in a small saucepan and bring to a boil. Gradually pour into the hot pot while cooking the meat and vegetables.

Learn

DAIKON

Mild, juicy white radish.

SAISHIKOMI SOY SAUCE

Condiment made from soybeans, wheat, grains, and sea salt; fermented 2 times.

SHIMEJI MUSHROOMS

A cluster of brown or white mushrooms with a nutty flavor.

SANSHO POWDER

Powder made from berries with a lemongrass-like flavor and minty, woody notes.

TAKANOTSUME

A very strong red chili.

FOR 4 PEOPLE

2 duck breasts
1 bunch of watercress
2 bunches of green onions or 1 leek
● 3½ ounces / 100 g fresh shimeji mushrooms
● 2 takanotsume chilis
● 1 daikon radish

FOR SERVING

½ daikon, top part (page 281)
● Soy sauce
● Sansho powder
2 bowls Japanese short-grain rice (already cooked)

1 Soak the chili peppers in a bowl of water for 10 minutes. Cut the daikon in half. Pierce two holes in one half with a wooden chopstick and insert the peppers into the holes.

2 In a bowl, using a grater or a daikon oroshi, grate half the daikon. In another bowl, grate the half with the red chili. Tilt the bowl to drain the juice and set aside.

3 Cut off the base of the shimeji mushrooms. Wash the watercress and cut to a length of around 2⅓ inches / 6 cm. Wash the leeks and cut diagonally (1 cm thick). Arrange the vegetables in a basket or dish.

4 Cut the duck breasts into slices about 7 mm thick. Arrange on a plate.

FOR SERVING

Place a portable gas or electric stove on the table, then set a pot on the stove. Arrange the other ingredients around the stove. Heat the pot and add the pieces of duck without oil. Add the vegetables. Prepare a bowl of soy sauce for each person with grated radish and sansho for dipping.

When there are no more ingredients to cook, add the cooked rice to the pot and stir-fry, making the most of the cooking juices. Season with a little soy sauce and enjoy.

Understand
ANKOU NABE

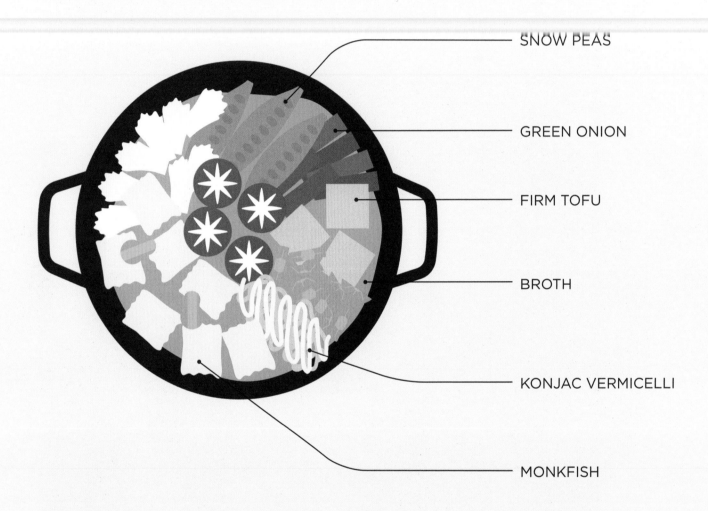

SNOW PEAS

GREEN ONION

FIRM TOFU

BROTH

KONJAC VERMICELLI

MONKFISH

WHAT IS IT?

Monkfish and vegetable hot pot with miso.

ORIGIN

In Japan, monkfish traditionally has seven edible parts. Among professional fishers, these parts are known as the "Seven Tools" and the most important aspect of making a delicious monkfish nabe is to include as many parts as possible.

TOTAL TIME

Prep time: 50 minutes
Rest time: 1 hour

EQUIPMENT

Clay pot or wok
Portable gas or electric stove
Small flower-shaped cookie cutter (optional)

WHEN TO ENJOY

This nabe is best cooked in January or February when monkfish season is at its peak.

TECHNIQUES TO MASTER

Rehydrating kombu (page 283)
Shimofuri (page 282) - blanching technique)

TIPS

- Add monkfish liver to the stock for a truly traditional version.

- The flavor and saltiness of miso vary according to type and manufacturer, so it's best to taste and adjust each time you use it.
– When blanching the fish with the shimofuri technique, be careful not to pour boiling water over the fish because the skin tears easily.

VERSIONS

In Kansai, the broth is miso-based. In Tokyo, the broth is made with soy sauce (shoyu).

VARIATIONS

- Replace the monkfish with cod.
- The carrot can also be thinly sliced, then each slice shaped into a flower using a small cookie cutter.

Learn

SHIITAKE MUSHROOMS

Plump fleshy mushrooms with a woody flavor.

KOMBU SEAWEED

Giant seaweed with a briny taste from the genus Laminaria.

FIRM TOFU

Its texture is semi-firm and chewy.

WHITE MISO

Soybean paste with very little fermentation (between 2 and 8 weeks). Mild and lightly salted.

SHIRATAKI

Translucent, gelatinous noodles made from konjac starch.

FOR 4 PEOPLE

- 1 pound 5 ounces / 600 g monkfish
- 1 block of firm tofu (10½ ounces / 300 g)
- 10½ ounces / 300 g napa cabbage
- 8 shiitakes
- 2 carrots
- 1 bunch of green onions or baby leeks
- 1¾ ounces / 50 g snow peas
- 7 ounces / 200 g shirataki

BROTH

- 4½ cups / 1 L water
- 6 tablespoons / 100 g white miso
- ⅓ cup plus 4 teaspoons / 100 ml cooking sake
- 3 tablespoons / 45 ml mirin
- 1 teaspoon grated fresh ginger
- 5-inch square piece / 15 g kombu

FOR SERVING

Shichimi togarashi
Yuzu or orange zest
Sliced green onions
2 bowls of Japanese short-grain rice

1   Rehydrate the kombu (page 283).

2   Cut the monkfish into pieces (1½ inches / 4 cm). Heat 1 L of water to 175°F / 80°C. Blanch the fish using the shimofuri technique (page 282): place the pieces in a bowl and pour the hot water down the sides of the bowl so that it does not come into direct contact with the fish. Then stir the mixture lightly with chopsticks. Leave to stand for a few minutes. When the surface of the fish turns white, rinse the fish pieces in a bowl of cold water and drain. Arrange the fish on a plate.

3   Coarsely chop the shirataki into 2 or 3 pieces. Then blanch in a pot of boiling water for about 2 minutes. Drain.

4   Cut the cabbage into 2-inch / 5 cm pieces. Peel the carrot and cut into 3 sections, then slice lengthways; detail some with a cookie cutter and cut the rest into sticks. Slice 2 stalks of green onions into 2-inch / 5 cm sections and set aside to serve. Trim the stems of the shiitake mushrooms and cut a star shape into the cap.

5   Cut the tofu into 1¼-inch / 3 cm cubes. Wash and remove the stems from the snow peas. Cut the remaining green onions into rounds. Grate the orange zest. Arrange the ingredients in a dish.

6   Place the pot on a portable gas or electric stove on the table. Arrange the ingredients on the table around the pot. Heat the pot over low heat and bring to a boil. Stir the miso through a small sieve into a ladle using a small whisk, then add the sake, mirin, and grated ginger. Add the vegetables and pieces of monkfish. Leave to cook, then skim. Serve with the shichimi togarashi, green onion rounds, and grated yuzu or orange zest. When there are no more ingredients to cook, plunge the cooked rice into the stock and cook for 2 to 3 minutes like a risotto.

ICHIGO DAIFUKU

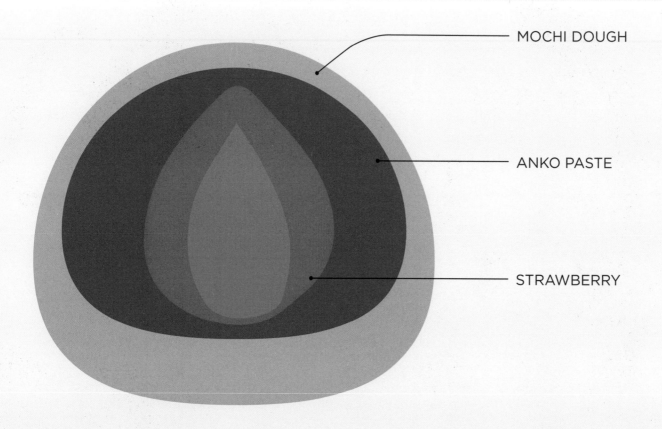

MOCHI DOUGH

ANKO PASTE

STRAWBERRY

WHAT IS IT?

A glutinous rice flour dough flavored with green tea and filled with sweet red bean paste and a strawberry.

ORIGIN

Strawberry mochi is a fairly new dessert; it was created in the 1980s as a variation of daifuku, a traditional dessert dating back to the 10th century and originally reserved for emperors.

TOTAL TIME

Prep time: 30 minutes
Cook time: 4 minutes

WHEN TO ENJOY

Mochi daifuku is a popular spring and summer (strawberry season) dessert much loved by the Japanese.

TIPS

- If the mochi dough cools, the mochi will be difficult to make, so it's best to work quickly while the dough is still hot.
- Daifuku mochi without strawberries can be kept for about 2 days in an airtight container. Do not put them in the fridge, otherwise they will become hard.

VARIATIONS

- Daifuku mochi can be made without green tea, in which case they are white on the outside.
- They can be made with or without strawberries, according to preference.

SUBSTITUTIONS

Replace strawberries with peaches, kiwis, or pears.

Learn

GLUTINOUS RICE FLOUR

Flour made from ground glutinous rice. It has a thicker, softer texture than other flours and is gluten-free.

ANKO

Sweet azuki bean paste.

MATCHA

Green tea whose leaves are ground to a very fine powder. It should be bright green. Be sure to find matcha from Japan.

FOR 8 MOCHIS

- ¾ cup / 250 g anko paste, store-bought or homemade (page 44)
  1 teaspoon matcha for decoration
  8 strawberries

MOCHI DOUGH

- 1 cup / 120 g glutinous rice flour
  ½ cup plus 2 tablespoons / 150 ml water
  ¼ cup / 50 g granulated sugar
- 1 teaspoon matcha
  ¾ cup / 100 g cornstarch

Make

1 Wash and dry the strawberries, then remove the stems with a knife. Divide the anko paste into 8 portions of 1½ tablespoons / 30 g each.

2 Spread out the anko paste on an 8-inch / 20 cm square of plastic wrap. Place a strawberry in the center and surround it with the paste. Form a ball using the plastic wrap. Set aside in a cool place.

3 In a bowl, sift all the ingredients for the mochi dough, whisk together, and cover. Cook for 2 minutes in the microwave at 600 W. Stir with a wet rubber spatula. Cover and cook for another 2 minutes, stirring to combine. The dough is ready when it becomes translucent.

4 Sprinkle cornstarch over the work surface and place the mochi dough on top. Divide into 8 portions using a scraper or knife.

5 Wrap the anko-coated strawberries in the mochi dough and press together with your fingers to form balls. Sprinkle with matcha and serve.

Understand

NERIKIRI

254

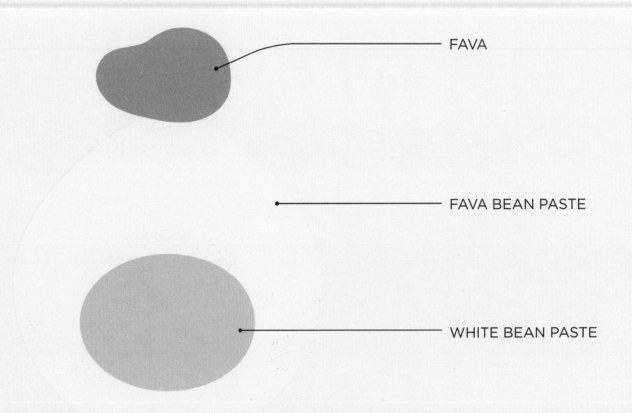

FAVA

FAVA BEAN PASTE

WHITE BEAN PASTE

WHAT IS IT?

Nerikiri is an attractive traditional cake made from white bean paste and fava beans. It is naturally pastel-colored, and its refined shapes are paired with the season (cherry blossoms in spring, maple leaves in autumn...).

ORIGIN

Nerikiri dates back to the Edo period when falling sugar prices led to the development of candy stores and pastry shops.

TOTAL TIME

Prep time: 1 hour
Cook time: 20 minutes

EQUIPMENT

Flat-bottomed sieve
Small rolling pin

HOW TO ENJOY

This traditional cake is served during the Japanese tea ceremony. It is also made at home - usually from sticky rice, sugar, and syrup. This simpler version takes advantage of the natural flavor of the beans and is therefore less sweet.

TIPS

- To test for doneness, smash a bean; you want it to be fairly soft.
- Pass the cooked beans quickly through a sieve while they are still hot to ease straining.

SUBSTITUTIONS

Replace the beans with sweet potato or kabocha squash.

Learn

FOR 8 PIECES

FAVA BEAN PASTE

6¾ cups / 800 g whole fava beans
    or 1 cup / 250 g cooked
1 teaspoon salt (for 4¼ cups / 1 L of water)
7 tablespoons / 50 g powdered sugar

SYRUP

3 tablespoons / 40 g granulated sugar
⅓ cup plus 4 teaspoons / 100 ml water

WHITE BEAN PASTE

¾ cup / 200 g canned white beans
6 tablespoons / 50 g powdered sugar

1 Peel the fava beans. Bring a pan of salted water to a boil, add the beans, and cook for 10 minutes.

2 To test for doneness, smash a bean. If it is fairly soft, it is cooked. Drain and set aside 8 beans for decorating. Press the rest of the beans through a sieve while they are still hot. Put them in a saucepan, add the sugar, and stir. Prepare the syrup by placing the sugar and water in a small saucepan. Bring to a simmer, stirring if necessary, until the sugar has dissolved. Leave to cool, then marinate the 8 beans reserved for decoration.

3 Drain the white beans, then blend, press through the sieve, and place in a saucepan. Add the sugar and cook over low heat, stirring to allow the moisture to evaporate.

4 Make 8 small balls of white bean paste.

5 Spread 2 tablespoons of fava bean paste (about 2¼ to 2¾ inches / 6 to 7 cm in diameter) on a square of plastic wrap. Place a ball of white bean paste on top and twist the plastic wrap to shape it. To finish, place a bean on top of the ball.

MUSHI PAN

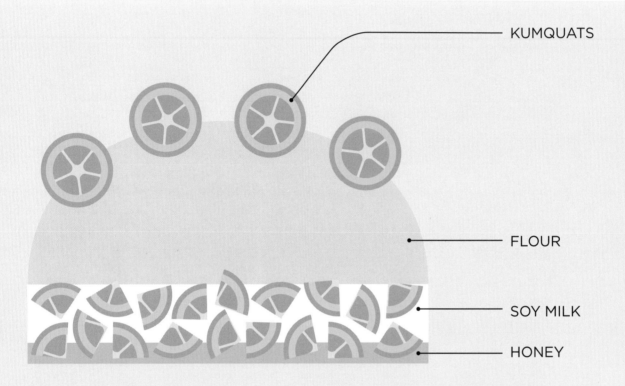

KUMQUATS

FLOUR

SOY MILK

HONEY

WHAT IS IT?

Steamed kumquat cake.

TOTAL TIME

Prep time: 15 minutes
Rest time: 15 minutes
Cook time: 40 minutes

ORIGIN

These steamed cakes appeared after the war when wheat became more widely available in Japan.

EQUIPMENT

Bamboo steamer basket
Bamboo skewer

HOW TO ENJOY

It can be eaten as a hot or cold snack.

TECHNIQUE TO MASTER

Steaming in a bamboo basket (page 284)

TIP

Covering the kumquats with parchment paper while simmering keeps them completely submerged in the syrup and speeds up the cooking process.

VARIATION

With matcha: replace the kumquats with 1 teaspoon of matcha powder and sprinkle with black sesame seeds.

Learn

KUMQUAT

A small citrus fruit with sweet, tangy flesh. Available during winter in Asian grocery shops and farmers markets.

FOR 1 CAKE

KUMQUATS IN SYRUP

- 3½ ounces / 100 g fresh kumquats
  ½ cup / 100 g sugar
  1 tablespoon honey
  ⅓ cup plus 4 teaspoons / 100 ml water

CAKE

2 eggs
1 tablespoon vegetable oil
⅓ cup / 80 ml soy milk
⅓ cup / 60 g sugar
1 tablespoon eau-de-vie of your choice
   (optional)
1¼ cups / 150 g flour
1 teaspoon baking powder

Make

1 Slice 2 kumquats to use as decoration. Set aside. Prick the other kumquats several times all over with a bamboo skewer to prevent the skin from tearing. Place them in a saucepan and add water until they are just covered. Bring to a boil, then lower the heat and cook for 3 minutes. Prepare a bowl of cold water. Drain the kumquats and plunge them into the bowl. Leave to stand for 15 minutes to reduce bitterness. Drain.

2 Dice finely and remove the seeds.

3 Place the kumquats, ½ cup / 100 g sugar, and ⅓ cup plus 4 teaspoons / 100 ml water in a saucepan and bring to a boil. Cover with parchment paper. Cook over low heat for about 1 minute. Remove from heat and leave to cool to room temperature. Set aside in a cool place.

4 For the bread, whisk the eggs, sugar, oil, and soy milk in a bowl. Sift in the flour and baking powder. Mix well to obtain a homogeneous dough.

5 Add the diced candied kumquats and the eau-de-vie and mix well.

6 Line a bamboo basket with parchment paper and pour in the mixture. Decorate with the kumquat slices.

7 Place the basket over a pot of boiling water (page 284). Cover. Wrap a tea towel around the lid of the pot to absorb any droplets of steam that could fall onto the bread.

8 Steam for approximately 30 minutes. Then remove from the basket and leave to cool.

Understand

OSHIRUKO
& SHIRATAMA DANGO

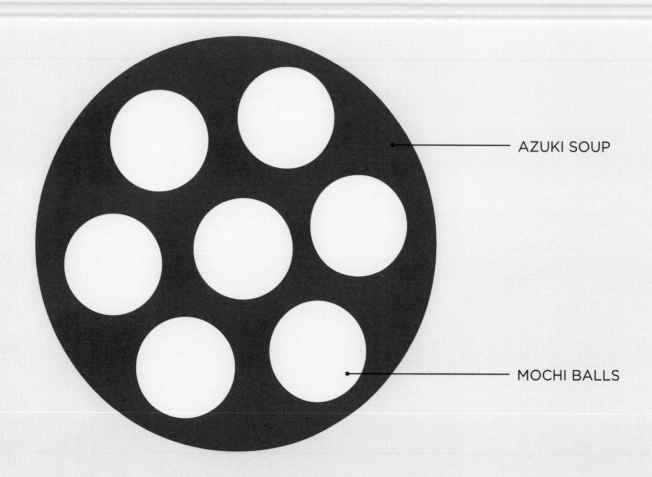

AZUKI SOUP

MOCHI BALLS

WHAT IS IT?
Sweet red bean soup with shiratama dango (mochi balls).

ORIGIN
Shiru = soup; ko = ingredients.

TOTAL TIME
Prep time: 15 minutes
Cook time: 10 minutes

WHEN TO ENJOY
Shiruko is a traditional dessert that is very popular in winter when mochi is commonly eaten.

TECHNIQUE TO MASTER
Making glutinous rice balls

TIP
In this recipe, the azuki paste is bought ready-made, but homemade azuki paste is even better (page 44).

VARIATIONS
Add pieces of kabocha to the red bean soup or replace the bean soup with kabocha soup (made with the same amount of sugar). In summer, enjoy the soup cold.

Learn

FOR 4 PEOPLE

MOCHI BALLS

¾ cup plus 4 teaspoons / 200 ml water
1⅔ cups / 200 g glutinous rice flour

AZUKI SOUP

¾ cup / 250 g sweet azuki paste,
    ready-made or homemade (page 44)
1¼ cups / 300 ml water

1 In a bowl, combine the rice flour and ¾ cup plus 4 teaspoons / 200 ml water, then knead. Shape the dough into small balls about 1¼ inches / 3 cm in diameter.

2 Cook in boiling water for about 3 minutes. When the balls float, leave to cook for another minute.

3 Drain then plunge the balls into a bowl of cold water (to prevent them from sticking). Drain again.

4 Place the azuki paste in a saucepan and pour in 1¼ cups / 300 ml of water. Bring to a boil, add the mochi balls, and heat for 2 or 3 minutes.

5 Divide into bowls and serve.

DORAYAKI

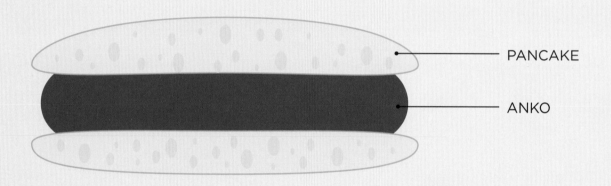

PANCAKE

ANKO

WHAT IS IT?

A thick, fluffy pancake topped with anko and covered with a second pancake.

ORIGIN

The name dorayaki comes from the legend that the batter was cooked on a gong instead of a griddle, dorayaki having a similar shape.

TOTAL TIME

Prep time: 10 minutes
Cook time: 10 minutes
Rest time: 30 minutes

EQUIPMENT

Nonstick skillet

HOW TO ENJOY

This cake is a very popular snack, found in all konbini (convenience stores) and traditional Japanese pastry shops. They are also made at home by families.

TIPS

- During the summer, place the batter in the fridge to rest.
- Be sure not to use too much oil for cooking, otherwise the cakes won't brown evenly.

ADDITIONS AND SUBSTITUTIONS

With chestnuts: place a chestnut in syrup in the middle of the anko or replace the anko with the same amount of chestnut spread.
With fruit: place a fresh strawberry in the middle of the anko.
Lighter version: whip ½ cup plus 2 tablespoons / 150 ml of heavy cream and fold the whipped cream into the anko.

Learn

GLUTINOUS RICE FLOUR

Flour made from ground glutinous rice. It has a thicker, fluffier texture than other flours and is gluten-free.

AZUKI BEANS

Small Japanese red beans with a mealy texture and a taste slightly reminiscent of chestnuts.

COOKING SAKE

Sake with added salt.

FOR 8 DORAYAKIS

BATTER

1¼ cups / 150 g flour
¼ cup / 30 g glutinous rice flour
1 teaspoon baking soda
3 eggs (about 150 g)
⅔ cup plus 1 tablespoon / 120 g sugar
1 tablespoon honey
3 tablespoons / 45 ml cooking sake
3 tablespoons / 45 ml water

HOMEMADE ANKO
(to make 1½ cups / 500 g anko)

1 cup / 200 g azuki beans
¾ cup / 150 g cane sugar

1   To make the batter, sift the flour, glutinous rice flour, and baking soda into a bowl.

2   In another bowl, beat the eggs and sugar until the mixture whitens. Stir in the honey, sake, and water.

3   Gradually add the eggs to the flour, mixing until the batter is smooth and combined. Cover with plastic wrap and leave to rest for around 30 minutes.

4   Heat a non-stick skillet and grease lightly with a paper towel. Place small discs of batter (about 3 inches / 8 cm in diameter) in the pan and cook over a very low heat. When small holes appear on the surface, turn the pancakes over and cook for another minute or so. Repeat the operation, greasing the skillet between each batch, to make 16 pancakes.

5   Spread 2 tablespoons of anko in the center 6 of the pancakes. Cover each one with a second pancake. Repeat until all the ingredients have been used up.

BLACK SESAME
ICE CREAM

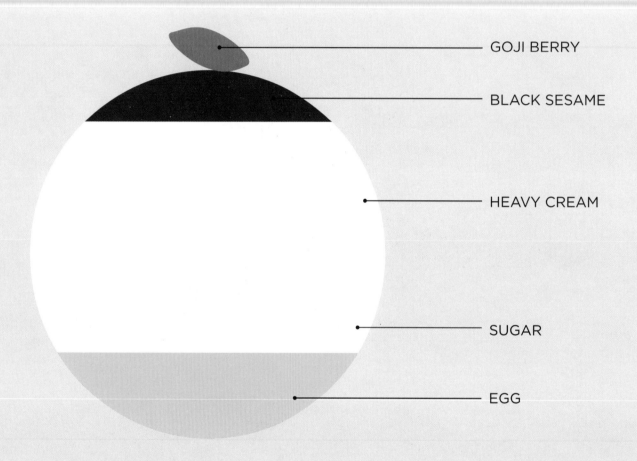

GOJI BERRY

BLACK SESAME

HEAVY CREAM

SUGAR

EGG

WHAT IS IT?

Ice cream made with black sesame paste.

ORIGIN

Ice cream, initially in the form of crushed ice (kakigori), dates back to the Meiji era, which is synonymous with the modernization of Japan.

TOTAL TIME

Prep time: 15 minutes
Cook time: 3 minutes
Rest time: 1 hour 30 minutes

EQUIPMENT

Ice cream maker

HOW TO ENJOY

Black sesame is the most popular ice cream flavor in Japan, along with matcha (green tea).

TIP

If you can't find black sesame paste, replace it with tahini (white sesame paste).

VARIATIONS

With matcha: incorporate 3 tablespoons / 20 g of matcha instead of sesame paste.
With white sesame: replace the black sesame paste with the same amount of tahini.

Learn

FOR 2 PINTS / 800 G

3 egg yolks
½ cup / 100 g sugar
2 cups plus 4 teaspoons / 500 ml
    heavy cream
6 tablespoons / 100 g black sesame paste
1 tablespoon sake (optional)

FOR SERVING

1 tablespoon black sesame seeds
1 tablespoon goji berries

1 Place the egg yolks and sugar in a bowl. Whisk until the mixture whitens.

2 Whisk in the black sesame paste and sake, if using.

3 Pour the mixture into a saucepan and add the cream. Heat for 3 minutes over medium heat, stirring constantly with a spatula.

4 Remove from heat and leave to cool at room temperature for 30 minutes, then chill in the fridge for about 1 hour.

5 Pour the cream into the ice cream maker and churn to the desired texture. Place in a container and freeze before serving. Garnish with black sesame seeds and goji berries.

CASTELLA

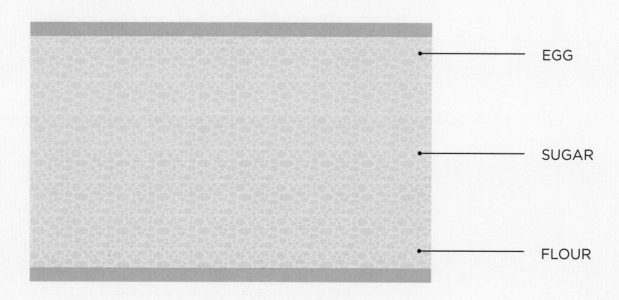

EGG

SUGAR

FLOUR

WHAT IS IT?

Oven-baked sponge cake made with eggs, flour, honey, and mirin.

ORIGIN

Castella was inspired by the pastries introduced to Japan by Portuguese immigrants living in Nagasaki.

TOTAL TIME

Prep time: 20 minutes
Cook time: 65 minutes
Rest time: Overnight

EQUIPMENT
Skewer
Mold (7 by 7 inches / 18 by 18 cm)

VARIATION
Sandwich some azuki paste between two sponge cakes to make a Siberia.

ADDITIONS
With matcha: add 5 teaspoons / 10 g of matcha powder with the flour.
With sesame paste: add 1 tablespoon of sesame paste with the honey.

Learn

MIRIN

A Japanese rice wine
used as a condiment;
it is sweeter than sake.

FOR 1 CAKE

⅔ cup / 160 g egg whites (about 6 eggs)
6 tablespoons / 100 g egg yolks
    (about 7 eggs)
¾ cup / 160 g granulated sugar
¾ cup plus 2 tablespoons / 150 g
    pastry flour

WITH HONEY

2 tablespoons / 40 g honey
2 tablespoons / 30 g mirin

WITH BUTTER

4 teaspoons / 20 g unsalted butter
2 teaspoons / 10 g milk

Make

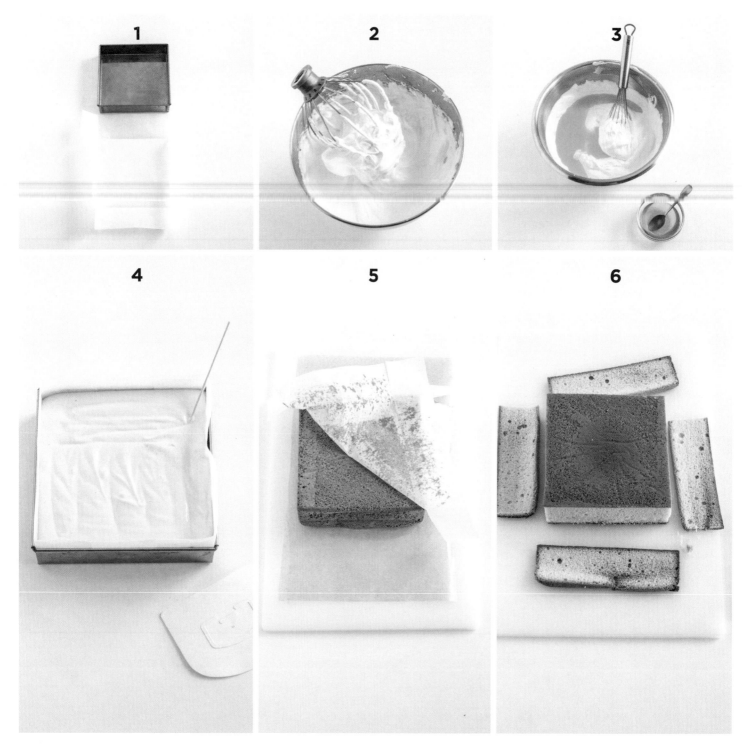

1   Preheat the oven to 340°F / 170°C. Line the mold with parchment paper. Chill the egg whites. For the honey version, heat the honey and mirin in a bain-marie or in the microwave for 10 to 20 seconds at 600 W. For the butter version, melt the butter with the milk in a bain-marie or in the microwave for 10 to 20 seconds at 600 W.

2   Make a meringue by beating the cold egg whites until stiff with an electric mixer. Add the sugar in three batches. Then beat on low speed for 1 minute. The meringue should be shiny.

3   Whisk the egg yolks into the meringue. Mix in the flour in two batches. Add the ingredients for the honey version into the meringue, or if you're making the butter version, first add 3 teaspoons of the butter and milk mixture to the meringue, then pour in the rest.

4   Pour into the mold and smooth with a spatula. To eliminate any air bubbles, use a bamboo skewer to cut the mousse 3 times vertically and horizontally. Smooth the surface well.

5   Bake in the oven at 340°F / 170°C for 20 minutes, then reduce the temperature to 285°F / 140°C. Bake for another 45 minutes or so.

6   Lightly oil a sheet of parchment paper with a paper towel. When the castella is cooked, place the parchment paper on top and turn the cake over. Unmold and leave to cool, then wrap in plastic wrap. Leave to stand overnight. Slice the castella, lightly oiling the knife between each slice.

MATCHA AND FIG
ROLL CAKE

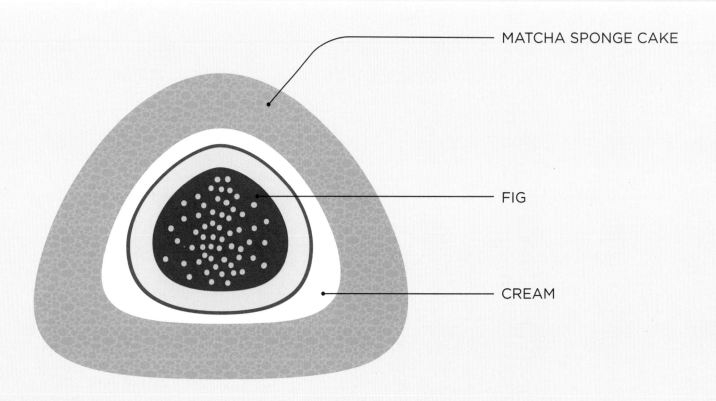

MATCHA SPONGE CAKE

FIG

CREAM

WHAT IS IT?

Matcha sponge cake topped with cream and figs, then rolled.

ORIGIN

Also known as a Swiss roll, roll cake does not have a single precise origin, although it probably originated in Central Europe in the 19th century: countries such as Austria and Switzerland were renowned for their Viennese pastries.

TOTAL TIME

Prep time: 30 minutes
Cook time: 15 minutes
Rest time: 3 hours

EQUIPMENT
Square mold (10 inches / 26 cm)

WHEN TO ENJOY
Light, creamy, and low in sugar, it makes a delicious afternoon snack or dessert with coffee or tea.

TIP
Before cutting the roll cake, leave it to rest for at least 3 hours to set.

SUBSTITUTIONS
- Replace the matcha with black sesame paste.
- Replace the figs with seasonal fruit: strawberries, peaches, cherries, grapes, etc.

Learn

●

MATCHA

Green tea whose
leaves are ground very
finely into powder.
It should be bright
green in color. Be sure
to select matcha that
comes from Japan.

FOR 1 CAKE

SPONGE CAKE

5¼ ounces / 150 g eggs (3 eggs)
⅓ cup / 60 g sugar
6 tablespoons / 45 g pastry flour
2 teaspoons / 5 g cornstarch
Scant ½ teaspoon baking powder
● 1 tablespoon / 6 g matcha
2½ teaspoons / 12 g milk
2½ teaspoons / 12 g unsalted butter

CREAM & TOPPING

¾ cup / 170 g crème fraîche
   (35% fat content)
Heaping tablespoon / 15 g sugar
Rum (optional)
5 figs

Make

1 Line the tin with parchment paper. Heat some water for the bain-marie for the egg mixture. Sift together the flour, cornstarch, baking powder, and matcha. In a bowl, beat the eggs with an electric mixer and add the sugar. Place the bowl in the bain-marie and whisk while heating until the mixture reaches a temperature of 105°F / 40°C. Preheat the oven to 340°F / 170°C. Heat the milk and butter in a second bain-marie. Bring to 140°F / 60°C for a stainless-steel bowl, or 160°F / 70°C for a glass bowl. Continue whisking the eggs. The mixture should be stiff and form a ribbon. Whisk for about 1 minute more at low speed.

2 Sift in the flour mixture in two batches. Mix until the batter is glossy. Add about 2 tablespoons of batter to the small bowl of milk and butter heated to 140°F / 60°C and mix well. Then fold into the batter and mix.

3 Pour the batter into the pan and spread with a spatula. Lift the tin to a height of about 4 inches / 10 cm and let it fall back onto the table to eliminate bubbles. Then bake at 340°F / 170°C for 12 to 15 minutes. Immediately after removing from the oven, lift the tin again to a height of around 4 inches / 10 cm and let it drop. Unmold and leave to cool.

4 Mix the sugar with the cream in a bowl. Prepare a bowl of ice water, and place the bowl of cream inside. Whisk until the cream rises. Add a little rum at the end. When the cake has cooled, turn it out onto parchment paper and remove the original parchment from the bottom of the cake. Spread the cream over the cake with a thicker layer at the front and a thinner layer at the back. Leave a little cream in the bowl.

5 Place the figs along the bottom section and roll the cake loosely.

6 Leave in the fridge for at least 3 hours. Finish by filling both ends of the rolled cake with the remaining cream. When cutting, run the knife under hot water and wipe dry with a paper towel before cutting the slices.

CHAPTER 3
ILLUSTRATED GLOSSARY

Tools

1 Japanese mandoline

2 Wooden brush for basting, wooden spatula for rice, kitchen chopsticks, wooden spatula, strainer

3 Japanese knives (from left to right):
- **Shotoh, small knife (3½ inches / 9 cm):** for prepping and cleaning fruit and vegetables
- **Shotoh, mid-sized knife (5 inches / 13 cm):** for cutting all types of fish and meat

- **Nakiri (6½ inches / 17 cm):** for cutting vegetables and udon
- **Santoku (7 inches / 18 cm):** multi-purpose knife (vegetables, meat, fish)
- **Gyuto (8 inches / 20 cm):** for meat and large vegetables
- **Sujikiri (9½ inches / 24 cm):** for filleting and slicing fish

4 Cookie cutters (available in a range of sizes and shapes)

5 Triangle-shaped onigiri mold

6 Grooved ceramic mortar for crushing sesame seeds (suribachi) and wooden pestle (surikogi)

7 Tweezers (kenuki)

8 Bamboo baskets (zaru)

Tools

9

10

11

12

13

16

14

15

9   Sushi mat (makisu)

10   Clay pot (donabe)

11   Rectangular skillet with straight edges (for rolled omelets)

12   Cast iron wok

13   Dutch oven

14   Portable gas stove

15   Steamer basket

16   Graters - in copper, stainless steel, and plastic (daikon oroshi)

Cutting Vegetables

1

2

3

4

DECORATIVE CUTS

In Japanese cuisine, there are many beautiful ways of cutting decorative vegetables.

1. Star-shaped: remove the stem of the shiitakes and make a star-shaped cut in the caps. Can be used for hot pots, etc.

2. Cookie cutter: cut thin slices of carrot, then shape each slice into a flower using a small cookie cutter. Can be used to decorate hot pots, bentos, etc.

CUTTING ON CHOPSTICKS

3. Place a radish between two wooden chopsticks on a cutting board and make 1 mm thick parallel cuts on the top of the radish until the knife touches the chopsticks. Turn the radish 90° and repeat to make perpendicular cuts.

4. Follow the same procedure for the cucumber to obtain a serpentine shape that can be cut into 1¼-inch / 3 cm sections. Then macerate using the tate shio method (page 282) for about 10 minutes, drain, and firmly squeeze dry.

CUTTING FOR COOKING AND GARNISHING

5. Bias cut: cut the leek on the diagonal (1 cm thick). Be sure to cut all the pieces uniformly for even cooking. Use for hot pots, simmered dishes, and stir-fries.

6. Shiraga Negi: (shiraga = white hair, negi = leek): cut the leek whites into 2½-inch / 6 cm lengths then cut in half lengthwise. Slice into very thin strips. Soak the filaments in cold water. Use as an accompaniment to grilled fish, in simmered dishes or salads, and with noodles.

Cutting Vegetables

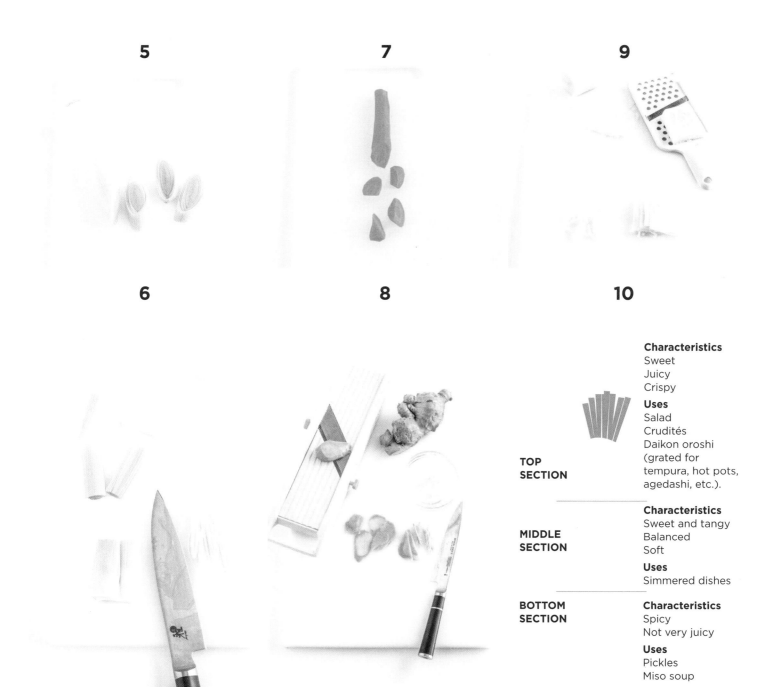

5

7

9

6

8

10

Characteristics
Sweet
Juicy
Crispy

Uses
Salad
Crudités
Daikon oroshi
(grated for
tempura, hot pots,
agedashi, etc.).

**TOP
SECTION**

**MIDDLE
SECTION**

Characteristics
Sweet and tangy
Balanced
Soft

Uses
Simmered dishes

**BOTTOM
SECTION**

Characteristics
Spicy
Not very juicy

Uses
Pickles
Miso soup

7 RANGIRI

Cut the end of the carrot or cucumber on the diagonal, turn it by hand so that the cut edge is facing up, then cut again on the diagonal. This cut is used for simmered dishes.

8 HARI SHOUGA

(Hari = needle, shouga = ginger): peel the ginger and slice thinly with a mandoline. Then slice into thin strips, soak in cold water and drain. This cut is used for decoration and as a condiment.

9 KEN AND TSUMA

Used to accompany sashimi.

Tsuma: a garnish used to embellish sashimi; edible flowers and seaweed such as wakame are often used.

Daikon ken: peel the daikon. Thinly slice lengthwise using a mandoline. Stack 4 or 5 slices of the daikon on a cutting board and cut into very thin strips. Repeat this process several times, then place the daikon slivers in a bowl of very cold water and drain. You can use the same method for other vegetables: carrots, cucumbers, radishes, kabocha (Japanese squash), etc.

10 DAIKON (JAPANESE RADISH)

Daikon is composed of 3 parts, each with different characteristics useful for specific recipes.

The top part is sweet, juicy, and crisp: for salads, crudités, or grated (daikon oroshi) for use as a condiment.

The middle part is sweet, balanced, and soft: for simmered dishes.

The lower part is spicy and not very juicy: for pickles and miso soup.

Preparing Fish

1

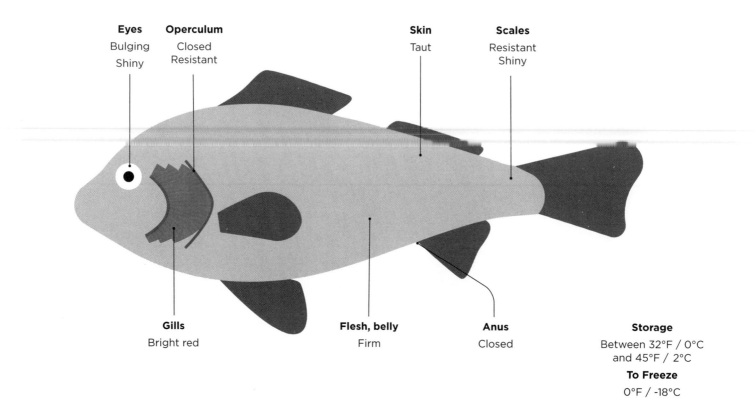

Eyes
Bulging
Shiny

Operculum
Closed
Resistant

Skin
Taut

Scales
Resistant
Shiny

Gills
Bright red

Flesh, belly
Firm

Anus
Closed

Storage
Between 32°F / 0°C
and 45°F / 2°C
To Freeze
0°F / -18°C

2

3

4

1 CHOOSING FRESH FISH

Favor whole fish over ready-made fillets. Ensure that: the eyes are bright and transparent, there is no blood, the scales are not peeling off, the color is bright and the abdomen is firm and elastic. If the surface of the fish is shiny and colorful, this is a good sign of freshness. The gills should be bright red because the blood vessels are concentrated there. If they are brown or blackish, the fish is not fresh. Fish varieties that can be eaten raw include tuna, sea bream, bass, turbot, brill, farmed salmon, scallops, and bonito. Fish varieties that are not suitable for raw consumption include cod, monkfish, pollack, whiting, and ray.

2 TATE SHIO

A traditional method of using salt water to remove sand from shellfish and wash seafood. This method is also used to season fish evenly or to prepare vegetables. Use a concentration of about 3% salt (1 teaspoon of salt for 1 cup / 240 ml of water).

3 SLICING SASHIMI

Position the knife on the right-hand side of the fish fillet and slide the blade gently up and down toward you to slice thinly. The aim is to cut by pulling the knife without pushing it. Then cut into pieces ¼-inch / 7 mm thick for the sashimi.

4 BLANCHING FISH (SHIMOFURI)

Pour hot water over the fish to eliminate any fishy odor. Once it turns white, clean it in cold water. Dry with paper towels. Use this method to remove grease, blood, mucus, etc.

Basics

1 TOASTING SEEDS

Put the sesame seeds in a small hot skillet and cook over low heat for 2 to 3 minutes until toasted.

2 STRAINING LIQUIDS

Strain a liquid through a sieve or strainer by lining it with a clean cloth to trap impurities and residue.

3 MIXING WITH CHOPSTICKS

Using chopsticks instead of a whisk to mix allows you to obtain a varied consistency and to leave some lumps intact.

4 DILUTING STARCHES

Stirring the starch vigorously into a cold or lukewarm liquid will dilute it completely and eliminate lumps. You can then incorporate the mix into a hot liquid.

5 TEZU

Mix ¾ cup plus 4 teaspoons / 200 ml cold water with 1 tablespoon white vinegar. Use tezu to moisten your hands when making maki and sushi. The tezu reduces hand temperature and prevents the rice from sticking. The vinegar also has an antibacterial effect.

REHYDRATING

6. Kombu: wipe with a damp cloth to remove debris without removing the white film (the umami component), then soak for 2 to 3 hours in lukewarm water.

7. Shiitake mushrooms: soak for about 1 hour in lukewarm water and squeeze dry. Use the soaking water in a broth.

8. Wakame seaweed: soak for 15 minutes in cold water, squeeze dry, and discard the soaking water.

9. Kikurage (wood ear) mushrooms: soak for 30 minutes in cold or lukewarm water, squeeze dry, and discard the soaking water.

Cooking Methods

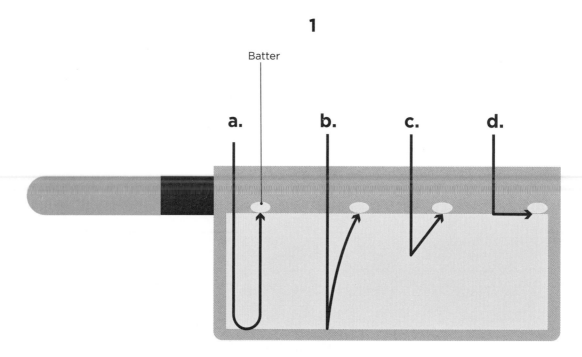

Batter

a. **b.** **c.** **d.**

a. Less than 300°F / 150°C: the batter sinks to the bottom, and then slowly rises to the surface.

b. 325°F / 160°C: the batter sinks to the bottom, and then immediately rises to the surface.

c. 340°F / 170°C: the batter sinks halfway, and then immediately rises

d. More than 350°F / 180°C: the batter immediately floats.

2

3

Beef Tataki

Tuna Tataki

1 PREPARING OIL FOR FRYING

Drop a small amount of batter into the oil to see if it is at the right temperature for the recipe.

2 FRYING TEMPERATURE

Firm vegetables: (such as pumpkin, sweet potato, lotus root, etc.) fry at 325°F / 160°C to avoid overcooking on the outside and undercooking on the inside.

Shrimp/fish: fry at 350°F / 180°C.

Karaage (fried chicken): start at 325°F / 160°C for the first round of frying and finish at 350°F / 180°C for the second, so that the batter is golden brown and crispy.

3 TATAKI

A Japanese cooking method which consists of searing the outside of fish or meat in a very hot skillet, or over a direct flame or charcoal; the center remains raw.

4 COOKING WITH A STEAMER BASKET

Arrange the ingredients in a small shallow bowl and set the bowl in the basket. Place the basket over a pot of boiling water. Bring the water to a boil on medium heat. For the chawanmushi (page 148), place the individual bowls directly on the basket.

5 OKAAGE

A Japanese cooking method in which ingredients are boiled or simmered and then left to rest in a colander (without soaking in water). The juice or cooking water is drained off while the ingredients cool. Because the water is drained and the umami in the vegetables does not escape, the vegetables develop delicious flavors.

Cooking Methods

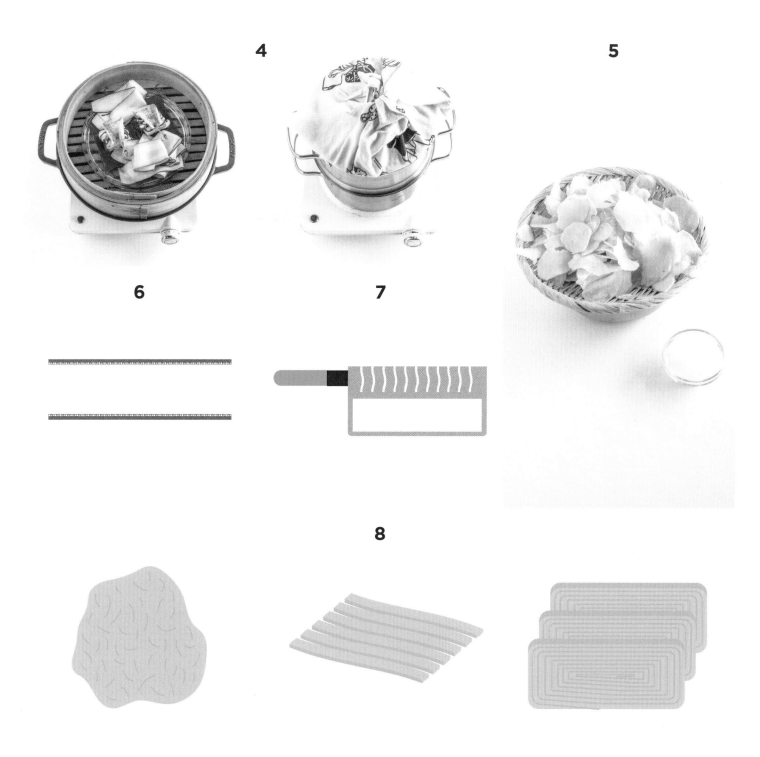

4

5

6

7

8

6 KOBUJIME

A method of sandwiching whole fish fillets or sashimi between pieces of kombu to add umami. Suitable for mild, white-fleshed fish.

7 NIKIRI SAKE

A method of removing alcohol from sake when it is used for seasoning and therefore not heated for the recipe. Pour the sake into a heat-resistant container. Place uncovered in a microwave and heat at 600 W for 50 to 60 seconds to evaporate the alcohol or bring to a boil in a saucepan.

8 COOKING EGGS

Iri tamago / scrambled eggs

Whisk the eggs in a bowl with sugar and salt. Pour into a small saucepan and cook over low heat, stirring with 4 chopsticks, to get small pieces. When the eggs are almost cooked, remove from heat and keep stirring for another moment.

Sliced omelet

Beat the eggs, add the sugar and a little salt. Pour into a hot non-stick skillet and tilt the skillet to distribute the egg evenly in a thin layer. Leave to cook for 2 minutes without flipping. Don't let the omelet brown. Slide onto a plate then slice into thin strips with a knife.

Rolled omelet

Heat a non-stick skillet over medium heat, pour in ⅓ of the egg mixture, and spread evenly over the skillet. Fold the omelette over onto itself. Oil the empty part of the skillet, pour in ⅓ of the egg mixture. Repeat the process (page 86).

Index of Japanese Ingredients

Thank you

To Audrey Genin! Thank you so much for your help and for the opportunity to create this beautiful book. Meeting you was a wonderful discovery, and I learned so much thanks to you!

To Aurélie Legay! Thank you for your advice, your patience, and your warm messages. Your presence was always reliable.

To Orathay Souksisavanh! Thank you, Mama, for all your help. Thanks to you, I was able to finish this book. We laughed and we ate, and I'm delighted to have worked with you.

To Pierre Javelle! Thank you for your sublime photographs. You're a samurai and the captain of our Team. You always fostered a positive, fun atmosphere! It was a delightful experience.

To Chimène De, for your precious and important work on the layout.

To Yannis Varoutsikos! For your designs and beautful illustrations.

To Olivier Derenne! Thank you for your support and your generosity in providing the ingredients for this book. Thanks to you, I discovered a great deal about Japan and found inspiration for writing the recipes. Your passion for great food is truly amazing!

To Nathalie Chabert! Thank you for your help, your kindness, and your beautiful materials from Zwilling-Staub, with which I was perfectly at ease. I'm always so pleased and so proud to work with you!

To Eri Uehara! Thank you for lending me your beautiful plates. I love the pure, zen, unique universe you create

To Rieko Koga! My lovely friend, I am always grateful for your support; your words have given me great courage and have brought comfort during difficult times.

To Kaori Tanaka! Thank you for your constant encouragement – when I'm happy and also when I'm feeling down. You've saved me, you are my rock.

To my mother! There are many of your recipes and memories of my childhood in this book. I grew up eating your delicious meals and sharing your love of cooking; that is my treasure. I am infinitely grateful to you.

To Luc Nguyen! A massive thanks for giving me your time and advice! ARIGATOU Luc!

Sachiyo Harada would like to thank the suppliers who contributed to the production of this publication.

ZWILLING, STAUB, MIYABI for the pots, woks, and knives.
www.zwilling.com

Nishikidori Specialty shop for Japanese ingredients.
www.nishikidori.com

Atelier Aonoto for the plates.
aonoto.strikingly.com

Published in the United States by Hardie Grant North America, an imprint of Hardie Grant Publishing Pty Ltd.

Food Styling: Orathay Sousksisavanh
Design: Yannis Varoutsikos
Layout: Chimène De
Proofreading: Aurélie Legay
Translations: Wendy Salters
Production Design: Monica Lo

ISBN : 9781958417911
ISBN: 9781958417928 (eBook)
Printed by Toppan in China, in 2024

Hardie Grant North America
2912 Telegraph Ave.
Berkeley, CA 94705
hardiegrant.com

Hardie Grant
NORTH AMERICA